Dmitri,

Enjoy the book.

Wishing you success,
Vitaly M. Golomb
April 2017

ACCELERATED STARTUP

*EVERYTHING YOU NEED TO KNOW TO MAKE
YOUR STARTUP DREAMS COME TRUE
FROM IDEA TO PRODUCT TO COMPANY*

VITALY M. GOLOMB

TIME
TRAVELLER
BOOKS

For information contact:
http://www.golomb.net

Publisher: Time Traveller Books
Book and cover design: Vitaly M. Golomb
Project editor: Haje Jan Kamps
Copy editor: Max Chittister
Dust jacket author photo: Dan Taylor

ISBN: 978-0-9984063-0-5

First Edition: January 2017

10 9 8 7 6 5 4 3 2 1

For my family, whose massive compromises have enabled me to learn the lessons in this book hands-on.

For my friends and mentors who have allowed me to learn from their trials and tribulations by osmosis.

And for the future generations of entrepreneurs whose passion inspires me. Your job is to keep this planet spinning.

CONTENTS

About the Author 1

Foreword by Dave McClure, Founder of 500 Startups 3

Prologue: Why Is Innovation So Important? 9

PART I - What Is a Startup and Is It for Me? 19

Chapter 1: A Brief History of Silicon Valley 23

Chapter 2: A Startup is an Experiment 31

Chapter 3: Choosing the Startup Career Path and Life Balance 37

Part II - The Birth of an Idea 45

Chapter 4: Who is the Customer and What is the Problem? 49

Chapter 5: Commercializing University Research 55

Chapter 6: Intrapreneurship in Large Companies 63

Part III - From Idea to Product 71

Chapter 7: Equity 75

Chapter 8: Finding a Cofounder 87

Chapter 9: Cofounder Relationships 93

Chapter 10: Building the Core Team—
          Business, Engineering and Design 99

Chapter 11: Prototypes and Minimum Viable Product—
An Exercise in Self-Constraint 107

Chapter 12: Working with Contractors 115

Part IV - Social Proof 123

Chapter 13: Advisors—The Masters and the Apprentices 127

Chapter 14: Your First Funding—Friends, Family and Fools 133

Part V - Everything You Need to Know About Accelerators 143

Chapter 15: The Accelerator/Incubator Explosion—
The Good, the Bad and the Ugly 147

Chapter 16: What Top Accelerators Look For 153

Chapter 17: The Application and the Interview 159

Chapter 18: Making the Most of Your Accelerator Experience 165

Part VI - Design Is the Product and The Technology Core 171

Chapter 19: Design Disciplines 175

Chapter 20: User Experience 101 183

Chapter 21: Naming, Branding and Psychographics 191

Chapter 22: Technology as a Core Competency 197

Part VII - Managing Time 203

Chapter 23: Busy Work vs. Important Work 207

Chapter 24: Agile Development 213

Chapter 25: Tools of the Trade 219

Chapter 26: Gathering Customer Feedback as Early as Possible.... 225

Part VIII - Raising Money 233

Chapter 27: Venture Capital and Angel Investors 101 237

Chapter 28: Making the First Impression 243

Chapter 29: Crowdfunding 251

Chapter 30: The Art of the Pitch... 257

Chapter 31: Conferences and Pitch Competitions 265

Part IX - Growth 275

Chapter 32: Measure Everything... 279

Chapter 33: The First 10,000 Users... 287

Chapter 34: Journalism in the Digital Age: A Blogger's Perspective 295

Chapter 35: The Sales Funnel, Elephant Hunting and Partnerships 305

Chapter 36: Dialing For Dollars... 313

Chapter 37: Building a Community... 319

Chapter 38: Industry Events and Trade Shows............................ 325

Part X - From Project to Company.. 333

Chapter 39: Transitioning From Startup to Company 337

Chapter 40: Going International 345

Chapter 41: Failing Forward 351

Part XI - Paying It Forward 359

Chapter 42: The Silicon Valley Way... 363

Chapter 43: Becoming a Mentor.. 369

Epilogue: Some Final Thoughts 375

Acknowledgements 379

About the Author

VITALY M. GOLOMB is a venture capitalist, serial entrepreneur, keynote speaker and author who has been involved with startups since his teenage years. He is a Global Corporate Venturing 2017 Rising Star and leads global investments at HP Tech Ventures, the corporate venture arm of Silicon Valley's original startup. He is a contributing writer to TechCrunch and a consistently top-ranked mentor at a number of startup accelerator programs in the US, Europe, and Asia. He lives in the San Francisco Bay Area and travels to over 20 countries annually to consult and guest lecture to corporations, associations and universities on entrepreneurship, innovation and design.

Vitaly M. Golomb is available for select speaking engagements.

Find the author online:
www.golomb.net
www.facebook.com/VitalyGolomb
www.twitter.com/VitalyG

Foreword

Startups are a pain in the ass.

In fact a proper Englishman might even exclaim,
"STARTUPS are an ASS!"

Indeed, most startups are rather foolish. Most of them die within a year or two. The ones that survive often don't produce anything magical and they often don't get very big. Even the ones that DO create amazing new stuff and become big successful companies result in a lot of pain and suffering on the road to success. Building a startup can be a non-stop rollercoaster of challenges and changes, likely to drive you crazy long before your startup donkey turns into a big beautiful Unicorn, and before you become a successful entrepreneur.

In short: most startups are Donkeys, not Unicorns - Silicon Valley slang for a startup company worth over $1 billion. They're exceedingly rare.

But here's the thing about entrepreneurs -- especially Silicon Valley tech entrepreneurs -- EVERY ONE of us thinks we are going to be a Unicorn, not a Donkey. We convince ourselves we're going to build the Next INSANELY GREAT startup, get rich and (Internet) famous, and we think adoring crowds will flock to us and follow us on social media. Awesome, let's get started! Except, it turns out most of us aren't going to be the next Bill Gates or Steve Jobs or Mark Zuckerberg. Most of us are more likely to be Homer Simpson, and we'd rather eat a donut and fall asleep watching TV instead of working hard to MAKE and SELL the donuts or TVs.

Rarely do most of us run the marathon long enough and well enough to make it across the finish line and certainly not without a few breakdowns along the way. Despite the potential for fame and glory, doing a startup isn't usually pretty - it can be tough to build the right product, find the right customers, raise or borrow capital, hire and grow a team, and make payroll. Startups are often a lot of work.

And yet, even with all the inherent challenges and failures, entrepreneurship can be a HUGE positive and global force for good - good for innovation, for making customers happy, for economic benefits, for creating jobs, for building bridges between countries and cultures, via commerce and community.

Even when startups fail to become Unicorns, they can still create inspiration and expose lessons for entrepreneurs. The pursuit of entrepreneurship is what drives us to create new products, to practice our craft and develop our skills, to work hard, to strive towards the sun in pursuit of an impossible dream... the Autonomous Hot Dog Delivery Drone! Well, maybe some startups are less inspiring than others ;)

Every once in awhile however, we get lucky and get it right.

Although the percentage of startups that scale and grow to thousands of employees and billions of dollars is small, the impact and returns of a single Unicorn can have outsize effects on driving innovation and market change. Silicon Valley happens to be very good at Unicorn Farming, and we have a LOT of Unicorns... and a lot of Unicorn Wannabes too!

A few major changes over the past few decades have provided even more rocket fuel to accelerate the Silicon Valley startup revolution.

More than a decade ago, companies like Amazon and Google started providing hosted computing services "in the cloud" that enabled startups to outsource a big chunk of their IT needs and costs. Free, open source software platforms for managing servers and databases also enabled cost savings. Previously, startups had to raise millions of dollars just to pay for their hardware, software, and IT services. Nowadays, many startups get up and running MUCH faster and cheaper by relying on other startups for critical functions like data storage, compute power, email delivery, voice, text, payment, and shipping & logistics.

Another big change over the past 20 years has been the massive consumer adoption of technology and the Internet by most people on the planet and the activation of more than 3 billion smartphones. Now we can start a company in weeks or months and use the Internet to quickly establish a connection and business relationship with almost anyone in the world.

The combination of reduced costs in building startups along with the speed increase / force multiplier of outsourcing tech services to the cloud, and access to millions (now billions) of customers online - all of these factors have created an EXPLOSION of startups and an astonishing acceleration in the pace of building and scaling businesses.

Lastly, the growth of VC funds, corporate investment, and the angel investor market has helped expand capital availability for startups.

However, access to capital is not universal and even in Silicon Valley raising capital can be tough. But with new fundraising platforms and services like AngelList, FundersClub, KickStarter, and more, I believe we will see even more startup capital in the US and around the world.

Governments, corporations, and academia all have their role to play in supporting, investing, and guiding the efforts of entrepreneurs and startups to drive innovation. Healthy startup ecosystems require more than just capital and entrepreneurs. The more substantial the number of participants and cash in the system the more likely the ecosystem is to succeed.

As we see further changes in tech innovation and our society begin to accelerate, startups are well-positioned to create value from chaos, bring both disruption and job creation, and improve personal and business relationships around the world. However, we still have much to improve - startups fail far too often, and access to capital is still a big challenge, especially outside traditional tech and finance metros.

While technology and startups may seem scary and chaotic and doomed to fail in most cases, it's the COLLECTIVE insanity and optimism of the Silicon Valley "hive mind" which I find fascinating. Although failure is common and widespread, with enough people working on startups we are bound to find success with a few of them. And with enough scale and success, perhaps even Unicorns can become more frequent and predictable.

We are still just at the beginning of understanding how to make startups more successful and more scalable. Certainly we still have much to learn in how to take the magic of Silicon Valley and replicate it in other parts of the world. But there's no question entrepreneurship is spreading all around the world, as well as more investors and capital too.

As we learn how to fail less frequently (or at least fail faster and more cheaply), and as we learn how to accelerate and scale faster and better, the benefits of startup innovation become more obvious and applicable to the rest of society. Imagine if we accelerate the pace of innovation in every country and city in the world to run at Silicon Valley speed and bring more jobs and products and benefits to everyone, not just entrepreneurs and VCs.

I wish you the best with your startup adventures and perhaps with a lot of work and a little luck maybe your Donkey might just turn out to be a Unicorn.

-Dave McClure
Founder & Dreamer & Troublemaker @ 500 Startups

Prologue

Why Is Innovation So Important?

Startups depend on coming up with a better, faster, cheaper way of solving an existing problem. Some startups find an entirely new idea that disrupts the way we think about a problem or market altogether. The drive to do something different, to make something that didn't exist before, has led pioneers to launch new businesses since before companies existed. Our current, fertile startup environment may be home to more of that activity than any previous period. Innovation itself, however, is hardly unique to today.

Human history has been marked by technological innovation ever since the first hominid stood up and figured out how to use a stone to knock a rabbit unconscious. From digging tools to plows, pottery to smartphones, the human story has been about attempts to use technology to tailor the world to meet our needs and to relieve the burden of manual labor. Innovation is simply part of human nature and has been from the beginning. Technological innovation may be

9

moving faster now than ever before but we're not the first generation to live through a technological paradigm shift.

Innovation has been so fundamental to the course of human history that it has provided the names we use to demarcate certain stages. We have the Stone, Bronze and Iron Ages in addition to the Agricultural and Industrial Revolutions. The term "Stone Age" today is synonymous with "primitive," but can you imagine what a huge leap in innovation it was at the time? Starting about three and a half million years ago and ending a few thousand years BCE (depending on what part of the world we're talking about), this period took humanity from rocks shaped into basic cutting tools through the mortar and pestle and other agricultural tools.

With some overlap, the Bronze Age followed the Stone Age. Bronze is an alloy of copper and tin. At first, the metals likely came from nuggets found at or near the surface, melted by cooking fires. Eventually, people learned to mine the metals and developed more advanced smelting techniques to improve the alloy quality. Moving from stone to metal let people create tools and weapons that were more precisely shaped and fitted to their tasks. In a pattern that would be repeated in subsequent technological revolutions, advanced tools enabled new developments in other areas. For example, metal axes and woodworking tools made it easier to cut and shape wood, which eventually lead to the design of wheels with spokes. These tools also made it possible to build large structures out of wood rather than stone.

Technology advanced further, bringing mankind into the Iron Age. Here, people invented the smelting of iron with carbon to produce steel. Working with steel and iron enabled the production of tools that were stronger than bronze tools of similar weight, or lighter and cheaper with the same strength. Among other benefits, iron and steel axes enabled people to clear land more quickly and easily than they could with bronze axes, enabling larger permanent settlements.

These developments also accelerated the agricultural revolution, in which humankind transitioned from hunting-gathering economies with temporary settlements to more permanent, larger communities. This transition was made possible by the ability to grow more food and feed more people, which allowed communities to sustain an increased population. In turn, these developments produced second-order innovations; for example, surplus food demanded sturdy, reliable storage containers, which led to advances in pottery. The ability to store food for the non-growing season was another factor encouraging the growth of permanent settlements, because it reduced the need for migration. A permanent large settlement also permitted specialization in labor; when people could focus on an individual niche, such as baking or toolmaking, they were also able to pursue technological innovation in each niche.

Domestication of animals provides another example of how the effects of technological innovation are not limited to just their first-order, direct effects. As humans domesticated animals for food, they were also able to use them for purposes other than just meat. For example, wool from sheep, goats and llamas provided the raw material for cloth and spurred the development of tools for shearing, spinning and weaving.

The same kind of feedback loop characterized the Industrial Revolution of the late 1700s through the mid-1800s. Beginning in Britain, this was a time when hand manufacturing was replaced by machine manufacturing and human and animal muscle power was replaced by the steam engine. At the same time, the telegraph enabled instantaneous long-distance communications for the first time. These developments opened up settlement in new regions including the American West, which in turn demanded still newer tools.

You've already spotted where I'm going with this. Today, we are in the middle of another technological revolution, started by the development of electronics and digital technology. This revolution has seen the invention of a communications and learning tool unparalleled in human history: the personal computer. It's also seen the rise of the Internet, which enables collaboration and communication instantly across the entire globe. More recent innovations in mobile technology have put all of those capabilities in everyone's pocket; once the province of science fiction stories, they're now within reach of even the poorest citizens of the world. These technological developments have and are having massive effects on society both within countries and globally.

Even these innovations, remarkable as they are, are about to be superseded by the wearable computing paradigm, started by products like Google Glass and smartwatches. The Internet of Things will turn every device into a connected sensor. With people connected all the time and sensors and devices communicating with our computers and themselves, we can expect yet another second-order period of innovation in devices to take advantage of these new capabilities. This is already apparent in the boom in electronic health monitoring tools, thanks to the combination of wearable computers and Internet-enabled exercise devices. New technology produces a revolution that, in turn, spurs the development of still more new technology. And with each technological paradigm, entrepreneurs that can see the future can solve the same problems over and over again, each time cheaper, faster and better.

Human history is the story of innovation, but it is worth pausing to discuss exactly what we mean when we say innovation. It's not the same as invention, which refers to the process of coming up with something entirely new, often through tinkering and experimentation. Innovation in business and technology can mean leveraging existing technology to answer a market need. The first steam engine was an invention; the steam locomotive and the steamship were innovations.

Most innovation falls into one of two categories. Continuous innovation, or the ongoing extension of current products or ideas, is a form of innovation that doesn't significantly upend an industry. An example of continuous innovation is replacement of telephone dials with buttons. By contrast, disruptive innovation (sometimes called discontinuous innovation) usually involves products or services that are so new and different that they have the potential to wreak havoc on existing industries or business models. Cell phones and Voice over Internet Protocol (VoIP) phones, for example, are bypassing the traditional communications carriers and forcing them to scramble to keep up with the changes. Uber made a serious dent in the taxi industry; in a bit over 7 years since founding, the company expanded to over 560 cities in over 80 countries, sporting a $68 billion valuation.

A product that results in disruptive innovation need not be something no one's ever seen before. It doesn't even have to be a new invention. It can rely on adapting existing ideas or technology to a new context in a process that has been called recombinant innovation. A good example is Apple's iPod. There were other digital music players on the market when the iPod was released in 2001, but fusing the iPod to the company's existing iTunes music software–itself not the first of its kind–made transferring songs from a computer and managing them on the player essentially frictionless. In doing that, Apple upended the entire music industry. This kind of recombination was Apple's founder, Steve Jobs, special skill: taking bits and pieces of existing technology and putting them together in a product that was more intuitive and easy to use than its sources. The ecosystem, and the network effects that came along with it, created a complete experience far beyond anything a single product could provide.

Like a shark that has to keep moving to survive, companies and industries have to keep innovating. The world of technology does not stand still and you don't want to be stuck with a big investment in bronze when everyone starts moving to iron. Even businesses and business models that look unshakeable (like the railroads, automobile manufacturers and phone companies once did) can find their foundations crumbling beneath them.

Similarly, trends and fads that have little to do with new technologies can disrupt an industry. Coffee roasting, grinding, and brewing technology has been around for a long time. But who would have guessed 20 years ago that coffee drinkers today would be willing to pay $5 for a cup and hundreds or thousands of dollars on coffee-brewing paraphernalia for the home? Innovation is what enables a business to be prepared to ride those waves as they come.

Continuous innovation is also what keeps a business relevant in the minds of consumers. A business school cliché is that most of the old railroad companies went out of business because they thought they were in the railroad business. When the automobile came along and started to make rail travel increasingly irrelevant, those companies had no answer. The innovative companies, by contrast, realized they were in the transportation business. That insight enabled them to stay relevant in the changing world.

Perhaps the most compelling reason for innovation is that a business that doesn't innovate opens the door for its competition or an upstart challenger. Trying to play catch-up once the initial wave of innovation has passed is never a good position to be in. It can be done successfully: Samsung and Google have managed to claim a place in the smartphone landscape once reinvented by Apple. But even Microsoft, with all its resources, was never able to make a dent in the iPod's dominance in digital music players. The less said about the Zune, the better.

Innovation isn't just about staying abreast of consumer demand for new products. Earlier, we defined innovation as "leveraging existing technology to answer a market need." In that respect, innovation enables a company to maximize its assets, both technological and human.

Don't make the mistake of ignoring innovation as a marketing advantage. Every business must ask itself "What makes us special? Why should customers come to us rather than our competitors?" If the only answer is "Because we're cheaper," because it is only competing on price, the company is at risk that someone will come along with a more efficient process or some other way to offer still lower prices. What then? On the other hand, a company that has managed to offer a unique value proposition isn't handcuffed the same way. Its customers will continue to patronize it even if they could go elsewhere cheaper, because the company is offering something the competitor doesn't.

Innovation helps a company develop such a value proposition. Once again, Apple provides an example. Its products are not the cheapest, but the company has established a reputation for high-quality, leading-edge computers for which people are willing to pay a premium price. Critics might argue that Apple customers are just paying for some perceived "coolness factor," but what the critics are missing is that being cool can be seen as value proposition in itself. Apple has established its reputation in part by constantly innovating in the technology that goes into their products. However, it has also innovated in its sales channel and customer service with the creation of Apple stores and Genius Bars. Innovative thinking doesn't have to be confined to products and technology. You can build a successful business by innovating on almost any aspect of the business model.

Startups have an advantage when it comes to innovation. Incumbents may have more resources, but they also operate under numerous restraints (golden handcuffs, if you will) that reinforce the status quo. When there is innovation in large companies, it often takes the form of improved processes and increased efficiencies in what the company is already doing. It makes sense that a business with an established model and customer base would not look for or encourage developments that stood a chance of disrupting the company.

Furthermore, once a business grows to a certain size, it has to develop a formal structure with explicit rules in order to operate at all. Having many employees and initiatives to manage requires multiple layers of management, and a new idea can get stuck in any one of them. As serial entrepreneur and investor (and, incidentally, one of the first venture capitalists I ever pitched) Ben T. Smith IV puts it, "these rules are 'The Box.' The goal of most enterprise innovation is to get close to the edge of 'The Box' without touching the lines."

Large companies also have to answer to constituencies beyond the people directly involved with the business operation or the product. Shareholders want to see a return on their investment and aren't eager to see their investments disrupted, even when innovation can take a long time to pay off. Also, public companies are required to report their results every quarter, and within companies, teams are often expected to present quarterly reports of their progress. That pressure further leads to impatience with the development of a new product or technology. Startups can work on their products without being subjected to such external influences.

Besides those formal restrictions, startups have an edge when it comes to innovation because of the kind of people they attract. Large companies, by their nature, tend to be staffed by people with some commitment to the status quo. And there's nothing wrong with that. It's appropriate for maintaining a well-established enterprise. BP isn't going to attract, and doesn't really want, employees who are obsessed with finding an alternative to fossil fuels. But the itch to try something new and challenge the status quo is what drives the innovators who get involved in startups.

While innovation in business is important for all of the reasons we've discussed, it's certainly no guarantee of success. For one thing, timing is critical. To the extent that innovation involves extending technology into a new context, success depends on whether the context is conducive to the new idea. Similarly, while innovation can help a business ride the waves of popular trends, it's possible to be too innovative and try to catch a wave that hasn't risen yet.

For example, Google is, for all intents and purposes, the only search engine out there, but they weren't the first. Far from it; there were at least fifteen attempts at creating search engines before Google came along. Google offered a superior alternative to the search engines of the time, but if AltaVista and Lycos hadn't already trained Internet users in Internet search, Google might not have attracted the positive attention it did. Similarly, when Netflix launched in 1999, consumers were already used to ordering products online; Amazon had launched four years before. Not only that, but the percentage of American homes with DVD players was starting to skyrocket. Those two factors created the context that let Netflix create an innovative business model.

Even the companies with the best track record for innovation can get the timing wrong. In 1993, Apple introduced the Newton, a handheld computer/digital assistant with handwriting recognition and an assortment of productivity tools. A mere five years later, Steve Jobs discontinued the product. It's certainly possible to list several flaws with the product itself that led to its demise: the handwriting recognition didn't work well at first (making the device the butt of jokes for cartoonists and comedians), it was too big and heavy and it was too expensive. But perhaps most importantly, it was offered to an audience that had no familiarity with handheld computers as constant companions. In 1996, when the Palm Pilot was introduced, it entered a marketplace that the Newton had already educated about the potential for a personal digital assistant. It also didn't hurt that the Palm was smaller and cheaper than the Newton. It's worth noting that the next time Apple set out to introduce a handheld computer, it combined the computer with a cellular phone, a device consumers were already familiar with; in turn, this familiarity with the iPhone provided a fertile marketplace for the iPad. In fact, as Steve Jobs revealed in 2010, the iPad was actually developed before the iPhone, but was shelved until the market was ready.

In sum, the ability to innovate and the willingness to embrace innovation are desirable and often necessary traits for any business.

Compared to established, large companies, startups are well positioned to embrace and leverage innovation.

In the following pages, we'll discuss approaches to coming up with new ideas, building organizations to take advantage of these ideas and turning ideas into fully fledged products.

PART I

What Is a Startup and Is It for Me?

Not a day goes by without you hearing about yet another tech billionaire. There are constant news stories of public companies gobbling up yet another promising young startup, making a small team of hardworking twenty-somethings millions of dollars overnight. It's hard not to think, "Damn. I'm at least as smart as those guys; why aren't I being interviewed on Forbes and TechCrunch, rolling in a small mountain of $100 bills?"

It's often said that entrepreneurs are people who work 80 hours per week to avoid working 40 per week. There's some truth to that. The freedom you get as an entrepreneur is real. But so is the relentless struggle, where the highs are few and far between. To say that founding and running a startup is frustrating and nearly impossibly difficult is a tremendous understatement.

But to the right kind of person, entrepreneurship can also be the most exciting, interesting and lucrative career decision you will ever make.

In this first section, we're going to take a closer look at what startups are and who runs them. Right out of the gate, we'll be taking a serious look at whether giving up a comfortable job to take a leap of faith into the unknown is a good idea. No startup is easy. With the right advice, both in the form of this book and in the shape of some heavy-hitting advisors, you can make the journey a lot easier.

What are you waiting for? Let's get to it.

Chapter 1

A Brief History of Silicon Valley

A **couple of hours' drive north** of Silicon Valley you'll find California's winemaking country. The grapes grow well because they have the perfect ecosystem: the perfect amount of sun, just the right amount of rain, warm days and cool nights. In Silicon Valley, you find a similar ecosystem. Not one that depends on sun, rain and soil nutrients, but on talent, money and experience.

A friend of mine was visiting from abroad. He made me laugh when he excitedly asked if we could take a quick tour and visit Silicon Valley. Of course, there's nothing preventing you from driving up Highway 280 from Cupertino (home of Homestead High School, where Jobs and Wozniak met), past Mountain View and Menlo Park, all the way up to San Francisco, but there's not a lot to see. It's pretty common to assume that Silicon Valley is a physical location where money is hanging from trees and innovation is flowing in the streets, but physically it's not much more than a series of sprawling industrial and office parks.

Geographically, the area spans from Santa Clara County in the south to San Mateo County in the north. Most people now include San Francisco, and a few startups will desperately claim that Oakland is part of Silicon Valley as well. Silicon Valley is the perfect storm for startups, not because it has office buildings (you can build those anywhere), but because it has a rich history and tradition of innovative hardware and software businesses. In this chapter, I'll take you on a brief tour of how we got here.

Silicon Valley was a hotbed for technology and innovation long before it started being called Silicon Valley in the mid-1960s. A lot of Silicon Valley's success can be traced back to the work of Frederick Terman. He was a professor in the engineering faculty at Stanford University, in the heart of Silicon Valley. His work focused on radio engineering, with a particular interest in vacuum tubes and circuits. He taught a number of the engineering luminaries of the time, encouraging more than a few of them to start their own companies, including Hewlett-Packard (HP) and many of the other first wave tech companies that called Silicon Valley home.

During World War II, Terman headed up a team of more than 850 researchers at the Radio Research Laboratory at Harvard, developing technology to help defeat German radar installations. After he returned to California, he was appointed dean of the Stanford School of Engineering, overseeing the creation of what would become the Stanford Research Park. That turned out to be a brilliant move. The combination of an engineering-focused university and a high-tech business park created an early focal point for businesses needing access to smart ideas and cutting-edge technology. Terman also ensured that the university continued its focus on technologies that would be useful to the military to ensure a steady flow of research grants. At the time, the technology in question focused on electronics.

If you know your world history, you know what happened next: the Cold War took hold. Instead of a war with men and machines, the 50s, 60s, and 70s were a war of technology and subterfuge. This meant that a significant amount of money was being spent on signals intelligence-related R&D. At one point in the 1960s, more than half of the money invested into the Stanford Research Institute (established by Stanford University trustees in 1946 as a center of innovation to support economic development of the San Francisco Bay Area) came from the Department of Defense. More than a third of Stanford's research funding at the time was earmarked for classified research into electronics.

By the time the Korean War started in the 1950s, Stanford was uniquely equipped to help the CIA, NSA and other military branches with their top-secret Cold War efforts. In parallel, Terman continued his mission to change what universities were all about. Instead of remaining a purely academic university, Stanford started encouraging its students to start companies. It invested in technology transfer to make it easier for students to take their ideas into the private sector. And finally, it pushed for professors to consult for companies and even take seats on their boards.

Stanford was on its way to becoming the epicenter of technology, which started a positive cycle of innovation. More high quality research meant the school attracted more smart students. The school's policy of encouraging students to start businesses and, in many cases, offering them the space to do so meant that there was a natural flow of students into the job market at these new companies.

Aircraft manufacturer Lockheed, in its desperation for smart engineering know-how, opened up a large manufacturing plant in Sunnyvale. The factory built, among other things, the Polaris submarine-based missiles that helped keep American citizens safe at night. Before long, the plant had more than 20,000 employees, many of whom were hired and relocated from all over the country.

With such a concentration of R&D activity, entrepreneurial souls and government research spending, it comes as no surprise that innovation happened at a steady clip. Around this time, a series of semiconductor companies were founded, including Shockley Semiconductor, which was founded by William Shockley. In 1956, the year he founded his company, he was also awarded a Nobel Prize for being the co-inventor of the transistor.

A group of Shockley's early employees, to this day referred to as "the Traitorous Eight," left to join recently founded Fairchild Semiconductor. It became the world's first venture capital (VC) backed startup. The company developed the first silicon-based transistors as opposed to Germanium-based ones, which were more common at the time. The new technology became the standard, and some of the technologies the company invented to create the new silicon chips are still in use today.

Fairchild Semiconductor, in turn, became an intense hotbed for technology and innovation. The company became known both for its own innovations and for its dozens of spinoff companies, which were referred to as "Fairchildren." These companies included Intel and Advanced Micro Devices (AMD), who went on to become some of the biggest players in computer microprocessors.

By the mid-1950s, a few of the first companies started maturing, offering their shares up on the public market. Successful IPOs by Varian and HP woke up a lot of investors and subsequent changes in the laws made it easier to invest in venture businesses for large funds such as pension funds.

Before the invention of the personal computer in the late 1970s, of course, there wasn't that much need for central processing units. Boy did that change. When it did, it transformed Silicon Valley once again. IBM built a large campus near San Jose. Here, the first moving-head hard disk drive, and a lot of other innovations necessary for the explosion in personal computers, were invented in the 1950s. I've already mentioned HP, headquartered in Palo Alto, which was a driving force for computing and scientific equipment. The company later branched into printers and many other categories that would later be spun off into Agilent and HP Enterprise. The founder of HP's computer business was Tom Perkins, who went on to found one of Silicon Valley's foundational venture capital firms: Kleiner Perkins Caufield & Byers. They had a pivotal role in funding some of the most important technology companies in the world, including AOL, Amazon.com, Compaq, Electronic Arts, Genentech, Google, Intuit, Netscape, Sun Microsystems, Symantec, and many others.

Steve Wozniak designed the first version of the Apple I while working at HP, and later became the cofounder of Apple alongside Steve Jobs. He initially offered the invention to his employer, but was turned down often enough that he eventually offered it to Jobs.

The other big shift that happened involved where the money was coming from. As I mentioned, Fairchild was one of the first VC-backed startups. The venture firm that invested in them was Venrock, which was a relatively new outfit that was investing private money from the Rockefeller family. Venrock, as you might have guessed, is a portmanteau of the words "venture" and "Rockefeller."

A number of other venture capital companies were founded around the same time, with initial capital coming from the funds' founding partners. Eugene Kleiner (one of the "Traitorous Eight" who founded Fairchild Semiconductor) and Thomas Perkins founded Kleiner-Perkins, one of the first venture firms to settle in at Sand Hill Road in 1972. They were soon joined by a number of others.

Sand Hill Road, or "Sand Hill" as it is often called, is a stretch of road that runs between Highway 280 and El Camino Real, alongside Stanford's campus. It became the center for venture capital activity, with the vast majority of investment firms having their headquarters there. Sand Hill is the Wall Street of venture capital. A Sand Hill address comes with a price; in the 1990s, during the first Dot Com boom, commercial real estate in the area became the highest in the world. These days, it has calmed down a little bit, but renting office space on Sand Hill will still cost you more than it would in central Manhattan.

Silicon Valley was sparked to life by vacuum tubes and radar technology and nourished into health by silicon transistors. It experienced a growth spurt when the personal computing revolution took hold, and nobody was prepared for what came next. With the Dot Com boom of the 1990s, followed by the tremendous rise in internet-based software of the 2000s and the rapidly developing app economy of the 2010s, software is innovating on a large number of fields. While a lot of the larger firms are still based in Silicon Valley, the newest generation of startups are running largely in the cloud.

Without a requirement for manufacturing or their own server rooms, the new generation of startups is light on equipment and big on people. As a result, they often settle in the cities at the outskirts of Silicon Valley. San Francisco, Oakland and San Jose are seeing a rapid upswing in the number of new startups. There is even some evidence that the money is following, with a number of VC firms opening satellite offices, or even their main base of operations, in San Francisco.

As the amount of money that was available started growing and the number of new companies that were founded exploded, Silicon Valley found itself facing some challenges. In a world where Apple, Google and Facebook are practically neighbors and thousands of exciting problems are waiting to be solved, finding, hiring and keeping skilled staff is no easy task. Wages for sought-after staff in software and hardware engineering have gone through the roof, which, in turn, has had a number of additional effects. A lot of the well-paid staffers want to live in San Francisco, the nearest big city. This is turning the main arteries running from Silicon Valley to San Francisco (280 and 101) into a traffic nightmare, and has a hand in rental prices spinning out of control across the Bay Area.

None of the apparent downsides of Silicon Valley appear to have much of a detrimental effect, however. The number of high-tech software startups is astonishing, and the truth remains that a lot of high-end talent is pretty well settled in or near Silicon Valley.

Even for startups that eschew Silicon Valley for their early years, there is a point in the development of a rapidly growing business where you simply run out of talent. Some will argue that there is a shortage of mobile developers (and wages would certainly indicate that this might well be the case), but that is nothing compared to the shortage of experienced managerial staff. The number of people with experience in successfully growing a company from a hundred to thousands of employees is small. Managers with the experience of taking a startup from a few million dollars of funding through an IPO or major sale are few and far between. Past experience might be Silicon Valley's superpower; whatever your company is trying to accomplish, there will be people here who've done it all before.

Should Your Company be Based in Silicon Valley?

The history of the development of Silicon Valley is directed toward its status quo: from signals intelligence via silicon chips to software. This history makes Silicon Valley uniquely beneficial for startups in those sectors, but that doesn't mean that it is right for every startup. There are a fair few outliers that are successful in operating a distributed business, and teleconferencing and cheap flights are making the world smaller by the day. For most companies, however, the benefits of having a home base that is geographically beneficial to your business far outweigh the potential benefits of being distributed.

I'm not saying this means you should get everybody a one-way ticket to San Francisco, however. There are many clusters of innovation around the world. Picking the right one for your business is crucial. Picking the wrong ecosystem isn't often the difference between failure or success, but picking the right one can make life a lot simpler. Keep in mind that in some industries, investors won't even consider you unless you have a base that's geographically close. If that is the case for your industry, proximity is obviously a huge factor.

It wouldn't take a lot of research to figure out where your industry is strongest, but here are a few questions to get you started: Where will your customers be based? Where are your competitors based? Where are the best universities in your industry? Where are your potential acquirers based? Following the money and the knowledge, you'll soon discover that New York and London are the powerhouses for financial services and technology. Tel Aviv is a frontrunner in security and communications technology. Texas is seeing strong growth in the medtech sector, while Sydney, perhaps in part because Australia is so geographically remote, has produced a powerful SaaS and remote working tech ecosystem. Sweden, Finland and Germany are emerging as gaming tech hubs. The list goes on, but I think I've made my point. Do your research and pick your future home base carefully. It makes a huge difference.

Chapter 2

A Startup is an Experiment

f you're not used to working within a startup, there are a few things you should become aware of as early as possible. Most crucially, a startup isn't just a small company being run by a small team of people, making a small profit. It isn't a tiny version of a large company. At the outset, you are not setting out to build a miniature Google, Uber or Airbnb.

The best way to think of a startup is as a science experiment of sorts. As a founder, you have a hypothesis, an idea for what might be an efficient way of solving a problem. The company you found is a startup, which exists to try to prove that hypothesis. It isn't necessarily a bad thing if the hypothesis is proven wrong: the company has created something, in the form of knowledge and experience. You have found a way that doesn't work, which is valuable as well. If you can figure out why the first experiment failed, but you still think the problem is worth solving, you can reformulate the hypothesis and try again.

To take a step back, think about why people are willing to pay money for something. If you look deep enough, it's almost always about alleviating pain or gaining pleasure. To avoid the "pain" of thirst, you might buy a bottle of water. To avoid the "pain" of not being able to contact your friends, you pay your mobile phone carrier. To avoid the "pain" of having to walk places, you might buy a car. Of course, each of these transactions could also have a pleasure element to them. If you enjoy Coca-Cola more than water, you might be willing to pay more for a can of Coke, or if you like attention, you might buy an extravagant sports car.

We'll be talking more about idea creation and where ideas come from in Part II of this book, but (spoiler alert!) some of the best ideas for companies come from a founder who is unhappy about something. Frustrated that your built-in car navigation keeps routing you right into traffic? Invent Waze. Annoyed that making a half-decent cup of coffee makes too much mess? Invent Nespresso's capsule-based coffee system. Tearing out your hair about how hard home video security is? Create a home security camera focused on easy setup and launch Dropcam.

I'm always delighted when a group of entrepreneurs are in a room having a group-rant about everything that sucks about things around them. Whenever that happens, I realize that the adage that "ideas are cheap" is so very true. If you pay attention, you can find hundreds of pain points throughout your day. Waking up in the morning is hard. Knowing whether you get enough sleep is tricky. Having to make coffee first thing is annoying. Realizing your car doesn't have enough gas to get you to work can ruin your day. Finding out that your first meeting is a phone call and you could have stayed at home instead of suffering peak traffic is frustrating. Scheduling lunch with a small group of friends is a nightmare, especially with a bunch of busy people always in and out of town. And those are just the tiny things I come across before my brain really gets going. If I were to carry a notepad around with me, I could probably generate 500 business ideas in a single day. You can, too.

The real question is whether the problem is one that's worth solving. Many are not. Yes, paper cuts are annoying, but are you willing to spend four years of your life designing a new type of paper that doesn't cut skin as easily, manufacturing it and then somehow bringing it to market? Dave McClure makes the distinction between "vitamins" and "painkillers."

Once you've identified a problem, the first point of business is to learn as much as possible about the problem. How often does it occur? How many people experience this pain? Do you think people would be willing to pay to have this pain removed? If, from the first round of simple questions, your idea seems like it is worth solving, it's time to start thinking about what your experiment is going to be. And that is when you need your startup.

I agree with Silicon Valley veteran, serial entrepreneur, investor, author and business school professor Steve Blank when he describes a startup as "a temporary organization used to search for a scaleable business model." Your series of experiments should be designed to get you closer to that goal.

The phrase "business model" gets thrown around a lot, and we should pause for a moment to talk about what it means. There are a lot of different business models out there and you are subjected to them throughout the day.

Let's consider an example. If you are into video games, you have probably bought a console, like a Playstation or an Xbox. How much do you think Sony or Microsoft actually made from you buying that console? It's actually a deceptively difficult question, not least because the price of components inside the console changes a lot in the years from when the console is launched to when it is discontinued. When the consoles are first introduced, they are usually sold at a loss; in other words, when you buy a newly launched console, you pay less for it than it cost the manufacturer to get it into your hands. Consoles don't turn a profit until the electronic components get cheaper over time; this can take a couple of years with each new generation. So why are they sold at a loss? At first, it is because the overwhelming majority of the profit is actually somewhere else. Most consoles use the "handle and razor" approach. This is a business model with a permanent part (such as the handle for a razor blade, a Nespresso coffee machine or a video game console) and another part the customer needs to experience continued enjoyment of the product (razor blades, coffee capsules, and video games, respectively).

There are many different business models for software. For example, look at mobile apps. Some are free mobile extensions of paid-for desktop software. Some must be paid for up-front before you can use them. Others have in-app purchases to unlock content, use a subscription model or are funded by advertising or partnerships.

It is possible for products that are virtually identical to have different business models, too. Famously, Coca-Cola is one of the top advertisers in the world. They spend billions of dollars each year to keep the company at the forefront of consumers' minds in virtually every country. In the United States, you are likely to order a Coke or a Pepsi by brand, and both companies are paying a lot of money to keep it that way. The no-name cola on your supermarket shelf next to the big brands use a different model. They would be crazy to take on Coke or Pepsi at their own game, so their strategy is different: they emulate the known brands and make their products cheaper. They don't have to account for the massive advertising budget of Coca-Cola or the like, and actually make a bigger profit at that lower price. Often, supermarkets are the ones that actually produce the generic products that range from sodas to cereals, from headache medicine to jeans and take the whole profit margin.

A completely different business model is the marketplace model. eBay, Amazon and Etsy are places for people to sell products of different descriptions. Freelancer.com, Upwork and Dribbble can be used to find freelance designers. To sell your car, you can use any number of online services. A marketplace is a company that connects buyers and sellers together, taking a cut of the profits. When done well, marketplaces are a license to print money, but it's also a tremendously difficult space in which to start a new business. Imagine an eBay where nobody bought anything, or an Etsy where nobody was offering their homemade trinkets for sale. Useless, right? Building the software for a marketplace is pretty straightforward, but getting people to use a new marketplace is incredibly hard. If nobody is buying, the sellers won't be selling there. If the sellers aren't listing their wares, then there's nothing to buy and nobody will buy anything. There is a reason Craigslist is still such a powerhouse in the US despite barely updating their website in 20 years: they have the community.

There are a large number of businesses in the "sharing economy" space at the moment. If you have a car you're not using, you can rent it to your neighbors using Turo or Getaround. If you want to make some extra money and you have a car, you can drive people around on Uber or Lyft. When you're out of town, you can rent out your apartment on Airbnb or Flipkey. All of these companies are great examples of an innovative way of creating marketplace economies.

A business model is a complete, detailed view of how your company operates. What resources (money, knowledge or staff) do you have at your disposal? Who are your customers (market segments), and how can you reach them (marketing channels)? What is the problem you are solving for your customer, why would they choose your solution over other options, how will you get your product to your customers and how is your business going to make money?

The amazing thing is that it is possible to innovate on almost every aspect of a business model. Salesforce, for example, decided that it was time to stop shipping CDs with software around. Instead, it started offering a sales platform based exclusively online, through the web. Today, that business model (called Software as a Service, or SaaS) is everywhere, but at the time, it was revolutionary.

Macro-economics also plays a role in business models. Before the age of smartphones, operating a business like Uber would have been impossible. Or would it? It is hard to imagine, but it wouldn't be impossible to design a system where a very good telephone control center could send a fleet of privately owned cars to passengers to be picked up all over a city. Work-intensive, for sure, but not impossible. In the UK, this is done through a fleet of minicabs: unmarked cars that come pick up you up and bring you wherever you need to go when you call. The challenge is that once this system gets big enough, it becomes almost impossible to manage, between drivers calling in to let you know they are free to take another passenger and passengers calling to book and cancel rides. There are only so many cars you could manage that way. Lyft's original business was basically the same system, but on mobile apps. The real innovation was utilizing people's private cars, and turning everybody with a smartphone into a driver. That is where the scalable part of Lyft's business model came in.

There were a number of players in the ride sharing space at the time, including Lyft. Uber copied the business model, and subsequently out-executed Lyft in a spectacular way. The result was that Uber found a way to make its service infinitely scaleable. When it did, Uber stopped being a startup and became worth a truly mind-boggling amount of money.

Your startup is the experiment that needs to bring all of these pieces together into a whole. Yes, your product is going to be important, but having a great product is meaningless unless you can find a way of creating a scaleable business model around it. Ideally, you want to create a perfectly oiled machine that means that for every hundred dollars you pour in the top, more than a hundred dollars falls out of the bottom. To find that magic recipe, you need to have a series of hypotheses and test them systematically by running a number of experiments.

Chapter 3

Choosing the Startup Career Path and Life Balance

f you're looking at a book of college courses, you may have spotted entrepreneurship on the syllabus. Once in a blue moon, someone will come along and encourage young people to consider a career in startups. Startups are the new garage bands, and even politicians are romanticizing life as an entrepreneur or a small business owner.

As you might have already guessed, I have some opinions on the matter. The first thing worth pointing out, which a lot of politicians and pundits simply don't get, is that there's an ocean of difference between starting a startup and being a small business owner. Don't get me wrong, there is absolutely nothing wrong with wanting to run a corner shop, restaurant or web design agency, but it is extremely rare that these companies bloom into true startups. And before you send me an angry email, McDonald's and 7-Eleven don't count. Yes, they are successful corner stores and restaurants, but the gulf between running a single taco truck and being Taco Bell is almost inconceivably large.

Thinking of your startup journey as a career isn't a bad idea, but be smart about it. My number one piece of advice is to start off by making mistakes on somebody else's dime. If you are fresh out of college, work at a couple of startups, or even in the corporate world, before you found your own startup.

Let me explain why with an anecdote a friend told me a while back. He was working on a monthly magazine. Every month, the entire editorial staff worked until 10pm as the deadline got closer and closer. Copy was filed at the last minute, designs had to be thrown together and when the magazine was finally sent to the printers, everyone needed a break. And they took one. Not by taking a holiday, but by just taking it easy in the office for a couple of weeks. Showing up at 10am. Leaving at 4pm. Taking long lunches. You can guess what happened next: when the deadline came around again, they had to work crazy hours. My friend didn't even realize this was weird until he started to work at a different magazine, where they had figured out how to spread the work out better. By being more organized, a lot of the staff didn't even know when the magazine went to print. It was a far better place to work as a result, even though the same size team delivered the same size magazine every month.

The reason for encouraging you to take a "real" job first is two-fold. There are a lot of things they don't teach you in colleges, and working in larger enterprises or established businesses can help you learn more about how relatively successful businesses are run. Along the way, you'll see a ton of things that will piss you off. You'll see meetings that are run poorly. Inefficient operational decisions. Processes that could be hugely improved by simply mapping them out and putting a big fat red X through the superfluous steps. The point is that in order to know whether a business is run smoothly or not, you need some points of reference.

Thinking of your startup journey as a career is helpful in that you can make some choices about what you need to do before you found your company. Maybe you're doing a bit of prototyping and hacking on the side of your normal job. Perhaps you go to events five nights a week to meet likeminded people, and to get inspired by other entrepreneurs. It's possible that you have loaded up your Kindle with books such as this one and a handful of others that are worth reading before you start your startup journey. If you know you're not a good manager, maybe you can take a course, read a book or take a job under a really good manager in order to learn how it's done.

In my mind, to think of yourself as an entrepreneur is to ensure you have the correct tool set. You need some good ideas, some solid skills, some great advisors and enough motivation to propel you in the right direction. Of course, you can do all of that as you are running your company, but you could also be strategic by training some of those skills, learning some of that knowledge and making some of those connections before you throw yourself into your first startup.

The other thing I feel obliged to point out is that yes, startup life can be really sexy when you're at the top of the pyramid, being interviewed on a big conference stage explaining how you built a billion dollar company. For every person on the stage, however, there are 2,000 sitting in the audience, scratching their heads, wondering how they get to be where the speaker is.

Being an entrepreneur is almost impossibly hard. The vast majority of companies fail, even though the founders work around the clock to make it happen. There is a culture in the startup world that says if the founder isn't working 16 hour days 7 days per week, he or she isn't trying hard enough. I've been there, and I completely understand the excitement and energy that comes from working on a startup, but the truth is that working 16 hours per day for many years simply isn't healthy. It definitely isn't sustainable.

Apart from the health considerations, working long hours with a laser-like focus on your startup is likely to make your personal life suffer. Some startup founders deal with this by ignoring their old friends and relationships and accepting that their cofounders are their only friends now. Others are able to find a work/life balance of sorts, carving out time for their friends and family.

The important thing is to go into the startup life with both eyes open. It will be a tremendous amount of extremely hard work. You will work long hours for next to no pay, especially in the early years. And there's a very good chance that your personal life will suffer as a result.

I have felt the burden of this myself, and paid dearly for it in my own personal relationships. Do I regret it? It's hard to say what could have been, but I can't think of many successful entrepreneurs who haven't compromised in a big way.

Is it worth it? That's really a question you can only answer yourself. There are a lot of great things about running your own startup. You don't have to ask anyone for permission, but there's also nobody to blame. You will be beating your own path through uncharted territory, doing something nobody has done before you, but there's no map. You don't have to ask anybody when you can go on holiday, but you will probably be filled with anxiety about the idea of taking even a week off.

Being an entrepreneur is definitely not for everybody, and you're going to have to think long and hard before you pull the trigger on founding a startup. At the minimum, you need to ensure that your expectations are in line with those of your cofounders and your significant other.

Your startup journey will be unpredictable. There will definitely be triumphs worth celebrating along the way. (I do recommend celebrating even the small victories as they happen, by the way.) But there will also be moments where you'll struggle to make sense of anything. It's incredibly valuable to have family, friends and loved ones in the loop, so you can reach out for some moral support when the going gets tough.

If you think the stresses and pressure of running a successful startup are bad, try running an unsuccessful one. To paraphrase an old joke: Ben Horowitz, serial entrepreneur and cofounder of Andreessen Horowitz, once said, "As a startup CEO, I slept like a baby. I woke up every two hours and cried."

I don't want to talk you out of being an entrepreneur. Honestly, if you're a born startup person, everything I've written so far will sound like a challenge and you're already leaning forward on your chair shouting, "Bring it on!" Nonetheless, it's important to be aware of some of the pitfalls so you can be prepared for them.

The stress aspect especially is worth highlighting, and if you know you deal poorly with stress, then starting the journey by finding some good coping mechanisms is a very good idea.

The most important advice I share with my mentees is to have a clear separation between founders as human beings and their startups. Especially when you are working long hours on getting something off the ground, it is easy for those lines to start blurring. It can feel like you are your startup and that any successes and failures reflect on you personally. This has resulted in some terrible tragedies, including a number of suicides. Occasionally coming up for air and focusing on activities that aren't your startup is very important to helping you look after your mind and body. Get some exercise, or go out for dinner with friends and avoid the topic of work for an evening.

I can't stress enough how important it is to eat healthy and to get some exercise from time to time. A few years back, I started doing a 10-15 minute workout routine just about every day, no matter if I'm at home or on the road. Startup founders must build good habits. One thing worth considering is doing meetings while walking. Yes, it feels weird to take a meeting on the road, but if you're just having a catch-up or potentially even a job interview with someone, there's no reason to sit in a poorly ventilated meeting room. Grab a cup of coffee and stretch your legs for an hour. The additional blood flow helps, and your brain, heart and fitness tracker will thank you for it in the long run.

The final thing to keep in mind is that if something bad does happen in your business, it doesn't mean you've failed as a person. As I've already mentioned a number of times, running a startup is incredibly hard, and failure is going to be part of the learning process. Your company can bounce back from some failures. Others, it may not. The important thing to remember is that your startup is an experiment. Some experiments fail. If your experiment fails, take a break, brush yourself off and try again.

And if you ever find yourself in a situation where things are becoming too much to handle, take a step back. Talk with your family and your friends. Get some professional help if you need it. Ultimately, you are making the choice to sacrifice a lot for your startup, but it isn't worth dying for.

Part I—Questions to Ask Yourself

I like to finish each section by taking a closer look at the things you may have learned, or you should have a quick think about before you move on to the next chapter. Hopefully you've now got a bit of an idea what startups are, what they do and what it might be like to run one yourself.

Here's an activity that's worth trying: for a week, carry a notebook with you. Write down absolutely everything that annoys you, causes you pain, or makes you think it could be done better. Think about your commute. Think about the tools, services and infrastructure you use. Consider the places you eat, the things you do and how you do them. As we'll be discussing in a later chapter, problems and challenges you run into at work are particularly valuable, so pay extra attention to those.

At the end of the week, you'll probably have a notebook full of problems. Now, think about each of those problems one by one. Is there an obvious solution to each problem? If so, why is nobody doing it? If not, what would be difficult about doing it? Who would be best positioned to solve that particular problem? Would you (as a person, as an employee of a company or as the company itself) pay to have this problem resolved? In the process, you'll cross out a lot of problems because you can't solve them, they're already solved or you're not in the right position to solve them. But maybe there are a few remaining where you think you could heal the pain.

Another exercise worth thinking about is spotting business models out in the wild. For each of the products and services you use each day, think about their business models. What resources does the company have available to them? How are they utilizing those resources to make money? Can you think of a way you could disrupt that industry by using a different business model, or by changing something fundamental about how the industry works?

One thing I didn't cover in depth in Chapter 1 is the names and brief histories of the top venture capital firms. If you're planning for your startup to raise funding, invest an afternoon in looking into where the big VC firms came from. Start with a quick Google search for "top VC firms" or similar, brew yourself a cup of coffee and spend some quality time with Wikipedia. I promise, it won't be a waste of time. A crucial part of raising money is to do your homework thoroughly. Knowing some of the differences between the top VC firms is a great place to start.

Finally, spend a bit of time thinking about your mental health. If you come from a macho culture, just think of this as putting together a good defense. How do you deal with extreme situations? Have you ever been depressed, and if so, how did you deal with it? How do you deal with stress, and do you have a good idea for how you can identify and help reduce the effects of stress? If the answer to any of those questions is "No," try talking it through with a friend, or perhaps even consider seeking some professional help. Walking into a therapist's office and saying, "Hey, I don't really suffer from stress or depression, but I'm about to start a company and I think I may be at risk for both. Can you help me find some coping mechanisms for when the going gets tough?" would be met with enthusiasm and encouragement. Prevention is the best cure, after all.

Part II

The Birth of an Idea

In Part I of this book, we talked about innovation, invention and the highs and lows of running a startup. If you're still reading, you're probably anxious to get started. But in order to actually get a company off the ground, you need a solid idea. More importantly, you need a solid idea that's worth doing. In this section, we're going to discuss some of the challenges involved in finding that idea.

As I already mentioned, ideas are pretty cheap, but how can you tell a good idea from a great idea? And, if you're already in a bigger corporation, or you're PhD researcher at a university, how can you turn knowledge, experience and ideas into a business?

In this section, we're going to talk about ideas. Good ideas. Bad ideas. How to tell the difference. Strap in, this is the part of the roller coaster that goes up that first ascent!

Chapter 4

Who is the Customer and What is the Problem?

You've probably come across the term "elevator pitch." In the old days, you had the length of an elevator ride to pitch your big idea to the boss; it took about 90 seconds. It's not a lot of time and the tricky part is to say just enough to hook your listener into wanting to know more so you can get that meeting.

If you're struggling to put together a coherent elevator pitch, here's the secret: as you are embarking on your startup journey, you'll soon learn that all companies have something in common. At its heart, a business exists to solve a problem for a customer. Nothing more, nothing less. Your elevator pitch, then, is probably just a quick summary of what the problem is, who you are solving it for, how the company will make money solving the problem and why you are the winning horse to bet on.

For the purposes of coming up with a good idea for your venture, put the money part aside for the moment. As an investor, I can tell you that if you are able to find a problem worth solving and people who want the problem solved, you're most of the way there already. Figuring out where the money is going to come from becomes the final piece of the puzzle, like a sanity check.

At the end of Part I, you did an exercise where you wrote down the problems you run into throughout the day. That's part one of the puzzle, but if you only thought about things in your immediate surroundings (your commute, whether or not your trash was picked up that day or a better way to make coffee), you're leaving out a huge opportunity. Why? Because all of those things are so common that there's a lot of competition for solving those problems. Yes, if you're able to solve commuting for everyone, you're going to make a lot of money, but there are a lot of very bright minds stuck in traffic jams all the time and there are probably thousands of people thinking about how to fix them for a couple of hours per day.

To come up with truly innovative ideas, it helps if you have deep domain expertise in the field you are considering. The term domain expertise will come up a lot as you work on your next big idea. You need someone who understands the niche deeply. For example, if you're building a website to sell cars, what do you think is harder: finding a good web developer, or finding someone who truly, deeply groks cars? My bet is on the latter.

You can bend that to your advantage. Whatever you did at college, whatever your hobbies are or whatever your current job is can help inform your ideas to make them stand out from the crowd. This drastically reduces the competition for the number of people thinking about an idea. For example, if you work for SpaceX or NASA, and you know a lot about the challenges and pain points of sending stuff into space, you may have an advantage that 99% of people don't have. If you just had a baby and are thinking of a startup idea in the realm of parenting, be aware that the opposite is true. Having children is magical, bewildering and full of inefficiencies, so there are a lot of potential ideas there, but a lot of people are having children all the time, and you wouldn't believe how many parenting startups are popping up all the time.

Which brings me neatly to the customer. There are a lot of different customers in the world, and to fully understand how your company fits into the whole, you need to consider who your customers are (market segmentation) and how you can reach them (marketing), further down the road.

As a first-time founder, it is tempting to say "Everyone is a customer," but that is true only in very rare circumstances. Few investors would take you seriously if you said your product was for everybody in the world. Even if your product was something almost everybody uses, such as toothpaste, it would be nearly impossible to reach all of those customers. For one thing, rarely does everybody in a household buy their own toothpaste. Getting a household of six to switch from one toothpaste to another would involve identifying the decision-maker (Is it dad when he is doing the shopping? Is it the daughter, who bought an Amazon Dash button so the family just presses the button to re-up on toothpaste?), convincing him or her that what you are offering is better than what the family is currently using and then dealing with the distribution channels to get the toothpaste to where they want to buy it.

For a lot of problems, people are fiercely loyal to their existing solutions. For the problem of needing to view websites, for example, you might use Chrome, Internet Explorer, Firefox, Edge or Safari. I won't judge. Convincing someone to switch from one browser to another is incredibly difficult. Trying to convince someone to switch from Canon to Nikon (when they already have a lot of lenses for their cameras) or from Apple to Android (when they've bought a number of apps) is similarly problematic. In economics, this is known as a switching cost and you should definitely consider whether your idea will incur pain in the process of switching. Indeed, if you think part of your marketing will involve convincing people to switch from an existing product, it may be worth devising a Minimum Viable Product (MVP) that can test how willing people are to switch. Keep this rule of thumb in mind: people will only switch if the new solution is twice as good at half the price.

I also think it is a good idea, early on, to figure out how often someone experiences the problem in question. For example, if you are creating a fantastic tool for wedding planning, you might find that you'll have very high marketing costs. Yes, you might be able to rely on word-of-mouth marketing (people about to get married are likely to get advice from people who were recently married), but you're unlikely to see a lot of repeat customers. The vast majority of people get married just the once. And repeat offenders usually don't do it too often.

The best problem/customer combinations out there are a problem that is very specific, and a customer who is clearly defined.

Let's try an example. Here is a great, succinct elevator pitch: "Car rental is too confusing. Our solution is to bring customers who are cash-rich but time-poor a luxury car wherever they are, whenever they need it, within 15 minutes."

"We do this by partnering with large car rental companies so we have all the cars we need" explains the outline of the logistics for how you plan to do this, and "We make money by charging a 30% markup on the car rental price, and a $50 delivery fee" explains how you're planning to make money. It tells a succinct, clear story that helps define your customer (wealthy people who need a car now), the problem (the hassle of renting a car) and the money side of the business model. Of course, you're already thinking like an entrepreneur, and you will be able to shoot a ton of holes in this business idea, but the key is to get a conversation going.

We'll be talking about measuring your startup later on, but for the sake of completeness: If you're able to follow up your elevator pitch with some compelling numbers, trust me, you've landed yourself a meeting with a potential investor. "We facilitate 3,000 car rentals per week and are turning over a million dollars per month with a 25% profit margin," or "We only do 200 car rentals per week at the moment, but we've grown 15% week over the past 18 months" would do the trick very nicely.

One of the reasons why it's so important to be clear about who your customers will be is that marketing becomes a lot more targeted. Marketing to "everyone" is easy. Television adverts and billboards go a long way, but they are extremely expensive. If your customers are a clearly defined group, such as mountain climbers, people who own a 3D printer or people who have pet hamsters, you have a fighting chance at devising a marketing plan that reaches those people directly.

Remember also that even if your vision is huge, there's no harm in scaling it down for the purposes of your experiments. You need to win the beachhead before your army can take the hill. Bezos had huge ideas for Amazon, but the company famously started as a bookstore. Page and Brin wanted to change the internet, but Google started its life as a search engine. Both companies were able to prove early ideas and started generating large amounts of revenue before they started branching out into other products.

This focus is a tremendous luxury startups have that bigger companies don't, and applies to both the product side and customer segmentation. If you prove that you've created a product that fixes one problem, it is easier to expand it to fix more problems later. Similarly, if you have a proven track record of marketing to one market segment, you can always find a way to raise more money to take on more markets.

Of course, some business models can get almost impossibly complicated. They solve many different problems for a great number of customers. Facebook, for example, now has a number of customer segments, all of whom have different needs and requirements from the platform. A grandmother wants to know what her grandkids are up to. A party planner organizing a birthday party wants to distribute information before, during and after the event. An advertiser wants to target adverts at specific subsections of the population. All of these are valid problems that Facebook solves for different customers. Also keep in mind that "If you're not paying for the product, you are the product." Nowhere is that more true than with Facebook: it is offering its users up to advertisers with a thousand different ways of slicing and segmenting the audience.

In the example above, note that not all of the customers are paying for the product. The grandmother and the event planner probably don't pay. That still makes sound business sense, when you think about it; in the process of interacting with the Facebook platform, they are creating a deeper profile that the advertisers can use, turning Facebook into a more valuable advertising platform. Incidentally, this is also why Twitter is struggling on the advertising side; Facebook knows a lot more about its customers, and can price its advertising rates accordingly.

Many of today's most successful companies seem as if they are doing everything for everyone. Sony, Microsoft, Samsung, Google and Amazon all have a huge number of different touch-points across the industries they are upending. They also operate in a broad number of customer segments and geographical areas. They all have one thing in common: they started with a single product that solved a single problem for a single customer segment in a single market. And then they started growing.

Startup founders often think too big. When that happens, I tell them to focus their ideas down to something more manageable. Occasionally, though, I experience the exact opposite: a founder solving a problem that is so small and specific that it isn't worth the time. Don't get me wrong: there's a lot to be said for tinkering away with smaller problems and learning new skills in the process, but unless you are fixing a problem that a sufficiently large portion of the population is experiencing, you're not really building a company; you're scratching an itch.

Chapter 5

Commercializing University Research

C hapter 4 discussed the advantages of having deep knowledge about a particular market. One of the ways to get this knowledge is to leverage research, technology and knowledge gathered during the course of university research.

Not all universities are great at picking the right projects to fund or approve for research; in fact, some are comically bad, pouring huge sums of money into technology that is outdated before the research even begins. Some (and it doesn't take a lot of research to find which ones) have a golden track record at funding PhD programs that put a dent in the world.

There are a great number of examples of extremely successful companies that started as a direct result of university research. For example, Frederick Smith wrote a paper on overnight delivery services. He only barely passed the course, as the professor didn't think the idea was feasible. Smith went on to found a company to try his ideas, which worked out pretty well. The company is still around; it is called FedEx.

A better known example is Google, which started as a PhD project at Stanford, eventually growing into one of the most valuable web businesses in the world. In order to use the technology Sergei Brin and Larry Page invented at the university, their company has to pay royalties to the university. To date, Google has paid out more than $300 million to its alma mater.

If you are interested in photography, you may have come across the concept of "light field photography," a revolutionary technology that enables photographers to re-focus the photograph after it has been taken. Its inventor, Ren Ng, started the Lytro company based on his PhD research.

Quite a few of the big breakthroughs that have shaped the world around us stemmed from deep research at universities. The internet as we know it today, for example, is the descendant of Advanced Research Projects Agency Network (ARPANET), which developed technologies in parallel with the US military and universities. More recently, new Wi-Fi and Bluetooth standards are the direct results of university research. Personally, I'm also pretty excited about breakthroughs in material science. You may have heard of Graphene, a close relative of graphite with a ton of interesting applications, many of which haven't been realized yet. There's also Sugru, which is a type of silicone rubber that was developed based on university research and was brought to market seven years later as a product for doing small repairs around the house.

In the above examples, all the founders had exceptionally sharp business minds and were able to bring their inventions and technologies to life. Of course, there are many fantastic research projects where the researchers lack the business acumen to bring their products to market. In addition, commercializing research can be tremendously expensive. While turning research into businesses is nothing new, historically educational institutions have been poorly prepared to spin up companies to take advantage of the new innovations. As such, university research tends to focus on the early, explorative stage, rather than building commercially viable proofs of concept. And that's where our opportunity lies.

Let's face it: PhD's aren't for everybody. On average, it takes about eight years to complete a doctorate, and doing so takes a tremendous amount of dedication and motivation. If you're not beyond fascinated by your field of study, you're not going to make it. Even if you are, a PhD is a real accomplishment.

I don't recommend starting on a doctorate solely to found a startup at the end of it. The great news is that you don't have to. Some of the most fantastic founding teams consist of a technologist with a deep understanding of the subject matter, an excellent marketer who can bring the product to life in the marketplace and a business person who can drive the business side of the effort. If you feel your strength is more as a business innovator or as a marketing wizard, tapping into the expert knowledge of university research is a pretty sharp idea!

There are real opportunities to be had by by partnering up with the academic world. You've probably already reached this conclusion, but it's worth repeating: academic research is often at the bleeding edge of its field. Working off the back of research breakthroughs or technology innovations discovered in the course of academic research is a great way to find ideas for businesses worth starting. Not only will your new business partners have a deep understanding of their own research, it is also likely that they've stayed in tune with other developments in their field.

In a way, academic research isn't all that different from starting a startup. Research students on a PhD level are surrounded by some of the best people in their field. Students are only responsible to themselves, and if they happen to discover that the thing they are studying is negative (that is, their research hypothesis was false), that is still a success. In academia, proving a hypothesis wrong isn't failure;

it is success. Come to think of it, startups could learn a lot from that mindset.

I'm not saying you should get in your car and kidnap the first research academic you see, of course. As we'll be discussing later, cofounder relationships are complicated, and it's often better to go into business with people you know very well. Business is often both about the long game and about opening as many doors for yourself as possible. Armed with this knowledge, why not familiarize yourself with some of the work that's going on at research universities in your area? I find the dogged determination that goes with committing yourself to hard research incredibly inspiring. Being a guest lecturer or enrolling in university yourself are two ways of exposing yourself to research, but those are not the only way to get to know people. Many universities run free, open lectures on interesting topics, or it's possible to take a course or go to other events at universities, then do what you always do as an entrepreneur: network, network and network.

The main thing you gain by commercializing academic research is access to defensible technology, developed by some of the keenest minds in the industry. These are researchers who know the problems in their respective industries inside and out and will be able to rattle off half a dozen pain points in their industries in a heartbeat.

There are a few things you need to know before you put yourself on a path to commercializing university research. The most important is that most universities have a contract with their students that means the university has at least a partial claim to the work that is being done on university time, machines and campus. On the flipside, most universities will have business development units that are designed to facilitate bringing university-conceived research into the world.

Some universities have their own incubators that are designed to help turn inventions and technology into businesses. Incubators often teach business skills and help companies with the resources needed (such as office space or advice) to incorporate a new business. As an existing or would-be entrepreneur, you could do a lot worse than introducing yourself to your local university incubators. Perhaps you can offer some of your business skills to some of the teams in the incubator, and from there, who knows what might happen.

Be aware, too, that many universities have "technology transfer" programs. These are similar to incubators, but tend to be more focused on licensing patents and technology to much larger companies.

Other universities have formalized their research and development efforts, running expansive educational programs to facilitate and grow their research efforts, sometimes in collaboration with other universities. Facilitating PhD-level research based on grants from its own research funds or private or government foundations ("contract research") is one of the main ways universities, governments, or corporations steer research towards their overall goals. Many companies you'll be familiar with (including Intel, Microsoft, Pfizer and Ford) have extensive grant programs for research in fields that they feel are particularly commercially viable.

Seeing where the research grants are going, by the way, can be a leading indicator of where institutions are focused. If you suddenly see heavy investment in a particular direction or field of research, it often means that you're a few years away from seeing a number of companies spawning in that field.

There are a number of venture capital firms that either pay extra attention to, or focus exclusively on, research that comes out of universities. These firms frequently start out as angel investors or angel groups focusing on the universities where the investors started their careers. If you're looking to commercialize intellectual property that is particularly strongly linked to a specific university, doing your research to see which angel investors are focusing specifically on that university can be a foot in the door and your first step towards raising some money to get your company off the ground.

Regarding money: there have been a number of crowdfunding

campaigns that have successfully leveraged ideas in the university research space. We'll talk about raising money from the crowd in a later chapter in this book. For now, I just wanted to highlight that more and more universities have their own crowdfunding platforms (or have partnered with existing platforms) to help connect business ideas from students with alumni who might be in a position to help fund these nascent startups.

If you're considering bringing products or services to market based on university research, there are a few pitfalls to be aware of. I already mentioned licensing; different universities have different licensing requirements when commercializing research done at the institution. Everything is negotiable, of course, but it's worth baking the licensing costs into your business models to ensure that the idea still makes sense once that side of the financial picture is taken care of.

The other thing to look out for is patenting. Even if the researchers have a patent pending, or have had a patent granted on something, they come in various degrees of usefulness. Most universities have solid patent lawyers retained, but you can't be too careful. There are a few horror stories out there of patents that are all but useless. If the viability of your business is based exclusively on whether or not you will be able to defend a patent, get a lawyer to look over the patent in detail, and have deep pockets. Defending patents is notoriously expensive, and there are plenty of patent trolls out there who'd love to take a bite out of your business.

The final heads-up is that while the academic world is usually very good at keeping an eye on what's going on in universities and colleges around the world, researchers aren't always fully up to speed on what's happening outside of academia or, as we like to say, "in the wild" real marketplace. A lot of the research that happens in labs at companies and within the military is kept a secret from the world at large. As a result, it's possible that similar work is already being turned into products elsewhere. That is true for every business idea you might have, of course, not just those resulting from university research, so it is always worth doing your due diligence before you throw yourself into a new project. Having said that: competition isn't a bad thing, so don't let finding a competing product or service deter you too much.

Chapter 6

Intrapreneurship in Large Companies

Sridhar Solur is the Senior Vice President of Product for Comcast, where he leads the team responsible for all devices, data and services omnipresent in tens of millions of US homes. Previously, he spent over 20 years at HP, where he conceptualized and developed several new products and services that ended up in customers' hands all over the world. He has been able to do the impossible on a consistent basis: drive innovation at large companies. He is a dear friend, and I thought his unique experience would be invaluable for those looking at intrapreneurship as their path. So, I've asked him to share his learnings with you.

* * *

With my years of experience in corporates, it may be curious to ask for my advice for a startup book. It is true that I may not be a startup guru, but I have created several products from the ground up. Building new businesses inside the expansive walls of Fortune 50 companies is much easier, and in some ways much harder, than building a conventional startup from scratch. Some of the ventures I spearheaded clearly failed. Others wallowed in mediocrity, and in retrospect perhaps we ought to have killed them off sooner. The last two, however, have done very well indeed. Two hits in a row is far from being a winning streak, but they have given me a ton of experience. I've started spotting some patterns that could potentially help intrapreneurs, and for this book, I'm delighted to share them with you.

When creating a new business within a large, existing company, the most important thing is that you have to solve a "Tier-1" problem for your customers. The good news is that identifying one of these Tier-1 problems is relatively easy.

As Vitaly mentions elsewhere in this book, incumbents have a huge challenge. One of the unfortunate truths about working in the corporate world is that on this side of the fence, we try to offer solutions that work for 90% of the population. That makes the most sense; that's where the big money is. The last 10%, however, is served by smaller providers, including startups. The problem is that sometimes the market shifts so fast that suddenly the small solutions are the best ones. When that happens, things can move very quickly. When the 90% dwindles to 80 or 70%, it is panic o'clock in the boardroom. That's what I mean by a Tier-1 problem.

The thing is, you don't have to be a market maker or a clairvoyant to spot the movements of the markets as they happen. One way to stay ahead of the curve is to follow the disruptions and create businesses to shore up the incumbent business. For example, in the years from 2008 to 2011, the adoption of mobile devices created a wee bit of panic in the printing industry. At HP, we created Cloud Print (marketed as HP ePrint at the time), which became the foundation for printing from mobile devices anywhere. I would argue that any startup could have created what we made, but they didn't have the special sauce that we benefitted from in being part of HP. We had direct access to C-level executives of the printing companies who were feeling the pressure from mobile devices. Long story short, the technology is now available in more than 50 million devices. Huge disruptions cause major reshuffling in a sector (sometimes referred to as "wake turbulence"). Keeping a close eye on disruptions as they happen means that you can leverage the strengths and scale of the corporations to further innovate in a space.

At HP, we saw the big moves happening in the smartwatch industry when the Apple Watch hit the market. As a response, we created technology to help popular watch makers like Movado and Titan create their own smartwatch technologies, embeddable into devices that look more traditional than the miniature smartphone approach chosen by Apple and Samsung.

Music, phones and wristwatches have already been upended. Television is going through a big shake-up. Self-driving cars and electric automobiles are going to have an enormous impact on the way we move and commute. All of these changes are forcing large companies to innovate or die.

The key to making intrapreneurship work is similar to how you would get a startup off the ground. Focus, segmentation and careful targeting are they keys to bringing your innovative products to market. Take our smartwatch example. Every major tech player was coming out with a smartwatch and carpet bombing it through all of their distribution channels, so we needed to take a different approach. Instead of loading up the cannons, we reached for a sniper rifle, as it were. For starters, we created products for specific target segments. In the US, for example, we picked "Urban Hipsters." We selected Michael Bastian, a designer who's popular in that particular demographic, to design and brand the watch. Instead of pushing the new products out through the tech press, we announced on Women's Wear Daily (WWD), broadly considered to be the Reuters of Fashion.

By going all-in on fashion and lifestyle press, we ended up with a completely different approach to the market, with launch events in New York and Los Angeles. For distribution, we picked the sample-sale site GILT.com. The results were delightfully refreshing. We produced a limited edition version which sold out in three hours. Production could not keep up with sales throughout the holidays and we ended up with over 1.1 billion impressions and more than 95% positive sentiment on social media. HP's Michael Bastian smartwatch had more media impressions than any other HP product that year. Our experiment was a resounding success and we secured many more collaborations with fashion brands and watch companies the next year. Consider all of this in sharp contrast to the other products, created by mainstream tech companies, marketed the traditional way and available in all popular distribution channels. The main take-away is to be insanely focused on your target segment when you start. Learn, and then grow much like you would with a new startup where this behavior is forced due to constrained resources.

To have success as an intrapreneur, you need to be good politician inside the company. Having a good understanding of organizational culture and dynamics is pivotal to being an intrapreneur. Great ideas can come from anywhere and staying open to great innovations from all angles is crucial. When ideas come top down, there can be magical alignment with armies of resources being allocated to the product and business. Everyone from corporate strategy- armed with charts, graphs and business plans-supply chain, dev and marketing will all march to the same drum beat. You may succeed in delivering a great product but when you fail, you fail miserably... It is like running hard on a treadmill and not going anywhere. HP and Microsoft's foray into Smartphones are examples of this scenario. There are also times when products created with executive epiphanies are totally uninspiring. I'm sure I don't have to list the bland operating systems and me-too tablets/smartphones. Look at any heavily-discounted holiday sale and you will see numerous failed one-hit wonders.

Flipping the script happens too. Bottom-up or democratic innovations happens when a person or group of individuals look at a problem from a human factors point of view. Sometimes, the innovations stem from the skills and resources available, based on what that team can uniquely do. In this scenario, when products/businesses succeed, they change the world by creating a product with passion and a soul. It is usually quite difficult to develop a business plan for these products/businesses. Example of products that fall into this category are Flipboard and Nest.

The biggest successes I've seen, however, are projects where top-down and bottom-up innovation come together. The resources and enthusiasm to commit comes from the top, whereas the passion and product/market fit trickles up from below. Having a strong product manager who can navigate the politics from both sides is the key to success. You'll occasionally find bottom-up projects that fail because the people behind them refuse to adapt to the market realities, just like top-down projects sometimes falter because people fail to see the reality of the big-picture. Communication is usually one of the most important factors, here propagating information through the organization is absolutely critical.

One big element to be aware of is organizational inertia. In my experience, this is by far the biggest challenge when incubating and growing new businesses in a large company. This problem is exacerbated when there are few synergies with the mature businesses and it gets even worse when the new business cannibalizes the mainstream. You'll sometimes find that the corporate, mainstream business has a hammer in its hand and every problem looks like a nail. The propensity of the system to force you to adopt existing processes and technologies relevant to a mature business, to a new idea/startup can be catastrophic. One small but crucial example: In the early days of HP's smartwatch, the Operations/Supply Chain business units kept recruiting traditional PC and Tablet ODM's to build watches. We ultimately went with a real watch assembler, which was of course the right decision, but it is new and can be hard to swallow for the larger, established organization.

Startups will often say that big businesses can't innovate. There's some truth to that, but you can definitely overcome the biggest hurdle of all: the organization's incompatibility with change. Think of it as antibodies: there will be people and business units within the company that will shun the innovations. It can get vicious and deeply political, but it isn't impossible to navigate this path. The best way to overcome organizational inertia and corporate antibodies is to be customer focused above all. Be data and user research-driven on adoption. It takes fearless and open communication with the executives of the company, along with a dose of inclusivity and humility.

Zuckerberg is now running a huge corporation, but Facebook has been able to incorporate the "move fast and break stuff" mantra in to how it does things. Zuckerberg knows that unless Facebook innovates constantly, someone else will innovate them out of existence. That's as true for Facebook as for most other large companies. It will cause a lot of friction if the internal startup starts gobbling up market share from the parent corporation. Ultimately, think of it this way: It is always better to have a subsidiary or spinoff take some of the parent company's market-share than to allow a startup to flank and disrupt your core business.

Part II—Questions to Ask Yourself

Understanding where ideas come from and evaluating them for usefulness is a core part of being a successful entrepreneur. As I mentioned, there are a million ideas for businesses out there, but not all of them are worth pursuing.

For your business idea, start by identifying who your customer is. We'll talk about personas for design later on in this book, but think about it like this: if you were to draw up a portrait of your ideal customer, who would it be? What is the problem you are solving for them, and how are they currently solving that problem?

Next, consider which incumbents are competitors in your space. I don't mean to suggest that you join a corporation to try and change it from within, but it is helpful to have half an eye on the innovation that's being done from within. If your company sufficiently threatens the livelihood of a large corporation, it is possible that this company might be a potential partner further down the line, or maybe even a potential acquirer of your company. Write up a list of who might be well positioned to create your innovation in house.

Similarly to the corporate exercise above, you should be aware of which universities and research institutions are active in your space. Google Scholar and other search engines can help you do some background research here, which might come in handy further down the line. Knowing what the cutting-edge research is in your vertical is useful. More interestingly, though, is knowing who is doing it. Maybe the leading-edge scholars in your field would be potential team members or advisors in a few months.

Part III

From Idea to Product

Once you have a feeling for who the customer might be and what the problem is, and you have an idea for how you can solve the problem, the real fun begins: it's time to start building a product.

Let me kick this section off with a prediction: you will wait too long to launch your product.

"But Vitaly," I hear you complain, "the customer will want it to be perfect!"

It is a completely natural reaction to want perfection in what you do. But not yet. Not for a long time yet, in fact. The problem is this: you might think you know what the customer wants. The customer might tell you what they think they want. But I'll bet you a sizable stack of dollars that they are wrong. And so are you.

Reid Hoffman, one of the earliest PayPal employees, founder of LinkedIn and now a well-respected VC, puts it best: "If you're not embarrassed by the first version of your product, you launched it too late."

Before you reach for the "launch" button, however, there are a few things worth nailing down. You need to figure out who owns your company, put together your cabal of cofounders and recruit your early core team and contractors.

Chapter 7

Equity

The reality of the startup life is that it takes money to pay the bills (including your employees' wages, of course) while the company gets to the point of breaking even on expenses. In many cases startups are "pre-revenue," working on their business model and/or reinvesting every nickel into maximizing growth for years. This is where high-growth tech startups and lifestyle businesses differ significantly. While a restaurant or consulting business has to be profitable quickly and therefore might need a relatively small amount of money to get off the ground, a startup will often need a lot more money to fuel growth before it tips into the black.

Costs include rent on any office space the company needs, the cost of equipment for the people working there, expenses related to materials for prototypes if the product involves hardware, costs for travel to trade shows or to demo the product to potential investors and a lot more. Software licenses, web hosting, outsourced work, marketing: these are all expenses a startup can incur before it has a product ready to show to customers.

This is why founders of startups spend so much time and effort raising money from investors. At first, this money may come from personal savings as well as from family and friends who believe in the founders. Later, bigger amounts can come from angel investors investing their own money and professional venture capitalists managing funds comprised of other people's or institution's money. These investments are done through convertible notes (a type of loan we'll discuss shortly) or by selling partial ownership in the form of shares in the company, also known as equity.

In its most basic form, equity works like this: if there are four founders on your startup team, each of you might own 25% of the company. The specific allocation might vary depending on what each member is contributing to the business. At this point, there is no way of knowing what that means in terms of dollars. The market hasn't had a chance to value your company yet. After showing some results and a need for your product in the market, you may get an investor interested in providing a certain amount of funding to your company in exchange for a certain percentage ownership.

Imagine, for example, that an investor offers to pay $100,000 in exchange for a 10% stake in the company. That means two things. For one, your business is now valued at $1,000,000 ($100,000 is 10% of $1 million). That is its "post-money valuation." It also means that, as new shares were issued in order to raise the capital, you and your fellow founders each now have only a 22.5% share of the business, because you're splitting the remaining 90%. If your company grows as you hope it will, of course, that 90% will end up being worth a lot more than the 100% you were sharing before.

Percentages are a natural way of thinking about company ownership, but as the company matures, that starts making less and less sense. In practice, this exchange is facilitated by issuing and selling shares of stock. When you incorporate the company, your lawyer should help you create a document that authorizes and issues a certain number of shares in the company (say, a million shares). Initially, if we were to use our example of four founders, each would "buy" 225,000 shares for some small value each of maybe $0.001 per share. 100,000 shares stay authorized, but are not yet issued. After you agree to bring in the investor, you can then issue and sell those 100,000 shares to the investor at $1.00 each. There are certain mechanics involved in board approval of authorizing and issuing shares as your company grows, but don't worry about that as part of the first steps.

It is crucial that you work with a legal firm that specializes in startup companies as soon as you begin formalizing the project. You need to make sure you are set up properly to manage eventual investment and have agreements in place between the founding team covering industry standards like vesting. This is covered in greater detail in Chapter 7, but the short version is that you want to ensure that a funding deal doesn't fall apart as a result of the company taking too long to get its house in order.

Most startups will deal with four types of investors. We have already mentioned the first type: friends and family. The next step up from there are so-called angels (working alone) or angel groups (working together) investing their private wealth. If your company outgrows its angel investors, the next step is venture money. Venture capital (VC) firms are professional investors who make a career of buying pieces of startups they think will do well. The fourth kind, accelerators, generally act like a combination of a venture capital firm and a business school. They make bets on teams and projects much earlier than other investors would, but the price of that bet is not low. When they invest (they don't always), accelerators don't provide as much funding as venture capitalists. Instead, they'll take a small portion of equity in your business, usually in the three to ten percent range, in exchange for a relatively small amount of capital (typically in the tens of thousands, but in some cases up to $150,000). They also provide a concentrated education program in the form of mentoring sessions and workshops with industry and subject matter experts. The programs typically last three to six months, and some charge tuition for that rather than providing funding at all.

Different Types of Stock

Your employees and (should your company be listed on the stock market) your public investors will usually be issued common stock in the company. Your investors, on the other hand, will most likely take their equity in the form of preferred stock. Because early investors are taking additional risk, preferred stock comes with certain rights, which you will negotiate at the time of the investment. They might include such things as a representative on the Board of Directors or various forms of protection for the investment. The rights asked for can vary widely, depending on which round of financing you're in, how much funding you're after, and so on.

The sales of preferred stock can come in several rounds of funding efforts, usually called Series A, B, C and so on. There's no hierarchy or relative dollar figures implied by those terms; they're just convenient shorthand. If you are lucky enough to take your company all the way to the public market, all of the preferred shares will convert to common stock, with preferred rights erased, and be treated the same at the initial public offering (IPO).

It has become quite common to do the first few investment rounds as convertible notes. This is a loan instrument that, counter-intuitively, won't be paid back if things go according to plan. After a major round of funding, the note is usually converted into shares of preferred stock, with a discount. In other words, whatever the value of the note is, it buys more than its face value of equivalent stock. This is why, ideally, the note doesn't get paid off; hopefully the company gets valued highly enough that it's better for the investor to convert it to stock. Complicated? Not really, but we'll delve into more details in Chapter 14.

Employee Stock / Stock Options

Other people besides investors who might be granted equity in your business include your founding team. They are the largest (or only) stakeholders to start with, although they will likely not end up that way. Early employees are often compensated with a share of the business, to make up for the fact that startups often can't afford market salaries yet, or (in many cases) any pay at all.

There's a downside to giving employees straight, unencumbered equity, however. Granted, shares are considered income for tax purposes, and their worth is based on the company's "fair market" valuation. After a strong investment round that results in a high valuation, employees could find themselves rich in stock but without enough money to pay the taxes they owe. Not a great situation for anybody concerned.

The more common approach, which avoids the tax issue, is to grant employees stock options instead. Options give employees right to buy shares at a certain price (the strike price). This means if the value of the stock does eventually rise as the company does well, the employees can exercise their options and buy stock at the lower strike price. Generally, employees are required to stay at a company for a certain amount of time before they earn the right to use all their options, becoming vested in a certain percentage per year. The industry standard is a four-year vesting period with a one-year cliff.

This means that employees have to stay with the company for a year, at which point they vest one quarter of their options. After that, they vest the remainder in equal monthly shares.

When employees exercise their options, they now have equity in the form of common stock, worth more on paper than they paid for it. How and when they choose to do that is an area fraught with tax implications. Any employee would do well to consult with a financial professional before making any decision regarding options. Because of their restrictions as compared to the preferred class, the common shares are also valued much lower on paper than the preferred shares in each round.

Determining the amount of equity each employee should receive is a matter of weighing several factors. A company doesn't want to be too free with granting ownership, because it dilutes everyone else's shares. You should balance the risk a particular employee is taking, how much they've sacrificed to take the job, what they're bringing to the role, how long you can expect them to stay and so on. You and your cofounders are taking the biggest risk. After all, it is likely you all quit your other jobs to work on the startup. That should be reflected in your ownership stake in the company. Eventually you'll bring in more management, who will be crucial to the success of the company (if they aren't, why did you hire them?), so you'd expect to grant them a share of the company as part of their compensation packages. As you work your way down the totem pole, more junior employees usually receive much smaller stock options. In many cases the differences from level to level are by orders of magnitude (for example, 1–2% for management versus 0.1% for junior staff).

At this point, you might be wondering where all these stock shares come from in the first place. It's up to your Board of Directors to decide when and whether your company can issue new stock. As mentioned before, the creation of new shares means that every already existing chunk of equity comes to represent a smaller percentage of the whole. The process is known as "dilution." The same number of shares becomes a proportionally smaller part of the company. That's not a bad thing; the plan is for the company to continuing growing and become more valuable. Or, put differently: it's better to own 10% of a $1 billion company than 30% of a $1 million company.

To avoid having to go through the process of creating new shares and diluting everyone's equity for every new hire who's in line to receive stock, companies usually set up a pool of stock options with each round of financing, somewhere in the range of 10% to 20% of the total shares outstanding. They then draw from that options pool to provide options to new employees. If an employee leaves without exercising his or her options, the options go back in the pool. Your lawyers will help you keep track of who owns shares and all of the other attached terms by managing your capitalization table, usually referred to as the company's "cap table." This is one of the first things new investors will ask for to understand the ownership interest in the company and to make sure that the founders and senior team still have enough "skin in the game" to keep them interested in pulling all-nighters to increase the value of the company.

Finally, there's common stock, which is equity owned by the public; this is the kind of shares that are traded on the stock market. Sale of common stock to the public doesn't happen until well into a company's existence, however. A company needs permission from the Securities and Exchange Commission (SEC) to make an Initial Public Offering (IPO), which is a long and tedious process.

The preferred stock that your investors receive generally comes with certain restrictions or investor's rights, which are subject to negotiation. Typically, with each equity round of investment, the lead investor will ask for a seat on the Board of Directors. Directors may find their fiduciary duties at odds with the personal or financial goals of the founders, so board composition is a very sensitive topic to be taken very seriously. Companies can be forced to sell earlier than the founders expected, or management can be replaced altogether. Famously, Mark Zuckerberg managed to keep complete control of the Facebook board before going public. If he didn't have that control, considering the number of risky and controversial decisions he made in Facebook's early days, the board would have likely replaced him with a more experienced CEO.

In some cases, investors can ask for some kind of antidilution protection, which is triggered if stock is later offered at a lower price than what the investors paid. In that case, the investors may have the right to convert their preferred stock to common stock at a ratio greater than 1:1.

Though you don't typically hear about it on TechCrunch, quite often if a company is not performing well but needs money to keep going, a later round of funding might value it lower than an initial round did, usually referred to as a "down round." That would leave first-round investors with equity worth less than what they paid for it. In this case, a new investor might insist on a recapitalization, or a reworking of who owns how much of the company.

Incidentally, the potential for a down round is one reason you don't want your company to be valued too highly in an early round of financing. Enticing as it might be to get the highest price you can as early as you can, an aggressive valuation sets a high bar for later rounds, and if the investors are left disappointed, it can trigger investor protections or simply scare off future investors who otherwise like the company. It can also affect the morale of employees. If, after a new valuation, the company ends up with a share price lower than the employee's strike price, they would stand to lose money if they exercised that part of their compensation. Obviously, that wouldn't be a great incentive for staying at the company.

By this point, you may be wondering how all these percentages and shares get turned into real money. After all, you're not working and starting a business so you can accumulate a lot of paper.

The real pot of gold at the end of the startup rainbow is a "liquidity event." This happens when a company is acquired by a bigger company such as a Facebook, a Google or a Microsoft. The usual way this happens is that the buying company pays cash for all the shares of the startup. That means your stock, no matter what its previous valuation, is now turned into real money at whatever price is negotiated with the acquiring company.

To help smooth the situation around an acquisition, many stock options programs have an acceleration clause. Acceleration is a process in which your employees' stock options get fully vested. This protects them in case the acquiring company doesn't want to retain all the acquired company's employees. In this circumstance, they won't suddenly find that they've wasted all the months they've spent waiting for their options to vest. At the same time, the acquiring company won't want to see all your employees get fully vested and able to exercise their options on the day of acquisition, because that removes a prime incentive to stay with the new company. For these reasons, a common element of a startup employee's contract is double trigger acceleration, which means two things have to happen for them to become fully vested earlier than planned: the company has to be acquired, and the employee has to be laid off without cause within a year after acquisition.

If you're lucky enough to successfully sell the company, as a founder you should be prepared to wear "golden handcuffs" and plan to stick around for several years to "earn out" a big portion of your shares. This is done because, in most cases, the product at the very least has to be transitioned and integrated into the acquiring company, and often a big part of the value being acquired is the knowledge and experience of the team itself.

No matter how big a check the acquiring company writes, not everyone gets rich. The money is distributed according to a hierarchy. First in line are the creditors to whom you owe money. Once your debts are discharged, holders of preferred stock come next. Generally, they have the choice of being repaid the money they invested or having their preferred shares converted to common stock. Some holders of preferred stock might have participation clauses, which means they do both: they get paid back their investment, but also see their shares converted to common stock.

Though selling to a larger company is a more likely outcome, most founders start their startup journey with the goal of building a strong, independent, and industry-leading firm that will endure for decades. In this case, the exit scenario or liquidity event for the company's investors is to sell stock publicly on the stock market after an IPO. At that point, and with the permission of the SEC, your Board of Directors creates new shares to be sold to the public. IPOs often end up setting a share price at a level much higher than any of the existing equity or option owners paid for their shares (or have the right to pay for their shares), as the public essentially places their bets on the continued success of the company. Equity owners can then start selling their stock through the stock market and realize their gains. Their equity has been diluted, but their individual shares can be worth a lot more.

Employees usually have a restriction of a six-month "lock-up" period after the IPO before they can trade their shares publicly. This is done so the company is not competing with its employees to sell shares at the IPO and can raise the maximum amount of money from the public market. There is also the basic principle of supply and demand, where flooding the market with more shares than the public is ready to buy will certainly devalue them.

IPOs are generally only undertaken by relatively established, large, fast-growing companies. In the absence of an IPO, there are a few other ways for employees and investors to sell their stock. There are private or secondary markets in which sophisticated investors can buy stock directly, such as SecondMarket and SharesPost. With the company's permission, equity holders can sell their stock on these markets without the stock being available publicly. However, potential buyers will demand that a company disclose a lot of information about its finances before they will take a chance on its stock. Companies are often reluctant to do so; one of the advantages of being a private company is the ability to keep more of the inner workings of the company a secret to the outside world. Therefore, secondary markets aren't an easy way for employees to liquidate their assets.

A less common approach is for a company to have its own stock auction, in which employees can sell some of their vested stock to outside investors who want a bigger piece of the company. There's also a new approach pioneered by some innovative growth-stage venture capital firms, where the firm directly buys chunks of stock from employees at some very large companies. Both of these approaches occur well into a company's life cycle, and neither of them are ways your equity holders should count on to achieve liquidity.

For the company, these mechanisms provide a pressure relief valve and a way for early employees to get partially cashed out while they are patiently waiting for the stock to be traded publicly or for the company to be acquired for the maximum price.

Whether it's to attract investors or compensate employees, you will almost certainly eventually give away part ownership in your company. You must understand this part of company formation, if for no other reason than that if you are lucky enough to attract professional investors, you will be negotiating with people who have done this numerous times before, while it may be your first. This is where experienced advisors and attorneys can show their value instantly. Equity distribution is just one aspect of the relationship among the members of your founding team, so in Chapter 8, we're going to take a closer look at another important aspect.

Chapter 8

Finding a Cofounder

Quick! Name an example of a successful startup that only has a single founder. Chances are you can't. Even if I'm wrong and a name does bubble to the top, you've stumbled across one of the rare outliers. I started my last company, Keen, by myself, but I probably wouldn't do it again. I was able to raise money, but in retrospect, I wasted a ton of time by being wrong, without even realizing it. I made mistakes on the strategy of the company, on product decisions, and on hiring. A cofounder would have gone a long way towards making things easier.

The early days of a startup are a team sport. You will need someone to bounce ideas off. They will be able to help you carry the burden and to help you keep going. Without support, your chances of making it dwindle rapidly. The pattern for startups is strong in this regard. Without a cofounder, accelerators will put you at the bottom of the pile. Investors won't take your meetings. The question isn't if you need a cofounder; you do. The question is how you find them.

Most founding teams consist of more than one and fewer than five people. Two to three is perfect. As you know, the goal of the startup is to confirm or refute a hypothesis through a series of experiments. Your founding team should have the skills required to design and execute those experiments. Of course, the perfect founding team depends on what your company is trying to do. Getting the user experience right is a crucial part of the experiment. In some companies, you'll need a strong user experience designer as part of the founding team. In other startups (for example, an API-driven company), user experience is almost irrelevant.

As I'll discuss in Chapter 12, it's possible to build a lot of your product with outside help. Keep your founding team focused on the basics. You'll need a founder with domain knowledge and understanding of a customer's pain points. You will also need a cofounder with enough technical knowledge to develop a prototype. That's it.

Freelancers, contractors and agencies go a long way for a lot of things you might need to do early on. Early stage companies can keep things simple. They do not need marketing, design resources, finance people, public relations, human resources or business development roles. It's helpful if the founding team members have experience in one or more of these roles. At the heart of it, you're building a prototype. Once you've built your prototype and proved that you can solve a problem, you can raise some money and hire the people you need. Ignore everything else.

Once you have an idea for what roles you need on your founding team, the hard part begins: finding people to co-found the company with you.

It is possible to co-found a company with friends or family. A word of warning here, though. Lifelong friendships and family ties can be problematic in some circumstances. There will be dynamics at play other than just the business. Imagine that you fall out with your sister-in-law over a business venture that goes wrong. You won't just have to deal with the business fall-out; there are two families that will have an opinion on what happened, causing a huge amount of extra stress. I'm not saying you should never do it. Just make sure that if you do, you go into a cofoundership with those close with you with both eyes open.

In my experience, the best cofounders are people you have worked with before, preferably for a long time. This is one of the key reasons why starting a company straight out of university is a challenge. Studying with somebody and working with somebody is a different experience. The great thing about co-founding a company with coworkers is that you've seen them in different circumstances. You know how they communicate, you know their skill set and you have seen them interact with other teammates. Maybe you've seen them pitch something in a meeting. You have seen their work ethic and ability to perform under pressure. You know whether they are good at solving problems. All of this is important to know about a potential cofounder.

If the coworker and friends and family wells prove to be dry, you're facing an interesting challenge. Of course, it would be possible to found a company with someone you don't know well. For all of the obvious reasons, that's a road fraught with dangers. If you can, try to use your network. Getting an introduction to your future cofounder from someone who knows you both is good. It is far better than striking up a conversation at a cafe with someone over a GitHub sticker on their laptop.

The hardest thing about convincing strangers that your idea is incredible is what we discussed in an Chapter 2: ideas are cheap and abundant. Chances are if you are meeting technical cofounders at a conference, at a meetup, or via a friend, then they too have an incredible idea already in progress.

Ironically, the best way to find a great cofounder is to already have traction. If you don't have a cofounder who can code a prototype of your idea, learn to code and write it yourself. Yes, learning to code takes a while, but it takes less time than you might think, and there are plenty of online courses to help you out. Even if you fail to build a good prototype, it doesn't matter; at least you now have a real example of what it is you are trying to do. In my experience, if your vision for what you're trying to accomplish is strong enough, asking for help is a great way to get a conversation started. You may go through a number of developers before you find someone who can add something to what you're doing, and chances are that when you do find your cofounder, he or she will throw all your code out and rewrite it from scratch anyway, but who cares? At that point, the first part of your mission is complete. You have your cofounder.

When you start having conversations with potential cofounders, there are a number of things worth talking about with them. A lot of the conversations will be to find out whether you're compatible. Chapter 9 will go into more detail about the relationship between cofounders.

Ideally, you need to find someone who agrees with you on some crucial things, such the overall vision and mission of the company. Much more important than agreement, however, is disagreement. You'll have many of those. The crucial thing is how you are able to discuss and handle disagreements. Challenging your assumptions and decisions is one of the cofounder's most important roles. There is a goldilocks ratio there. If your potential cofounder disagrees with everything you say and do, things won't end well. If your potential cofounder agrees with everything you say and do, run away; he or she either doesn't have opinions (which is terrible) or is hiding them from you (which is worse).

Your cofounder should be someone you can trust, who can work well with you and who can compromise from time to time. It also helps if you like and respect each other as people. You're going to be spending a lot of time together. Being able to laugh together and spend time together outside of the startup office is key. Similarly, it's important that you be able to pick a fight. As part of your cofounder screening, discuss something important, vigorously. It'll happen many times in the future, so you may as well try to figure out whether you're able to have it out and still get along.

Skills-wise, you'll want a team of people who complement each other. Write up a list of what you're good at and the skills you're missing for your startup to be successful. It doesn't matter if there is a little bit of overlap, as long as you are able to stay out of each other's way in those areas, but it's paramount that your cofounders fill the gaps in your experience and vice versa.

The criteria vary from person to person, of course, but my key indicator for whether a cofounder relationship is going to work out is whether I think I can learn well from the other person. I look for people whose skills I admire in a particular field and who I feel would be a good teacher. Not because I necessarily need them to teach me their skills, but because I find that great, patient teachers make great cofounders.

There's nothing wrong with doing a trial with your cofounder, by the way. Work together on a smaller project, do a hackathon or volunteer on a project together. Nothing replaces the experience of actually having worked together; if you're going to be tied to this person for the next decade, you can afford a few weeks' delay while you find out whether you're a good match.

Chapter 9

Cofounder Relationships

We've already established that you probably can't found a startup on your own. Now that you've found someone to start a company with, it's going to be smooth sailing, right? Unfortunately, no.

Some people like to compare a co-founding relationship to a marriage. They will explain how, through sickness and in health, through good times and bad, the cofounders will need to trust one another and rely on each other. All of that is true, with one major caveat. In a marriage, if things should go horribly wrong for one of the parties and they feel they cannot continue, there is a legal mechanism that can bring a marriage to an end. No couple goes on a first date thinking about divorce, but it sure is a relief that "until death do you part" isn't the only way to terminate a relationship. For cofounder relationships, things are more complicated than that.

If you paid attention to Chapter 7, you noticed that vesting arrangements are in place to ensure that it's possible to leave a company behind. If you do so before you've vested all your shares, you'll lose the unvested portion of your equity stake. The shares you do keep could prove to be problematic for the company you co-founded further down the line. Early-stage investors typically aren't big fans of shareholders who have a significant stake in a company but are no longer involved. Nonetheless, this scenario isn't that big of a problem.

Things get really complicated when a co-founding team disagrees about the direction of the company. I have seen companies implode over disagreements about key decisions. Imagine there is a fundamental decision that needs to be made, but there are four cofounders with an equal equity split. When the cofounders spend all their time and energy playing Machiavellian games to try to oust each other from the company or building alliances to get their way... let's just say, it isn't pretty. It certainly isn't productive. And while the company is busy ripping itself apart from the inside, competitors who aren't facing these issues are moving ahead at full steam. In fact, cofounder conflicts are often a major reason for startup failure.

Running a startup is incredibly intense; it can include near-space highs and subterranean lows. You need to adapt to brutal amounts of change in a short period of time. Unfortunately, it isn't discussed often, but in my experience, it is relatively rare for the full set of cofounders to stick together until the end of the startup, whether that means a closure or an exit. Numbers from Y Combinator suggest that even in startups conforming to their high bar, 20% will lose a founder along the way.

Earlier in this book, I advised you to take a long hard look at whether the startup life is for you. I hate to go over the same ground again, but much of the same advice applies about your cofounders. Think long and hard about whether the people you're about to start a business with are a good fit with each other and with you. I have a number of friends that I would start a business with in a heartbeat, but that is because I've seen them in action in leadership positions, not because we are friends. The corollary is even more true: I have friends that I love dearly that I would never consider starting a venture with (or hire, for that matter, which is yet another lesson I learned the hard way).

You should know your cofounders very well indeed before you set out on your startup journey. It is crucial that they have your back when the going gets tough. They have to be able to stand the pressure as well as your can. They have to be fantastic communicators. Above all, they have to be honest and open about their dreams, ambitions and goals in life. I believe it's usually better to start a company with people you know well professionally rather than socially (in other words, start a company with coworkers rather than with friends or family).

I'm a strong believer in communicating early and often. It is easy for the co-founding team to keep their heads down and get shit done, especially when the company is in its early stages. That's great, but don't forget to do frequent check-ins, both on day-to-day decisions that are being made and for regular realignment on the overall goals and objectives of the organization. All the early stage companies that I advise or serve as a board director have regular check-in sessions every two weeks or every few months, with the founding team covering the basics. You can get some really good discussions going with a few simple questions. Who are we, what do we do and who do we do it for? What are the assumptions we are making about the market we operate in? Where do we want to be five years from now?

Some of the biggest potential conflicts are around ambitions of the individual cofounders, and the feelings those ambitions evoke. Some cofounders (Steve Wozniak, for example) are happy being "in the shadows," leaving the public work to other cofounders who revel being in the limelight (such as Steve Jobs). Even if this is the case, however, be aware that these ambitions could change. There are plenty of examples of founders who burn out from being at the front lines, but continue delivering great code in the back end, and vice versa.

The broader conversation is that there can only be one CEO of the company. Job titles don't matter much when the company is young, but trust me, that will change as the company gains traction. If two people assume they'll be carrying the CEO crown, things can get nasty. Have these conversations early on and re-visit them regularly to ensure everybody is on the same page.

It is important to avoid the tension that builds up when someone feels they are being treated unfairly for a prolonged period of time. The equity split is a classic point of contention. If there are two or three of you, it might seem most fair to split the company in halves or thirds. That isn't always the case, and in fact, a lot of founders who've founded a company in the past will shy away from equal equity splits. It's a discussion to have up front. If you get stuck, Foundrs.com offers a great tool that can be helpful for determining a possible equity split. I wouldn't necessarily recommend following the tool's advice blindly, but it's certainly a starting point for discussions.

Another thing to plan for is founder salaries. Irrelevant, perhaps, when the company doesn't have any money to pay wages, but what happens when the company raises a big round? If one founder is happy grinding away on ramen noodles and an air mattress while another has a mortgage and a family to support, there could be different expectations for what happens post-fundraising.

Some people never ship code until it's perfect, others let "good enough" be good enough. Some founders are most efficient when they also have a couple of side projects on the go. Some founders have skills that overlap, and end up stepping on each other's toes a lot. Some founders can't take setbacks, while others thrive on them. Some thrive on constructive criticism, while others cannot separate criticism of their work from criticism of them personally. It is obvious that people are different, but it's crucial that the differences between you and your cofounders are compatible, or at least tolerable.

The solution to almost everything about cofounder relationships is communication. Talk about the big challenges you're facing together, how you're going to solve them and how you like to work. Figure out how you're going to work together. I cannot stress how important it is to spend some time on this early in the relationship, and on an ongoing basis.

Even with all of this advice, you might experience a cofounder meltdown as part of your startup career. The groundwork for making sure that this doesn't bring the whole company down is done early on. If the worst happens, the incorporation documents, shareholder's agreements and other legal frameworks you put in place early on will be what helps keep the fallout to a minimum. Get solid legal advice early on. It's a good idea to have a what-if conversation as well. What happens if Anna disagrees with the direction of the business? What happens if Bart should be hit by a bus? What happens if Charlie's mom gets ill and he has to move to Australia to help deal with that?

Communicate early. Communicate often. Keep your fingers crossed that it won't get to the point that lawyers need to pick your company apart and put it back together again, but know this: should it come to that, you'll be far better off having proper documentation in place.

Chapter 10

Building the Core Team— Business, Engineering and Design

You have your idea, and your co-founding team is running at full speed trying to validate it. The next step will probably be to start building your broader team.

As a new startup, one of the things your peers, your family and your friends will judge your success on is how many staff members you have. Especially in Silicon Valley, there are a ton of companies with three or four cofounders, which might not sound that impressive. Perhaps it is tempting to hire a few people to show the world that yes, your startup is real! Resist that temptation. In the early days, the fewer employees, the better. Managing people takes up a lot of time, employees are expensive and the bigger the team, the slower the decisions. I believe in "hiring for pain." Start building your prototypes and get the big questions out there in an effort to get some answers. You'll probably start running into the limits of what your founding team is able to do very quickly. That's OK. You are a small team, after all. When the pain becomes unbearable, it's time to start hiring. Slowly.

The first few hires are particularly important, which makes sense. When you go from three to four people in your startup, that's a 33% increase in the size of the team. This means that the first few employees have a huge influence on your product. Crucially, they also impact the company culture and how things get done. Don't underestimate how important this is. Changing company culture further down the road is incredibly hard. Sam Altman, president of Y Combinator, often emphasizes the importance of this by reminding people that a bad hire early on can be enough to bring down the company completely.

To identify where your startup's gaps are, you'll need a solid grasp on what makes a great product team. It typically consists of at least three roles, often jokingly described as the Hustler, the Hacker and the Hipster.

The Hustler is the (usually outward facing) driving force behind the company. Part product manager, part marketing wizard and part sales maven, the Hustler has comprehensive domain knowledge. He or she has a deep understanding of the product, the customer and the market your product will be operating in. The Hustler will be out there doing customer development to shorten the feedback loop between the technical team and the customers. He or she will be drumming up sales, driving app installs, and signing up test customers to drive early growth for the product. Above all else, the perfect Hustler is a people person who's probably a good talker, but definitely a great listener.

Next is the Hacker, who is the technologist of the team. The Hacker's skill set depends on what type of product you are building. If you're creating hardware, you'll want someone who is comfortable with a soldering iron and embedded code. Creating an iOS app? The Hacker needs to breathe Xcode. In addition to the tool set, the Hacker needs to be able to work fast and think out of the box. This is particularly important in a small startup, as there are probably a dozen different ways to solve almost every challenge you run into. Chances are that the first few runs you have at a problem will turn out to be suboptimal solutions. That is OK, but you don't want to spend any more time than you have to in the experimentation phase. The ideal Hacker is able to flip the switch between rapid prototyping and creating perfect production-ready technology. If you have to pick between one or the other, the choice is easy: you are a startup. Pick speed every time.

An important note about Hackers: get someone who is able to operate particularly well within your team. As impressive as it is to hire a senior engineer from a big company, be sure that he or she can deliver. Especially in large companies, senior engineers quickly become delegators rather than doers. There are people with incredibly impressive resumés who haven't committed a line of code in years. There is a place for that skill set in some companies, but a startup environment might not be it.

The final hero in the startup collectable cards deck is the Hipster, who is the all-important designer with some extra skills. Hiring great designers is incredibly hard, because great design is more than pretty pictures and well-chosen colors. Good designers will pick the right colors and put buttons in the right places. Great design, however, is invisible and is all about understanding the psychology of the customer. Keep this in mind when you are interviewing for your Hipster team members. They should be able to show off what they have designed, but the why behind the design is far more important. Ask them to narrate what the problem set was that they were working to solve in each portfolio project and why they made certain design decisions.

Remember also that design is a multi-disciplinary art form, and few designers are able to cover everything. A user interface designer will probably not be great at designing product packaging, for example. An acclaimed games character designer is probably not the right person to put together a style guide for your web developers.

I know all of this sounds obvious, but I find it is worth mentioning, because a lot of companies make the mistake of thinking, "Oh, we have a designer," and then throwing all design tasks at a single person. When the team is small, it's possible that your design resource is best positioned to do all the design, but don't hesitate to outsource or hire additional talent to deal with more niche aspects of design.

Hustlers, Hackers and Hipsters are stereotypes, here to help illustrate concepts, rather than job descriptions for actual people. If you're hiring a small team, getting three people who have a broad skill set falling roughly into the three H's is a great starting point, but you'll probably soon find that three people is not enough. Maybe your Hustler quickly turns into a full-time salesperson, or perhaps the Hacker is great at developing iOS apps but doesn't have the skills to build the Amazon AWS backend architecture to help keep a scaleable application up and running.

As your company starts growing, you might find that the people who are indispensable in the beginning of the process need to start changing. At the beginning, it is important to have generalists who can wear multiple hats, but plan to bring on specialists as the team grows. The best Android developer you can afford today might be able to build the first few versions of your app, but when your company starts growing rapidly, you might need a slightly different skill set. People who are able to work well independently don't always work well in a bigger team of designers or developers. However, there is no right way of emphasizing the future when you are hiring. There are fantastic engineering managers who have a magic touch when it comes to getting insane amounts of productivity out of teams of developers, but who aren't the best coders themselves. That's not someone you will want on your team from the start, but you might need him or her further down the line.

Having to hire for current business needs or needs you know you will have in the future is a difficult choice. Keep in mind that, more often than not, your staff will surprise you positively. I've experienced more than a few times that a relatively junior developer turned into a complete rockstar down the line, or that a more experienced designer who had never managed people before turned out to be a natural leader. Sometimes it goes the other way, though, so as I mentioned earlier, beware. There is nothing as dangerous as thinking you are getting a top-shelf ninja of epic proportions. It is possible that their skills are woefully out of date, that they haven't kept on top of the current development methodologies or that they are simply not very good coders. It's probably a moot point. Especially when your startup is young and unknown, it's extremely difficult to attract top-shelf talent. If you're on a limited budget, it can be hard to convince people to take a chance on you.

I'm not saying you should settle for mediocre staff, though. Quite the contrary; a so-so team is never going to build a great company. AirBnB famously took six months to hire its first employee. After it started hiring, it only employed two new staff members in its first year.

This is where the founding team becomes your key asset. When you are just starting out, you have an idea and a vision for where you are going. In addition to building a prototype of your product, you'll be doing a lot of pitching to investors. This practice will come in handy for attracting staff, too. As a young startup, you probably won't be able to get the attention of the cream of the crop, much less be able to hire them. Don't let that stop you. The Apples, Googles and Facebooks of the world don't have a monopoly on great talent. In fact, while the big startups you've heard about undoubtedly have a lot of smart people, not all of those people are a great fit in a small startup where you really have to roll up your sleeves and work long hours in constant crunch mode.

So, where do you find your first few team members? The best place to start looking is people you already know. The process, in fact, is very similar to finding your cofounders, except with (slightly) lower stakes. Think about the best engineers you've worked with, the most inspiring salespeople and designers you know and that HR person you were never able to say "no" to. People are far more than their resumés would dictate, and the only way to really cut through all of that is to hire people you've already worked with and trust.

After you've successfully hired your first few team members, tap into their networks for your next few hires. For every new staff member you add to the team, your company's network grows exponentially. It is also worth pointing out that your existing staff's incentives are aligned with your own. They want to work with smart people who get the job done, who are easy to get along with and who deliver high-quality work. This is the reason why a lot of companies have incentives for referrals that result in new team hires. Copy them and put incentives in place. It is worth every penny you pay staff to refer great employees.

As the company gets bigger, hiring gets easier, but finding the right people gets more difficult. You'll need more people, but your founding team's networks will be exhausted. This is why most of the top Silicon Valley companies have recruiters who try to ambush all new employees for their list of contacts. They know that it's a lot easier (and cheaper!) to hire from known referrals than trying to use recruiting agencies. It is also more fruitful than hoping that the pile of resumés they have on their desk results in a great new hire.

Many of the startups I talk to come to me asking what to look for in a great new hire. There are four key parts to this, and if your potential new staff member ticks all four boxes, you're onto a winner. They have to be innovative, able to come up with novel solutions to problems. At really big companies, you can get away with having meetings, creating spreadsheets and giving presentations without getting any real work done, but at a startup, your staff must be able to deliver and make real, tangible progress. They need to inspire something in you and their colleagues. And, perhaps obviously, but worth mentioning, you should want to spend time with them.

The silver bullet to finding the perfect staff members for startups is simple. Even if you've hired people before, chances are that you aren't that good at interviewing people for a role. That's fine, but find ways of compensating for that shortcoming. I believe in giving people a short trial period. Try them out for a day or two. If they make you want to work with them more, you have your answer. If you're thinking, "Well, that was OK, I suppose," you also have your answer. Don't sign on the dotted line unless you're sure. And remember: hire slow, fire fast.

Chapter 11

Prototypes and Minimum Viable Product—An Exercise in Self-Constraint

Throughout this book, I've mentioned a few times that a startup exists to ultimately cease being a startup. That is to say, the mission of a startup is to find a repeatable business model. The way to do this is to come up with a number of hypotheses that address things you are uncertain about with your business, and subsequently design the experiments to prove or disprove your hypotheses. The key to doing this well is to develop great prototypes and minimum viable products (MVPs).

Let's first talk about the MVP. The term "minimum viable product" was coined by Frank Robinson, who was working in the airline industry helping develop new planes for hauling cargo around the skies. A lot of the new craft he worked on turned out to be technical successes, but failed from a business point of view. It turned out that the planes did everything that was asked of them, but that they were asked the wrong questions. It made him wonder whether there might be a better way to develop products. Steve Blank, who developed the customer development methodology, and Eric Ries, who developed the Toyota Production System into a more universal model now known as Lean Startup, both continued to use the term, popularizing it further.

I have a confession to make here. I love the concept of MVPs, but I think it is the worst-named concept floating around in the startup ecosystem today. An MVP is neither a product, nor is it viable. An MVP is the smallest amount of work you can do to prove or refute a hypothesis. The best way to think of an MVP is this: you have a question. What do you have to do to get the answer?

People often get hung up on the "product" part of the MVP name. If you were asked to build an MVP of "a better television set," for example, you'd come up with a ton of different features a television would have to have to be a television, which is fair, but actually building that prototype would get tremendously expensive. It would also probably be the wrong way to go. A better approach would be to ask, "Better for whom?" The challenge in this task is that we all have a relationship with what a television is and a set of preconceived notions of what a television should be able to do. It probably needs a screen, speakers and remote control, right? But what if you were designing a television targeted at users who are hard of hearing? If you were designing a television that needed to be useable in hospitals with high infection risk, would that change the direction of your thought?

To design a great MVP, you must ask very specific questions, ideally with a true/false answer. I recently received a pitch from an early-stage company that was planning to make the sending of very large files (100 GB+) easier; for the sake of this book, let's call them Acme File Corp (AFC). The company founders were mostly engineers. Most of the founders' questions were about technical implementations and pricing. Both of those are fine things to test for, but I had some other reservations about the business.

The best thing you can do as a startup is to fail fast. I don't mean that I want your company to go under, but if you are going to fail, you should do so as quickly as possible. By failing fast, you save yourself a lot of work and hardship and you save your investors a lot of money. Put differently, if your company is going to fail anyway, you may as well ensure it does so in six months, rather than wasting two years of your life. The worst thing you can do is waste your non-refundable lifetime.

Designing your company to fail fast can feel weird, but the goal is to ensure that you are front-loading the hardest questions. In the case of AFC, I didn't think the product was the biggest challenge. File compression is a well-trodden path. Price experimentation is pretty easy and, again, there are a lot of marketers who are able to help here. AFC's real challenge was different. The companies sending enormous data files around are mostly in film production, big data and the backup space. AFC's hypothesis was that the companies who are sending enormous files around wanted to do so at a lower price point than other services, such as IBM's Aspera. At this point, alarm bells went off. I admit that even though I've been steeped in tech for most of my life, I've never heard of Aspera. That's not necessarily a bad thing; a lot of great companies fix niche problems, but it meant that AFC would need to make a very compelling case for who these niches are.

AFC hadn't built a first version of its technology yet, but I asked them to stop developing their product. They had proven enough of the technology that I was satisfied they would be able to deliver. But I had some different questions for them. Does anybody actually send 100 GB+ files? Who are these companies? What is wrong with the current ways of sending files? Why are they sending such big files? How are they currently sending those files? And, for truly enormous files, why aren't they just copying everything to a hard drive and using FedEx to send it to the destination? Sure, it feels low-tech, but shipping hard drives is a tried and tested way of shipping huge quantities of data around. If the file sizes get big enough, it can be faster than sending things over the internet, too. Or, to put it in computer terms: a FedEx truck has terrible latency but incredible bandwidth.

Designing great MVP experiments is hard, but asking the right questions can be even harder. This is one of the reasons I encourage startups to build up some advisor relationships very early in the process. Tech-first entrepreneurs and teams that are heavy on development often fall into the fallacy of, "If the only tool you have is a hammer, every problem looks like a nail." You can't code your way out of every challenge facing your business. Remember that you're not just trying to find a technology solution to a problem; you're trying to resolve all the questions that come up in the course of building a business model. It is sometimes easier for an outsider to spot the biggest challenges in a business, so don't hesitate to ask for a bit of help when creating your hypothesis.

How do you design a great hypothesis? In the case of AFC, there are a number of ways the company can lessen my worries. None of them involve writing much code. Yes, I'm sure IBM's Aspera is a pretty expensive service for sending huge files around the world. Its customers don't necessarily care, however. One of them is Cinema Cloud, which digitally transfer high-quality digital cinema files from a central repository to cinemas. Another is Courthouse Direct, which sends huge volumes of court documents between court houses. Another is PBS, which uses the service to transfer its programming to local affiliates around the US for retransmission. As a layman, I wouldn't have thought that any of those customers were price sensitive, and the question I would have is, "Do the current Aspera customers mind that the service is expensive?" The easiest way to get an answer would be to use IBM's case studies site, track down whoever is in charge of the file transfer between locations and do a customer interview. It is entirely possible that the answer would be, "We have our budgets set, we don't care how much the service costs and we trust IBM." There's an old saying in IT that nobody ever got fired for choosing IBM; if that is what is going on here, then AFC is dead in the water before they've even written a single line of code. No matter how good the product is, its target audience won't switch away from IBM, because nobody is willing to stick their necks out to make the switch to save a few dollars.

When coming up with an MVP to test a question, be open-minded. Dropbox famously launched its product as just a video. The company's question was whether anybody actually wanted anything like its service. 75,000 sign-ups to a "get more information" page gave them the answer: yes, this is a product that people might want. Perfect; this test answered the question without having to commit to building the product.

Another approach to a good MVP is to fake the product. There are many examples of companies creating a so-called "concierge MVP." For example, perhaps you are considering creating a website that gives customers recommendations for clothing they might want to wear based on the clothes they currently have. Building the technology wouldn't be particularly hard, but it would take time. If your question is whether this is something people would be willing to pay for, it is possible to put together a simple website with a payment form. After customers puts all their details in, give them the recommendations manually and charge them. Hiring people to recommend clothing will probably cost you more than you are charging your customers, but that's OK for now; this particular MVP isn't about efficiency, it is about whether or not people are willing to pay. If the answer is "yes," you can hire the coders you need to build out the automated side of the service. If the answer is "no," the interns you had sending out manual recommendations are almost certainly a lot cheaper than hiring a team of programmers to build a product nobody wanted.

You'll probably have seen companies launching in "closed beta," or with a waiting list. Companies do this because they want to create a constriction in the number of people who sign up. Consider the previous example, and you probably understand why. The company in question probably hasn't fully optimized everything about its service yet, or there are manual steps in the process.

Cheating or creating shortcuts is a crucial part of building a startup. If you aren't charging your customers yet, don't worry about integrating with a payment service. If you expect a couple of hundred customers, don't worry about adding password reset functionality; you can always do that manually if you have to. Don't build anything that isn't helping you answer your hypothesis. Yes, it creates a lot of technical debt, and you'll have to resolve these things further down the road, but that's OK, as long as you get the answers you need to make the decisions that are waiting for you.

This is not just true for the business side, of course. Test your market assumptions. Going back to the AFC example, their assumption is that sending huge files will continue to be a problem, but the internet is never going to have less bandwidth. Everything is constantly getting faster, and local internet connections continue to get better. Yes, using FTP for file transfer is an inefficient standard compared to some other solutions, but the rapid development in internet connectivity might just eat up the slack. If it does, does anybody care about efficiency?

On a product level, MVPs are also crucial. Developing new features takes up resources, which means that if you develop feature A, feature B has to wait. How can you be sure that the customer really wants this? Again, fake it if you can. One company I was advising had a few of its customers request to pay by invoice rather than on a credit card. The customers were incredibly loud about it, and the CEO of the company thought he had to let them pay by invoice, because he was dealing with some pretty big-name companies. I recommended they put a "pay on invoice" button on the next payment statement, and measure the number of clicks on the button. It turned out that less than ten percent of the company's customers wanted the feature. The company then raised the prices by 5%, and added a "Pay on invoice on NET 30 terms, but get 5% discount if you pay immediately by credit card" option. It turns out that even the most insistent customers would rather take the credit card deal and take the flak from its own accounting department rather than taking the price increase. Convincing the customers that they wanted to pay by credit card made the customers happier and, as it turned out, saved the development team several weeks of unnecessary work.

The reason I am so passionate about good MVPs and prototyping is that I've felt this pain myself, dedicating resources to fixing problems that the customers didn't have. When I started Keen, I had years of experience in the print industry. I thought I knew exactly what print shop owners needed. They're in the manufacturing business, so the number one thing they need is efficiency, right? It turns out that assumption was incorrect. For a lot of print shops, the thought process isn't in terms of manufacturing, but as a mom-and-pop small business. They care a lot less about efficiency than they care about getting more new customers. This is true even though they would be much more profitable if they were just running their businesses better. If you analyze it, it doesn't make sense, but this is how the industry works.

We took on a huge effort to develop a very sophisticated e-commerce platform that would require our customers to set it up and change the way they do business. There was a lot of reluctance on their part. At a certain point, we decided to just give them what they were asking for and built a marketplace. We essentially took on all aspects of marketing and order processing, while feeding work to local printers that signed up for our system for one reason only: to get new customers. They were happy to pay us as much as 30% commission. We made this course correction several years and millions of dollars' worth of investment too late. The cost of this stubbornness was significant. I believe that if we had played our cards differently, Keen could have been a market leader in a $700B per year market, but instead the company sold to a competitor.

The keys to great prototypes are to be creative and to make sure that your question gets an unambiguous answer. If it doesn't, try a different experiment until you do get a clear answer, even if it isn't the answer you were hoping for.

Chapter 12

Working with Contractors

You've followed my advice on how to find a good cofounder and how to properly manage your cofounder relationship, so you have a great team. However, it's pretty unlikely that you have all the skills you need in your core team, so you'll have to reach a bit further. That's where contractors and freelancers come in.

Let's face it, you're not going kick off your company by hiring in-house counsel or a team of accountants, but that doesn't mean you don't need both roles as part of your company from the start. Finding a good accountant and a solid lawyer are important steps to make sure your finances are in order and your company formation paperwork is rock solid. It's also remarkably handy to have somewhere to turn when legal or financial questions invariably turn up.

Even if you have solid technical skills in house, you'll often find that you aren't able to develop as quickly as you want. Working with contractors, freelancers or agencies is a great way of increasing your company's capacity for getting more things done, but there are a few pitfalls and things to be aware of.

Before you run out and hire the first agency you can find, be aware that the work you get from contractors is only as good as what you're able to manage efficiently. It's also dangerous to outsource work that is core to the business. To understand the distinction, consider that unless your company is specifically in the legal or finance field, lawyers and accountants are auxiliary functions required by your business. If you're a software startup without any software skills in-house, I strongly suggest you hire someone who is able to manage the external relationships. The person managing the teams of contractors will need to be able to determine whether you are getting what you paid for, at the very least, but it is also helpful if they can have an opinion on the quality of the work that is delivered. The most horrendous example I've ever seen of this going wrong was for a software startup with a hardware component. The company was extraordinarily well set up for delivering software, but they trusted an external supplier for their hardware. The company poured almost half a million dollars into the external agency before it finally showed the work in progress to an electronics engineer. Suffice to say that if the first piece of feedback received from an expert is, "Oh my god, who did this?" you're about to hit some rough seas.

Of course, sometimes you do have to trust people to deliver, but I've seen contractors underperform enough times that I now stand by a firm, "Trust, but verify" approach. Whatever you do, don't engage with contractors if you don't have the tools or skills to verify that what they are delivering is of the quality you need.

There are a lot of large development agencies out there, many of whom are well respected. The problem is that some agencies will use their A-team for pitching, but the people actually doing the work are the C-team. If you are engaging with an agency, make sure that the people you were promised will be the ones doing the actual work. Even if you're working with a reputable company, though, there is another big challenge: price. You will be paying a premium for working with a team that is already established and operating like a well-oiled machine. For a lot of startups, hiring a complete dev team just isn't financially viable.

The good news is that you don't necessarily need to. Especially in the early days, it is most efficient to hire contractors who can accelerate what you are already doing, rather than taking on brand new pieces of work. The best things to outsource are discrete tasks or projects. For example, translation from one language to another or creating mock-up designs are great tasks for contractors because they are finite in scope and easy to define.

There are a number of sites that can help you find reputable freelancers to help you out. Upwork.com (which used to be called Odesk or Elance) is a fantastic resource for sourcing freelancers for almost every aspect of the beginning of your business. Copywriting, coding, design work, administrative work, bookkeeping, desk-based research and customer service can be outsourced pretty easily if you just need an extra pair of hands when the going gets tough. I've also often found that using a freelancer for a while in a particular role helps inform what I need a role to be, so it can be a great pre-hiring exercise to find out exactly what you need done in your business.

One thing freelancers are particularly good for is building things that are designed to be thrown away. For example, Chapter 11 discussed the possibility of creating a video MVP. It is unlikely that your founding team has motion graphics or video expertise, but that is where sites like Upwork excel. The same is true for creating a logo for your company, or writing up the first round of marketing copy for your website. Yes, you can probably get in-house people to do a better job further down the road, but remember that you're still committing to dogged determination to answering your early questions; don't waste your time on perfection when "good enough" is good enough. It does mean you acquire some technical debt in the process, but factor it in and worry about that later. Staying focused on answering only what you need to answer right now is helpful.

Contractors usually work to either a specific quote or on an hourly basis. There are advantages and disadvantages with both. If you are working on a fixed price, it is likely that the scope and delivery time of the work is fixed, too. That is great from a budgeting point of view, but in my experience it often means that the quality of the work suffers. See it from the contractor's point of view: if they deliver amazing work, they don't get paid any more than if they deliver mediocre work. On the other hand, there is an incentive to work fast. If you are asking for 10 articles for your website and the contractor is on a fixed price, there is no point in the contractor drawing out the process. The problem, of course, is that it means you have to agree (usually in writing) on a specific scope of what you want. That works great for small, well defined pieces of work ("translate this article into German"), but gets complicated for more nebulous tasks that involve some experimentation. If you specify that payment in an iOS app should be via Apple Pay, but you later discover that your customers don't typically have Apple Pay in their countries, you'll need to change the scope of the work, which often gets expensive.

For early-stage startups, staying as lean and agile as possible is vital. As I will be discussing in more detail in Chapter 24, writing up detailed scopes of what you want is wasted work. You do need to have an idea of what you want your contractors to do, of course, but planning the next three months worth of work in detail isn't the way to get that done. Working on a per-hour basis can be a great way to go with contractors that you trust to deliver high-quality work in a short period of time.

You'll be unsurprised to hear that you can find the best contractors the same way you find the best cofounders and your core team: use your networks. There are a lot of extremely talented contractors floating around the ecosystem, and they are usually easier to find than full-time staff, which makes sense. Unlike your future employees, who may well be happily working along in their existing roles, freelancers have to market themselves, just like any other business. If you can't find contractors via your network, there are a number of sites that help match-make between startups and freelancers. It's a rapidly changing market, so I'm hesitant to make specific recommendations, but ask around or take to your favorite search engine. The perfect contractors are out there.

I'm sometimes asked if it's possible to run a startup entirely on freelancers and outsourced staff, to which the answer is almost always, "No". There are examples of startups that relied heavily on outsourced teams (such as Slack, GitHub and Upwork), but those teams were led by great in-house product managers and CTOs.

One of the things you are creating when you're building a startup is skills. Your team is building up an in-depth knowledge of the industry you are operating in. That domain knowledge is an important part of your competitive advantage. By the nature of your relationship you have with your contractors, you can't prevent them from working for your competitors, which could be a risk. You'll also have heard of companies that are bought mostly for the team in a so-called "aqui-hire." This practice reflects just how valuable a great team is, especially if the team has specific niche knowledge in a particular industry. If you are working on the power of freelancers alone, you'll never build up that level of knowledge in your team, which might hurt the valuation of your company further down the line.

You should also limit the outsourcing of core parts of your business. If you're a hardware startup, you should have hardware skills in house. If you're a software business, you need coders. If you're a publisher, you can probably get away without having people who build printing presses from scratch, but you should at least have editors and talent scouts on the payroll. Either way, you need to ensure that the people leading the effort, at the least, are part of your company. They can, in turn, outsource part of the workload. You can still use contractors to build prototypes or to backfill staff that you haven't hired yet, of course, but the skills that make your company's core intellectual property should be in house in the long run.

I always find that a good measure for whether you should hire resources or outsource them is how you would feel if that freelancer wouldn't be able to work with you in the future. If they walk of the door at the end of the contract with so much knowledge that its loss would be damaging to the company, it's a sign that perhaps it is a role you should have in-house.

A final word of warning: make sure that everything contractors do for you is done under contract. I've seen situations where a freelancer created a website and a logo for a company as a favor, without a contract. As a result, that freelancer technically still owned the copyright to the work. When a potential investor wanted to see the signed contracts where the freelancer handed over the rights for the work done, it put the contractor in a very strong bargaining position. The contractor still owned the logo, and because the company wanted to close its series A quickly, was able to negotiate a 10x higher fee for the signed contract than would have been possible otherwise. It's rare, but it does happen, and it is good to get into the habit of making sure that all work is done under contract. It will save you a lot of headaches further down the road.

Part III—Questions to Ask Yourself

A lot of Part III was about being brutally honest with yourself. You have a great idea, but who is going to help you determine whether the idea can turn into a viable business?

The first exercise should be to take a long, hard and honest look at yourself. Grab a piece of paper and write down what you are great at. What do you know about your chosen industry that not many other people know? Are you a great salesperson? What are your technical skills like? What do you know about the legal issues that affect your business? How good are you at hiring people? In fact, are you much of a people person at all? What do you know about your company's potential competitors? How are your marketing and communication skills? Are you best at creating five-year plans, five-week plans or a plan for the next five hours? How would you do in pitching your company to an investor? Would you be able to pitch your company to a large audience from the stage of a trade show?

The purpose of this exercise is to figure out what your real strengths and weaknesses are. Once you know them, draw up a picture of the exact opposite. If you're an expert coder who is introverted and terrible at interviewing and hiring people, what would a business expert who is extroverted and great at attracting staff look like? Do you know such a person? If not, how could you go about finding them? The idea here, of course, is to build up a picture of your perfect cofounders.

The other thing I'd like you to do is to think about your product and customer. What are your assumptions about your product? How sure are you that those assumptions are correct? Can you think of a way to test your assumptions? What are the biggest risks to your business? How can you test whether these risks are likely to impact your business? Do you know what your customers want you to do to help fix their problems? Are they willing to pay for it? Are you sure? Actually, scrap that. Even if you are 100% sure that your product is the perfect solution to your customer's problem, you should design a MVP and test it anyway. You never know what surprises your customers have in store for you.

One great way of putting the above together is to write up a list of the ten biggest assumptions around your product, market and customers. Run that list past a trusted advisor and see if he or she agrees that these are, indeed, your biggest challenges. Come up with hypotheses around each assumption, and design an MVP that will determine whether your theories are correct. Now, take a look at each MVP; do you have the team in place to execute your experiment? If not, what skills do you need and do you need to hire or find freelancers to complete this?

It's a lot of thinking up front, but trust me: every hour you invest in asking the right questions about this phase of your business will save you a week further down the line.

Part IV

Social Proof

Until this point, your startup has been little but words: ideas spoken in coffee shops, by the water cooler at work and over a couple of beers in the local pub. Perhaps you have some mock-ups and some rough ideas, but let's face it. None of it is real. Yet.

That is about to change dramatically. In Part IV, we are going to look at two forms of social proof. It's only two short chapters, but this is where many companies find they stumble. You're taking the first step beyond your proverbial garage to see whether your idea will survive its first contact with the real world.

It is said that if you can convince others to believe in you, it is a vision; if you cannot, it is a hallucination. The two forms of social proof I'll focus on are both about selling the vision. First, I'll talk about how you can find advisors who can act as a sounding board for your fledgling company. Second, I'll give you some insights into how you can raise your first, albeit tiny, round of funding. If you succeed in both, it is an indicator that you are onto something. Discovering that people are willing to give you money (which is a renewable resource) and time (which isn't) is a milestone worth celebrating, so let's find out how it's done...

Chapter 13

Advisors — The Masters and the Apprentices

One of the main advantages of being part of a vast ecosystem of skills is that you don't have to create your company in a vacuum. There are a lot of people who have skills and experience that you can tap into, and a wealth of information you can use in your favor. And you should take advantage of both. It is a lot cheaper to learn from someone else's mistakes than to learn from your own.

One of the most inimitable things about Silicon Valley is its multiple generations of tech mentors. There are thousands of people who have been there and done that. People who received invaluable advice when they were first starting out are often eager to take what they've learned and pass it on to the next generation of entrepreneurs.

For first-time founders particularly, advisors will play a crucial role. Even if this isn't your first rodeo, don't underestimate the usefulness of advisors. You may have learned a lot from your first venture(s), but things are always changing. New tools are always popping up. Even if you don't need any specific advice, it's likely that you could benefit from having a couple of enthusiastic cheerleaders in your corner. A good advisor can help open doors and advise you on the niche for your new company.

This chapter is mostly about making a meaningful connection with mentors you look up to and who you aspire to learn from. I think it's far more valuable to get advice from advisors who have built companies before and who know what you are going through, than relying solely on industry experts.

I have had many advisors in my time, some who turned into dear friends. They are sounding board for ideas and confidants you can go to when things get tough. Being able to vent and get some advice on what to do is incredibly helpful.

Note that there are different types of advisors, too. Some give advice to the entire company or founding team. Others, you may want to keep to yourself, getting personal advice on how you deal with challenges and setbacks personally, including things such as how to resolve specific matters with your cofounders. I have seen advisors call bullshit on what founders thought was a great idea. As you can imagine, sometimes that turns into a heated argument, and advisors can be wrong like anybody else, but the value of seeing the broader picture, asking the right questions and challenging your assumptions and decisions cannot be understated.

Good advisors or mentors are connected people who can guide you in the way you think about your company and the strategies you pursue. This covers all sorts of topics, including getting investor money, signing up customers and specific, tactical advice on the presentation or sales techniques, etc.

There are many lawyers, accountants and others in the startup ecosystem who are willing to give your company advice. Outside Silicon Valley especially, there are huge machines in place to help startups. Be aware that this machinery doesn't always have your company's best interest at heart. Many of the companies offering help use advice as lead generation for their businesses. That is fair enough; the product they are selling is knowledge, after all.

When you're very early in your startup journey, you're in a challenging position. It is unlikely that your advisors are willing to sit you down to explain what equity is, for example, but you really do need to know. You're well on your way in reading this book, so clearly you're thinking in the right direction.

Just like your cofounders, it is important to interview your advisors to see how you get along with them. The most effective advisors are best seen as extended members of your little startup family. Being able to be frank and honest with them is crucial. The best way to find out is to just get started; run some of your current challenges past a potential advisor, and see what sort of advice you get in return. Look at their past experience and what roles they've had in startups, both as insiders and from the sidelines. Also be on the lookout to see whether they're able to give advice that's helpful to you and your situation. Some advisors will happily talk your ear off about situations they've experienced in the past, but if they're not identical to your challenges (and, let's face it, no two situations are ever the same), the advice might be of limited helpfulness.

After you get up to a certain level, you can draw a lot more advantage from your advisors. A word to the wise, though: don't abuse the advisor relationship. Personally, I operate with a two and a half meeting rule. I'll take two meetings with startups I mentor via accelerators with no strings attached. At the third meeting, we'll talk about what the future relationship is going to be. Most advisors will expect a bit of equity in exchange for offering their time. Having a little bit of skin in the game goes a long way towards ensuring that I'll prioritize returning your phone calls and emails quickly.

The Founder Institute operates a great Founder/Advisor Standard

Template (look for "FAST agreement"). It's a simple agreement setting expectations for how much help the startup is expecting to receive in exchange for how much equity in the company the advisor will receive. Best of all, because it's a fair agreement, it means you don't have to get lawyers involved.

Be aware of advisors who try to negotiate hard for equity or payment. If an advisor is in this to get rich, I'd question his or her motivations. I have a lot more respect for advisors who work with a small number of startups they believe in, and who do it for the right reasons. To find out, just ask them! Ask why they'd be interested in advising your company and what they are hoping to get out of it themselves. A lot of advisors will want to invest in your company. If that's the case for you, it's a particularly good sign; if they believe in your company enough both to get their hands dirty and to put up some cash, it's a very strong signal that they believe in what you're doing.

Remember that part of the reason for using advisors is for their networks, so don't be shy about asking how they can help on that front. If they are golf buddies with half of the VCs in Silicon Valley and play poker with a number of your prospective customers, they might be particularly well suited for your business just for their little black books. Again, not all advisors are fully truthful about how close they are to the people they say they can introduce you to. Ask potential advisors about who else they are advising. I wouldn't necessarily call it a reference, but ask if it's OK to talk to the other companies they work with about them. It's usually fine, and they'll just confirm how much value they got out of the advisor relationship. If that isn't the case, ask yourself why.

Some advisors will ask for cash to help you out, or to be paid for their time. That works for some companies, but I'm generally not a big fan. There's a name for an advisor that charges for their time: a consultant. With that role comes other expectations and requirements. In my opinion, you wouldn't expect to also give a consultant equity.

An important skill to learn is when to engage your advisors. It's no good to only call them when everything is about to explode. Some advisors do enjoy helping to fight fires, but ultimately, you need to get them involved early enough to avoid disasters, not just to recover from them. It's tricky, but you'll get the hang of it. I find that scheduling regular check-ins with advisors is best, even if you have nothing in particular to discuss. In a startup, you'll always have something that's challenging your existence, and I guarantee that on any given day you'll have something on your mind that you could use some additional advice on. It's the nature of running a startup; embrace it, and use the help you have available.

Having said that, advisors, and especially good advisors, are very busy people. They might be reluctant to schedule random coffee sessions with you on a regular basis. If that's the case with your advisors, try going the other direction by scheduling meetings around a very specific topic. "I just want to talk" is easily cancelled as a meeting. "I am thinking of hiring a new VP of engineering and I need your advice to help choose between two great candidates" is a specific topic that is harder to ignore. More importantly, you could send their resumés to your advisor; perhaps they can use their network to find out more about your candidates, or maybe they want to challenge you on whether you really need a VP of engineering. Either way, you're much more likely to have a productive meeting.

If you ever get an advisor that tells you point-blank what to do, possibly even without having taken the time to really grok the full problem, beware. As a founder, you probably already have all the answers. Even the best advisors in the world cannot dream of having the in-depth understanding of your business that you do. You do this twenty-four hours per day, seven days per week. The best advisors are coaches who are able to ask the best questions. Some of the most inspired advisory sessions I've ever had, I never actually offered advice. By asking a lot of questions and digging deep into the issue at hand, I was able to help the founders of the company reach their own conclusions. That's the real power of an advisor; as a sparring partner and well-informed third party, a great advisor can unlock your full potential and decision-making power.

One final word of advice: sometimes, your advisors will let you down. Maybe a conversation wasn't as helpful as you had hoped, or perhaps they weren't as well prepared for a meeting as you had hoped. Or perhaps they said they would do something, but failed to deliver on time. It happens because we're all busy people, but don't let it fester. Advisors are grownups; they've seen it all happen before and because they have a small stake in your company, they should care passionately about how you are doing. Sometimes they can take on too much work, advising too many companies. It's happened to me in the past, with advisors I've worked with. If that happens to you, don't be shy about pointing it out to your advisors. They, too, are human, and will be grateful to be reminded of their commitments. Sometimes, a friendly nudge is all it takes!

Just like your team and cofounder shares, advisors' shares should be placed on a vesting schedule. This is typically over a two or four year period. Advisors become more valuable when they can see the changes happening in the business over a period of time. Ensuring that an advisor's shares vest over time ensures that your advisors stay committed to helping you on an ongoing basis. Just like with cofounders, if it turns out an advisor doesn't work out or decides not to stay involved for whatever reason, it means that there is a mechanism for ensuring that the advisor doesn't end up with an unduly large share of the company.

Of course, once you've been through the mill a few times, it's your turn. Towards the end of this book, we'll talk about how you can take what you've learned, and turn yourself into a great advisor.

Chapter 14

Your First Funding—
Friends, Family and Fools

As you starting to spool up your startup, you're probably going to need a cash injection. Even if you, your cofounders and your early staff are willing to work for free to begin with, there'll be costs involved with building your first prototypes, travel and so on.

Occasionally, cofounders opt to "buy into" the company they are founding as a way to put some money in the coffers, in proportion with their ownership stake. I think that's a very bad idea, because it gets in the way of vesting. If one of the founders doesn't work out and wants to leave, but does not vest any of his or her shares and doesn't get the buy-in money back, you'll spend a lot of time and resources figuring out how to extract a founder. It's hard enough to lose a founder as it is. Don't mix money into it. Technically, there are ways of doing this, but I usually advise founders against it. If you invest all your money

133

and all your time into the company, the level of stress involved with the company failing is likely to impair your decision making powers.

You should have some clarity about how much you need to raise before you start hitting up people for cash. Having a specific fundraising goal is helpful for tracking progress. The best way to set a goal is to think hard about the worst case scenario of how long it will take you to cross a specific milestone, such as a beta version of the app or a specific MVP. Clearly define your milestone, calculate how long it will take you to get there and how much it will cost to do it. Add a 50-75% contingency on top, and don't forget what happens next: when your first funding runs out, you either need to be cashflow positive (which is unlikely) or have raised your next round of funding. Raising a proper seed round takes time, so don't get caught out. The CEO has two main jobs that no one else can do: hire the best people he or she can find to join the team and make sure the company doesn't run out of money.

You've probably already taken your own savings and put them in your startup pot, alongside your energy, blood, sweat and tears. Assuming you know people who have some spare cash sitting around, it is not very hard to raise money from your friends and family. Tell them what you are trying to accomplish, and ask them for money. What is hard is ensuring that both sides are completely clear on what that means and setting expectations to ensure you don't ruin a good relationship in the process.

So what can you do? As the old gag goes: raise from the three F's—Friends, Family and Fools. There's something to that. Before your company has built anything, there's nothing to verify whether the team is working. Not only do you not have product/market fit yet, you have no real way of knowing whether you will ever get that far. As such, the only people willing to invest are those who share your blood, your closest friends and, well, fools. At that point, they are investing in you personally, because they have faith in you, your skill in building a team and your vision for what your company might turn into.

It is possible to reach out to angel investors at this point, but honestly, unless you've already run a few businesses, I wouldn't waste your time. Angels who might be investing at this early stage usually fall into one of the F's discussed above. The reasoning is that professional investors aren't going to hand out money for charity or because you have a pretty face. They want a chance at getting a return on their investment. Without at least some progress or traction, there's very little data with which to make an investment decision.

The best type of investor to be looking for is always so-called "smart money." If you have the choice to take $5,000 from someone who can be an advisor, make introductions or has knowledge about the industry you are in and someone who just puts in the money, the former is obviously more valuable. At this stage, that is nice to have. It is better to be able to turn to your investors when you run into issues you'd like some help with, but if you can't, don't worry too much about it.

On the one hand, friends and family don't tend to be particularly sophisticated investors, so they may not be asking the hard questions that a professional investor would. But they also often don't understand what they are getting themselves into. As a result, it could create tensions. The vast majority of startups fail, and it is hard enough to deal with that, without also having to tell your best friend that the $20,000 they invested is now gone and that they are not going to get it back.

The most important thing, in my opinion, is complete honesty with the people you are raising money from. Even sophisticated angel investors typically won't be doing the same level of due diligence at this stage as they'd be likely to do with their usual investments. Show them the stats for how many companies fail. Explain that even though you will be doing your best, it is possible, maybe even likely, that this venture will fail. Remind them to not invest money in early-stage startups that they cannot afford to lose. And, most importantly, don't do a hard sell. Both as part of your startup journey and in life in general, you're going to need some good friends and close family to make it out the other side in one piece, and your relationships are worth more than a few thousand dollars of investment cash.

Make it very clear to your early investors that they are investing in your venture, not in you personally. It is easy to fall into a miscommunication trap here. You might think that your debt is forgiven if your company fails, but that might cause some tension at the next family gathering, when your uncle is asking, "So, about that money...." Even if there were clear agreements in place, family (and some friends) can be funny about loans and money, so make doubly sure that you've made it explicit that if your endeavor fails, the investment is gone. Or isn't gone, if you choose; if you want to personally guarantee a loan, that's a bad idea, but up to you. Just make sure there cannot possibly be any misunderstandings on this front.

You might find that friends and family are more eager to invest when there have been some recent high-publicity IPOs in the market. That should be a warning sign, and an opportunity to continue setting expectations. 75% of companies don't survive for five years, but that doesn't mean that the remaining 25% produce swathes of billionaires. There are a large number of companies that limp past the five-year mark before failing, or who achieve a relatively modest exit that means the investors get some or all of their money back.

When you are presenting your idea to your friends and family, treat it like a meeting with any professional investor. You will pitch your business a lot going forward, so you may as well put together a simple 10-slide deck now and get some pitch practice in. The focus of the questions from your early investors will be different than the questions you get from professional investors, but even complete outsiders will often have valid questions. I've been in pitch meetings where a profoundly "stupid" question actually caused a breakthrough in the mind of the founders. Having to re-explain a part of the business can be extremely valuable and help you gain a deeper understanding of your own plans. Either way, your earliest investors will appreciate being treated as "real" investors before the investment takes place, and being kept in the loop further down the line.

I mentioned "Fools" earlier, as a joke, but there are people who don't fall in the Friends and Family categories who might still want to invest, such as friends of the family, friends of friends or someone who is interested in what you are up to. I've heard some horror stories on this front, such as a startup founder who accepted a modest investment from an ex-boss. When the startup failed, the founder later heard that the ex-boss was spreading some extremely unpleasant rumors as a result. The warning here is that if you are accepting money on little more than a handshake, ensure that you know who you are accepting investments from. You don't want to later find that you are leaving a string of scorned people behind.

You'll occasionally come across a family member or friend who has done a bit of reading about startup investing, or who has seen too many episodes of Shark Tank, and who wants to over-engineer a deal. It's great that they want to be better informed, but the truth is that there won't be a lot of information to share with them at this point. In particular, if your early investors hint that they want a say in how the money is spent in your startup, walk away. They should be rewarded for having faith in you and your idea before anybody else, but in terms of complexity, the investment should feel more like a favor (on both sides) than a business deal.

Always put the deal in writing, and give your early investors good terms even if they wouldn't think to ask for them. A lawyer should put together the deal terms, both for peace of mind and because you'll want the paperwork for due diligence for other investors later. Early investors will likely invest using a convertible note, mostly because this sidesteps the discussion around valuing the company. Putting a value on a company is hard enough when there is data to take into account; before there is any, it's practically impossible. Don't waste your time engaging in a pointless discussion on that front. The other good thing about this particular investment instrument is that a good startup lawyer can throw together a convertible note in his or her sleep, making it cheaper than most other types of deals.

We'll get more into accelerators later in this book, but they are another group of investors to be careful with. A select number of accelerators are worth it, but others aren't. While the likes of Y Combinator, TechStars and 500 Startups are the Ivy League of accelerators, many are simply good at marketing themselves while providing little actual value. Worse, some fly-by-night accelerators will invest a small amount of money at arduous terms, pair you up with a poor advisor and leave you to figure it all out yourself anyway.

I know that this chapter is filled with doom and gloom, and I wish there was a way I could make it seem more optimistic. The truth is that the vast majority of early-stage startups lose their money and I've seen families and friendships hurt as a result. I do want to highlight that this rarely happens as a result of the company failing, however. It always is because the up-front communication wasn't good enough.

Let me end on a high note, however: there are many great reasons to invest in a friend's business. It certainly worked out for Eduardo Saverin, for example, who put some money into his friend Mark Zuckerberg's startup. If, as an investor, you go in with eyes open, you can learn a lot by investing in startups. The excitement is real, and while your investment doesn't automatically buy time or the right to advise the founding team, you did invest with a friend, and there are many opportunities to have great conversations about how a company is growing and blooming into a real business. I've learned as much from the companies I've invested in and the ones I'm advising as they've learned from me. Being part of the marathon, even just cheering on from the sidelines with a little bit of skin in the game, is exhilarating!

Part IV—Questions to Ask Yourself

Picking the right advisors is an exercise in self-awareness. The very best ones can amplify your strengths and help you work around your weaknesses. Your advisors will quickly suss out what your skills and deficiencies are, but are you aware of them yourself?

Take a deep look at your skill set and the skill set of your wider co-founding team. You've already mapped out what you are good at and what their superpowers are. Now it is time to revisit that, but from a whole-team point of view. When you do this exercise, pay attention to the different parts of the business separately. Do you know everything about your market? How good is your team at designing and executing MVPs? Do you have the necessary contacts to help you raise investment funds? Are you likely to need advice on hiring? Operations? Legal? Finance? When you have a good idea of where the gaps in your team are, use this as a guide for what to look for in your advisors, but bear in mind that some advice (especially early legal and financial) are services you can pay for.

With fundraising, the exercise is to put together an early deck. Chapter 30 covers this in more detail, but for now, focus on the questions rather than the answers. What are the unknowns and uncertainties you have around your startup? Those are the things you need to have answered. In effect, the money you are raising at this stage is to figure out whether you can get the company to a place where you're ready to raise more money. Staged financing is what separates scalable startups from traditional lifestyle businesses.

When you know the questions, it's time to build a timeline for how long you think it will take you and your team to get the answers. The timeline plus a simple budget will give you a goal for how much money you need to scrape together in your friends and family round. With a fundraising goal, it's time to get your founding team together and see whether you think it's realistic to raise that much money from your network. If it isn't, see if there's a way to get your answers for less money, or figure out whether there are other ways to raise money.

Good luck! Signing up your first advisors and raising your first money is a fantastically exciting phase of starting a business. This is where a lot of the learning to date comes together.

Part V

*Everything You Need to Know
About Accelerators*

I named this book Accelerated Startup because I believe that accelerators are an incredibly useful springboard for startups. You don't have to participate in one to have a successful startup, but there is a lot to be said for not stumbling over the basics. Business schools have their place, but for those choosing the startup career path, I think accelerators are the best way to learn.

Your accelerator experience will be incredibly intense. You'll learn faster than you ever thought possible. You'll come to some profound realizations about your business. You'll make friends for life. And ultimately, being part of an accelerator shifts the odds of success for your business. Before you dive in, your chances of success are one in a thousand. By the time you reach your last slide at your demo day at the end of your accelerator experience, those odds have shifted to one in a hundred. Your team will be stronger and more focused, your company will be more investable and hopefully you'll be able to steer clear of some of the big roadblocks all companies face.

In Part V we will take a look at what accelerators and incubators are. I'll guide you through the application process, and I'll give you the inside scoop on what you need to pay attention to in your application to maximize your chances of getting noticed.

When you finally do get accepted into the accelerator, throw a party and pat yourself on your back. And then strap yourself in for the ride of a lifetime. Accelerators are a rollercoaster, and those few weeks you'll be spending with your accelerator batch will zoom by. It's easy to suddenly realize it's almost over, so to make sure you make the most out of your accelerator or incubator experience, Part V will close with some tips on how to milk it for all it's worth.

Chapter 15

The Accelerator/Incubator Explosion—
The Good, the Bad and the Ugly

'm always surprised by how often the terms "accelerator" and "incubator" are used as if they were interchangeable. They are very different. An accelerator program usually has a fixed term and takes a minority stake in startups participating in the accelerator. An accelerator has a curriculum to help founders find their path through common issues and challenges (much like this book, in fact). They will commonly invest a small amount of money, typically just enough to ensure that the founding team doesn't have to live in a van down by the river or starve to death during the accelerator experience. The real strengths of good accelerators are the mentor pools and alumni networks that startups have access to during and after the program.

An incubator, on the other hand, typically doesn't have a fixed term. An incubator is often an experiment inside of a larger organization comprised of an autonomous group of smart people playing with ideas.

They would then spin out into a new company if the business looks promising.

The incubator model turned up in the mid 1990s, in the form of Idealab. Concepts were developed in-house or brought into the fold. The successful concepts were "graduated" into the real world as standalone businesses. Combining strong ideas and a solid start with an experienced operational team meant that many of these companies had an advantage in the world of startups. Rocket Internet, started by the three Samwear brother in Germany, turbocharged this model, taking over many hot regions around the world with e-commerce arbitrage and business model copycats in a few short years.

Y Combinator opened its doors on its first accelerator in 2005. Techstars followed in its footsteps the year after. Between them, they pioneered the accelerator model which soon produced a number of big hits, including Dropbox, Airbnb and SendGrid. Eager to participate in the goldrush in the following decade, hundreds of accelerator programs have popped up, of wildly varying qualities. F6s estimates there are now over 1,800 accelerator programs around the world.

Just like applying to a business school, you must do your research into the programs you are considering. Unfortunately, not all accelerators or incubators are what they seem. There are plenty of stories of promising startups who, led on by bad advice, wasted a lot of money running in the wrong direction. You would be unsurprised to learn that getting the wrong advice early in the life of a startup could be the beginning of the end.

As you know, quantity and quality are very different beasts. There is no shortage of accelerators, but that does not mean that it's easy to find one that is perfect for what you or your company needs. The vast majority of accelerators don't mean any harm, but an accelerator cannot run on good intentions alone. Some of them are being run by teams that have zero experience in running or investing in tech companies.

Top-tier programs receive thousands of applications for each batch. They have the luxury of being more selective than Harvard and Stanford's MBA programs. The flipside is that the other accelerators are fallbacks by definition. That doesn't mean you shouldn't consider other accelerators, however, especially if there are accelerators that focus specifically on your particular niche. For example, if you are operating in the quantified self or fitness space, the Nike accelerator might unlock opportunities you wouldn't otherwise be able to access. There are accelerators focusing on finance tech, health tech, media tech, marketing tech, advertising tech and much more. You might consider a lesser-known accelerator if its unique selling point is access to a large number of early customers because of its industry ties, or if it has access to mentors that are particularly suitable for your business. Be careful, do your research and definitely talk to people who've been through the accelerator in the past.

To understand why accelerators exist, follow the money. From the accelerator's point of view, it is able to do some serious spread-betting among promising young companies. The accelerators will usually take between 3% and 15% of a company's equity, which, when you think about it, is a clever strategy. Imagine if you could own 7% of most of the most promising startups coming out of an area. Most of those companies will fail, but as the accelerator, you can increase their odds by teaching them best practices and connecting them with experienced mentors. The companies that don't fail will bring a small return on investment. And then there will be the 1% of startups that turn into billion-dollar companies, which make it all worthwhile. Starting with a 7% chunk ownership of a number of unicorns adds up quickly, although to be fair, that 7% will be diluted significantly by the time the companies reach an exit event.

By understanding the accelerators' business model, you can also understand why it is so important to put all your eggs into the top-tier-accelerator basket. As an investor, are you going to go to every single accelerator demo day? Probably not. Would you miss a Y Combinator, 500 Startups or TechStars demo day? Hell no! This is true for many layers of the startup ecosystem. It is more prestigious to be a mentor at the best accelerators. It is easier to invest in companies that have had expert advice. For journalists, seeing that a company has been in one of the big accelerators ticks another box as to whether or not they will read a press release.

I'm not saying that it is a complete waste to be in an accelerator that isn't in the top five, but be aware that as you are comparing higher-end accelerators, the accelerator experiences get exponentially better.

Whichever accelerator you end up choosing, be sure to read the small print they put in front of you carefully. Most accelerators wouldn't make you sign anything unduly arduous; as we discussed previously, the accelerator model is only successful if the startups grow and thrive once they leave the accelerator. Having said that, your startup has to live with whatever equity deals it signs for the life of the company. Understanding what you sign is important.

The first data point worth looking at is the valuation. This is often where you'll find the first surprise, as valuations at an accelerator level tend to be extremely low. Y Combinator, for example, is at the high end of what's common. It currently invests $120,000 for 7% equity in participating startups, which works out to a $1.6 million pre-money valuation. As I said, that is at the high end—I've seen as bad as $15,000 in cash and $50,000 in "services" for 15%. That works out to a valuation of $500,000, which is nothing to write home about. Looking at accelerator deals on paper, then, should give you pause. If you're doing it just for the money, it honestly isn't worth it. Of course, accelerators typically also add value beyond money. Most accelerators offer office space, internet connectivity, social mixers and other events in addition to the structured program and mentoring. As such, you need to think about the non-monetary advantages of being in an accelerator.

Put in purely financial terms: if you think your company is worth $3 million today and you are looking to raise at that valuation, a $200,000 investment at 6% ownership would value the company at roughly $3.1 million pre-money. If an accelerator comes along, offering you a deal of $50,000 for 6%, it is short-changing you to the tune of $150,000. It makes financial sense to be part of that accelerator only if you think it will supply with more than $150,000 worth of intangible value in addition to the $50,000 it is investing into the business. If these numbers seem confusing; don't worry, we'll cover fundraising and the slightly counter-intuitive math that comes with it in a later chapter. Some accelerators are genuinely worth that much. Others are not. Choose wisely.

Your advisors will come in handy for helping evaluate the deal from an accelerator. You don't want to sign on the dotted line if the structure of the investment means that you become less attractive to other investors in the future. This might become the case if the accelerator insists on strange clauses as part of its investment. Deal standards tend to change all the time, so I can't give an exhaustive list of things to look out for, but your startup or legal advisors should be able to flag anything that worries them.

Some of the things to consider are pro-rata investment rights or beyond, which is often in accelerator agreements. This would give the accelerator rights to participate in future financings to preserve their percentage of ownership and sometimes the ability to increase their stake via warrants. Some also demand approval rights, usually in the form of a veto right in the case of certain decisions, such as selling the company. In some cases, these additional rights might make sense for a short period of time (say, until the company has raised a Series A). As I said: think carefully, and ensure you understand everything about the deal you are signing before you sign.

It's also worth considering the opportunity cost of being part of an accelerator. It takes time and effort to work your way through the accelerator program. The majority of companies report that the time and equity invested into an accelerator was worth it, but that isn't true for every company. For example, if you have investors lining up around the block, it may not be worth "giving away" a chunk of equity to an accelerator, if you can get significantly more money for the same amount of equity. If, as in the previous example, you're able to raise $150,000 more for the same proportion of your company, consider how much advice $150,000 could buy you. You know your own strengths, weaknesses and roadmap best. Personally, I think if you're given the opportunity to be part of a top-tier accelerator, you should grasp it with both hands. The biggest risk is not knowing what you don't know.

You should also research what happens once the accelerator program finishes. Some accelerators give you access to a powerful alumni network of mentors and fellow startups. These networks can help you raise money, get advice, recruit staff and much more. Much like when you graduate from business school, a good alumni network is a gift that keeps on giving and can be worth as much as the accelerator experience itself.

Chapter 16

What Top Accelerators Look For

Getting accepted by an accelerator is like getting into a top business school. It requires advance preparation, some demonstrated accomplishment, the potential for future accomplishment and success, a strong application, doing well in an interview and more. In fact, getting into a top-tier accelerator is nothing like getting into a business school; it is far harder.

There are hundreds of accelerators and incubators of various quality, with various business models, with locations in just about every major city. The world's top four accelerators are Y Combinator (Silicon Valley), TechStars (New York, London, Austin, Boston, Boulder, Chicago, Seattle and growing), 500 Startups (Mountain View and San Francisco), and Seedcamp (London); they each receive thousands of applications for their 3–5-month programs that take place several times each year. These programs each have a demanding application process and accept fewer than three percent of applicants.

By contrast, in 2016, Harvard accepted six percent of its applicants and Stanford five percent.

It's difficult, but it's not impossible, any more than getting into Harvard or Stanford is. But you need an understanding of what an accelerator is looking for and a plan for making sure you offer it. That goes beyond the quality of the product or service your startup offers.

The accelerator's selection committee usually consists of partners and mentors. They are the ladies and gentlemen you need to convince that your product solves a problem, and that the problem is worth solving in a large and growing market. They need to be on board that your product or service solves the problem in an obviously differentiated way, and, perhaps most importantly, that your team is the best group of people to take on the task.

The key to getting this right is storytelling. Think specifically about who you are telling the story to. Think like a consumer to help you figure out how you would "sell" your product. Most importantly, remember that the problem you're really trying to solve isn't just a technological one, though it may be partly that. It's not an appearance or interface one, though the interface is certainly part of a what makes a product successful. It's what the technology and the interface lets your customers do that is important. Be prepared to show that the number of people who want to do what your product lets them do is increasing, and discuss how that desire is not being met.

The problem can't be trivial, either. There's nothing wrong with a new game or a new smartphone shopping app. True, there's no shortage of them, but that doesn't mean a new one can't be a successful product. But you're trying to get the selection committee excited about your product, and showing that you address a meaningful problem is one way to do that.

In addition, focus on the ways your product is innovative rather than an incremental improvement on what's already available. Again, a "same but better" product can find success in the marketplace, but it's not the kind of pitch that will stand out in the application process.

You also want the selection committee to be excited about your team's ability to address the problem. Part of that is making sure you have a strong, balanced team behind your startup. Accelerators accept solo applicants only on rare occasions, and they are also wary of teams that are too large. Having more than three to five founders on your team suggests a lack of focus. It also raises the possibility that equity has already been distributed so extensively that the founding team will quickly get diluted past the point of caring much about the company.

More important than having the right size, however, is having a good balance of skills. You need someone with the domain knowledge to properly analyze your product's niche in the marketplace. Along those lines, there's no substitute for a team member having hands-on experience with the problem you are setting out to solve—experience gives a clear advantage over another average smart person. This will also likely be someone with marketing expertise, who can lay out how the business can scale, what kind of sales figures you can expect, how you're going to achieve them and so on.

You need a designer who can build a good interface, too. Remember that the engineering team often cares less about what the user experience is like, but that's a mistake. Jef Raskin, who started the Apple Macintosh project before famously being ousted by Steve Jobs, put it, "As far as the customer is concerned, the interface is the product." Today's consumers expect easy-to-use software that improves their lives. These same expectations are now infecting even the business world with the "consumerization of the enterprise." The impression your product makes in the first few seconds will be critical. This is especially true for mobile apps, where a user typically decides to keep an app or unceremoniously delete it in the first 30 seconds or less. Trust me, whether or not the app has a beautifully engineered database plays no role in that decision.

Perhaps most importantly, you need engineering expertise. At least one member (and preferably more than one) needs to be able to answer questions about how the product can be built and iterated in response to mentor or customer feedback. Accelerator sessions are short, so part of what they look for is a team that does a lot of work on their product in that limited amount of time. The last thing an accelerator wants to see is a team reach the end of the session with an idea that's still not ready for prime time. In fact, the top accelerators will expect you to have at least a first version live along with some initial customer feedback that confirms the market for the product and your initial unit cost projections. You need to convince them that your team has the engineering chops to quickly iterate the product based on customer feedback and guidance from mentors. They will only very rarely consider an applicant without engineers as part of the founding team.

Remember, you will be in a highly competitive environment, fighting for a place in an accelerator batch. Spots are limited, so you don't just have to be good. You have to be better than the other applicants. The other teams are all smart, and they're all convinced of the value of their product. After you've convinced the selection committee that there's a problem waiting to be solved, you need to also convince them that you're better than any other group of smart people at solving the problem.

If it's too early to rely on customer feedback, revenue or growth numbers to make your case, almost the entire evaluation comes down to the team. Your only tangible differentiator may be that one or more team members (hopefully on the product or engineering side) have worked in a related field or on a similar product. This experience indicates some familiarity with what's required to make a product successful in general. A track record of work at high-profile tech companies and/or time spent at highly regarded educational institutions likewise goes a long way toward convincing an accelerator that you're a group that can deliver the goods.

A lot of your competitors will already have their product ready to demo; others will already have some funding. Are you already testing your product? Do you have users? You have to be prepared to show that you have a real, realizable product that will work and that people will buy. Accelerators want to see that your group already has traction, or some signs of a foothold in the market. Building, testing, prototyping, beta testing, collecting user feedback: all of these elements will show that your group actually has something worth investing in. Even a solo founder has been known to get in if he or she, for instance, built a beta site, attracted users, and got positive customer feedback.

Don't lose touch with your passion; it is what will keep you going when you have more tough days than easy ones. That's part of what accelerators are looking for. You're asking them to take a chance on you, so that is where your story becomes crucial again. Convey that you think you're worth taking a chance on. If you don't believe that, why should they?

Remember what drove you to want to start a company in the first place, that itch that makes people want to create and own something, and let that come through in your presentations, no matter how many times it takes. The world of actual business is no more forgiving than the world of accelerators, so whatever you go through in this stage will prove useful later.

Chapter 17

The Application and the Interview

When you're thinking about applying to an accelerator, it's a good idea to start building relationships with people already connected with it. In my opinion, the biggest benefit you will gain from the accelerator program is the invaluable experience and feedback of its mentors. Accelerators publish a list of mentors on their websites as a top indicator of quality. Approach some of the mentors in advance, especially if they come from fields related to the one you're working in, to get advice and guidance on what the reviewers will be looking for in an application. You can do the same thing with the founders of companies the accelerator has accepted and funded in the past. Do your own reference checks with mentors and previous batch participants just like you will be vetted for fit once you make it to the interview stage of the process. Determine if the assistance provided and results meet your expectations. You should also have a firm understanding of the type of deals each accelerator offers, such as what percentage of ownership they will ask for in your company and whether their program provides funding in addition to advice; some even ask for tuition. You should not "over-engineer" the deal, especially at this early stage, but you should be well aware of current market standards.

If you can build these relationships as you develop your product, make a point of keeping your connections in the loop on improvements you make or how you modify your business model or marketing plan. Getting ready for an accelerator program is an iterative process, much like being in the program. If mentors show interest in your project, let them know how you're taking their advice or what kinds of traction you can show. In both cases, once you've established a relationship, ask a mentor or founder to write a letter of recommendation for your team that you can include with your application. It's one more way the process resembles applying to college.

Your application will usually include a video. It is said that most job interviews are decided in the first 15 seconds. If you're selected, the accelerator staff and mentors will spend many hours with you. Your video serves as a taste of what's to come, and is the fastest way for the accelerator staff to get to know you and get a sense of how you communicate. Many mentors, myself included, start the review by reading the company's tweet-length description and watching the video. For most applicants, that's the end of the review. I can't overemphasize the importance of these two elements; distilling your company into a tweet and creating a great video is hard, but it's worth doing well.

The video should feature your founding team explaining the reason for your product, the problem it solves and why yours is the best solution. The reviewers will be looking for a sense of your team's personality, will want to see how well you work together and see the passion you have for your product. Write a script of what you're going to say and rehearse until you're satisfied that your video communicates the drive that led you to follow the startup path in the first place.

At the same time, keep the video punchy and short. Use simple colloquial language and eliminate the technical, industry and business school textbook jargon. The reviewers don't have a lot of time to spend on your application. They're likely to be looking at a hundred or more each day. The old performer's advice is applicable here: give them enough to want more. Your goal is to make the reviewers like you enough to want to form a partnership with you. If they want more, they know what they need to do: accept you into the program.

If you make it to the interview stage, your odds of being accepted will be somewhere between one in five and one in three, depending on the individual accelerator program. Everything having to do with an accelerator is, as the name suggests, accelerated. When it comes to the interview, you will not have a lot of time to present your case (usually 10 to 30 minutes). As with your video, you want to make a succinct presentation of what your business is about in direct, easy-to-understand terms. You want to show the ability to stay focused throughout this process. A rambling presentation will raise doubts about your ability to focus on what you need to do to get your product ready for market. Make sure you rehearse what you want to say before the big day, and test drive your pitch with friendly investors or experienced friends as much as possible.

Part of demonstrating focus is being specific. What customer need are you addressing? How does your product help? To that end, avoid buzzwords and mission-statement-style sentences. Don't say, "We want to increase people's access to expert information about pet health," say, "Our product lets pet owners ask veterinarians questions 24/7."

It's a good idea for as many members of your founding team to show up for the interview as possible. Your video has stoked their curiosity about you, and now they want to meet you. Don't disappoint them. Answer any questions directly and succinctly. Don't handwave or try to sidestep a question, and don't pretend to know something you don't. It won't work. What you want to demonstrate is that you're ready and willing to work hard as part of the accelerator. Show that by working hard on your presentation.

Be prepared to lay out your competitive advantage and unique value proposition from the consumer's point of view. Your technology on its own, impressive and novel as it might be, isn't going to get you into the program. Remember, all those hundreds of other applicants are smart and have strong technology. They, too, passed the first screening, after all. Don't just talk about how your product offers more features than the competition, or how your team has more impressive resumes. Being incrementally better isn't going to make the breakthrough impression that you need. You don't get into Harvard or Stanford just by having better grades than most of the other applicants. You need to do something else to stand out from the crowd. Be surprising. That's what catches people's attention and sticks with them.

At the same time, you have to show humility and a willingness to be coached. You're not just applying for funding; you're applying to be mentored in developing your product into something that the accelerator considers worth funding now and angel investors and venture capitalists will want to fund after program completion. Crucially, you need to show that you're open to criticism and prepared to make however many iterations are necessary, quickly, to meet expectations and to help accelerate your company.

Part of the way you show this is to talk about your user feedback. Customers or testers have told you what they like and don't like about your product, and what they think is missing. Be honest about what you've learned—and even better, talk about how you have addressed it. That shows that you're not rigid in your concepts. You want to strike a balance between confidence and coachability.

Remember, too, that you'll be discussing your viability as a company, not just your individual products. Be prepared to outline your initial thoughts on possible business models, distribution strategy and growth plans. Who and what are the potential market for your product? Who are your competitors? How do you plan to beat them? Why are the dominant players in the market already in that position, and what will encourage your customers to choose your product instead? Do your homework on the value of startups with your team makeup, at your stage, in your region, with a similar market/business model. Gain as much expertise as you can on the various ways startups are funded. (This book will take you a long way.) Understand the typical deal offered by the accelerators you are applying for and make sure you are OK with it. If the interviewers ask you for a valuation for your company, be prepared, honest and realistic.

Getting into a top accelerator is difficult and the vast majority of applicants don't make it. Nevertheless, it's important to keep your confidence up. You might not get in on your first attempt, but that's okay. Remember any time in the interview that drew a raised eyebrow or skeptical look. If you've managed to capture the interest of the accelerator, they'll likely invite you to pitch them again. Keep iterating your product based on customer feedback, experiment with business models and user/customer acquisition and measure absolutely everything.

Chapter 18

Making the Most of Your Accelerator Experience

Being accepted into an accelerator program is a great milestone. You had to work hard to get your startup to the point that an accelerator was willing to consider you. You then had to work even harder to put together a fantastic application. Guess what? That was nothing compared to what's going to happen next. To get the most out of your accelerator experience, you should expect to do very little other than work on your startup. And yet, there are things you can do to ensure you get the most out of your accelerator experience.

Remember that the acceleration program will take three to six months. That doesn't sound like a lot of time, but when you're in the middle of it, it will really fly by. Everybody is going to be busy, but that's no excuse to miss out on some of the most valuable parts of the program: the things that aren't the program.

Before you enter the accelerator, it's helpful if you have a clear goal of what you want to accomplish. Do you want to double your number of users? Raise money? Launch a product? Get your list of goals in order and work towards them relentlessly.

Remember that an accelerator is so named for a reason. The program kickoff is just the beginning of the roller coaster ride. This usually isn't the time for aiming for perfection. Build prototypes, throw them away and build new ones. Sign up test customers and don't be afraid to make changes that would alienate those customers. Design the simplest MVPs possible and get your answers quickly. If there is any way to do something faster while you're in the accelerator, do it. Take shortcuts, build simple prototypes and focus on measurable goals. If you're not growing during an accelerator, it's a sign that something has gone seriously awry.

Beware of information overload from mentors, too. Especially in the early days of the program, when you get paired up with your mentors, you will get a huge amount of information and opinions. That is great, but remember that every mentor sees the world through his or her own lens. Some are eager to offer advice before they've fully understood the business they are advising on. Either way, your startup will probably experience "mentor whiplash," which is an abundance of help and advice that can sometimes be conflicting and counterproductive.

Remember that the mentors are there for a reason. They are probably very good at what they do. Listen with an open mind and try to see things from their perspective. Take in all the information that is thrown your way, then distill it into actionable advice. There's a careful balancing act here. Don't reject everything out of hand, but also don't bend over backwards to do everything a mentor tells you. No matter how much time you spend with your mentors, remember that you know your business best, so absorb the advice and implement the things that seem to align the best with the short-term goals you've set for the accelerator.

When you're in the thick of it, the demo day at the end of the accelerator experience will be on the mind of a lot of the startups. It's true that the demo day is important, but a good pitch is rarely enough to raise investment once the accelerator draws to a close. Traction, above everything, is what will get the investors to sit up and listen. Give them what they want by focusing on your metrics. Figure out what numbers will truly represent whether or not your company is being successful, then focus on those. If you fumble your demo day pitch but your numbers are good, you have a far better chance at raising investment than if your pitch is perfect, but your company has seen only modest growth during the accelerator program.

The single most important thing about your accelerator experience will be networking. You are among a group of people who have been carefully curated. Your fellow companies, the mentors and the crew operating the accelerator are all there to help each other. Don't hesitate to ask anybody for feedback.

The other thing to keep in mind here is what I told you back in Part III. You will get to know the people who are in your accelerator pretty well. Make a point of getting to know as many as possible. You wouldn't believe how valuable this network will prove to be over the years. Your team may be limited in cash but rich in certain skills you can offer to others as barter for things you need but can't afford to hire out at the moment. One startup up may have a great designer and the other a database expert; you can often scratch each other's backs.

You're going into the accelerator knowing that most of the companies won't make it; that's just a fact of life. However, the people who participate are all smart, driven and entrepreneurial. More than a few co-founding teams met each other at accelerators when they were working on other startups, and there is no shortage of examples of a startup imploding, but its team immediately getting absorbed into other startups who are in a rapid growth phase. Being remembered as someone smart, driven and helpful can't hurt when you're part of a startup ecosystem.

If your goal for the accelerator is to raise money, you'll be doing your research about potential investors (more about that in Part VIII). If there are investors who you think are a particularly good fit with your product and market segment, start building the relationship early, and ensure they are invited along to the demo day.

Part V—Questions to Ask Yourself

However you twist and turn it, being part of an accelerator is almost exclusively about storytelling. Your application, your interview and ultimately the demo day are about having a well-spun narrative to go with your startup idea.

First, get your elevator pitch nailed down. In 30 seconds, what problem does your company solve? Who does it solve this problem for? How will it reach its customers, and how will it make money? Of course, you're not going to need your elevator pitch for the interview or application process (although some do want a tweet-length pitch). Perfecting your elevator pitch will help express what your company is and does, and trust me—you will be explaining that to hundreds, if not thousands, of people over the next few months.

Next, try to figure out what you would do if you were accepted into an accelerator. Imagine your life six months from now; what five milestones have you hit? If you could only accomplish two of those milestones, which ones would they be? What help would you need in order to nail those two? What would have to happen to hit even just the most important milestone? What this exercise is meant to do is to tease out what's important to you and your company.

Look at your cofounders and the broader team. What are your knowledge and skills gaps? What are the most important things that you hope you can turn to others for? One final thought: if you aren't accepted into an accelerator, how would you still be able to draw some of the benefits from it? Can you work in a coworking space? Could you recruit some top-shelf advisors? Previously, you created a list of things you wanted to accomplish in the next six months. Sure, the accelerator would make it easier/faster, but how would you go about smashing those targets regardless?

Part VI

*Design Is the Product
and The Technology Core*

Today, consumers and businesses are met with increasing choices for products and services. Their attention spans, and therefore the time available to make an impression, are shrinking rapidly.

It is still possible to find products out there that are terribly designed and difficult to use. Bear in mind, however, that those are few, far between and rapidly dwindling in number. Ensuring that your products are designed well is not a luxury. In today's market, it is simply the price of admission to be able to compete and have any chance of standing out in the market.

You might be unsurprised to hear that without technology, tech entrepreneurship does not exist. This goes deeper than just the products themselves. Technology envelops everything you do in business. Picking the correct tools goes beyond just choosing the right development platform. All your business operations, including production, distribution, support, accounting and marketing, include aspects of technology. To succeed, you and your entire workforce need to be tech-first workers who are able to choose the right tools to make the day-to-day work of your fledgling company as efficient as possible.

More often than not, ideas and initiatives for a new product come from those who would not typically describe themselves as technologists. As we discussed earlier in this book, that makes sense: pure tech problems are exposed to the people who can solve the problems all the time. There are big wins to be had in areas where expertise is less common, but the professionals experiencing the problems might be less equipped technically to be able to jump in and create products. Part VI will provide core knowledge on the psychology behind design, design principles, marketing basics, how to manage the design process and how to use technology to turn designs into products.

Chapter 19

Design Disciplines

A **lot of what we used** to think of as design is about pretty colors and fonts that go well together, but over the past decade, we've come a long way towards determining what design is and what it is for. If you think "design" and your mind's eye automatically goes to a box of crayons and a few sheets of paper, we have a lot of work to do in this chapter.

Today, "design'" covers almost all aspects of a product, and many different specialist fields of design (usually done by people with different skill sets) will become crucial to the success of your startup. That isn't to say that "design" is a new thing, but to my embarrassment, the startup world has been lagging behind on this front for a long time. Design is in everything around you. It shapes how you live your life and how you interact with objects. Having a good understanding of why things are designed the way they are can be a huge advantage to a startup team.

Take something as simple as a door handle on a shop, for example.

If you pull a door, only to spot a sign that says "Push," you might feel pretty stupid for having tried to move the door the wrong way. I would argue that you shouldn't. If a door looks like it ought to be pulled, but cannot be opened that way, it is a design flaw, and an easily solved one, at that. Instead of a handle, the designers could have put a flat plate on the door. As a functioning human being, you would instinctively realize there is no way of pulling a flat metal plate, and you wouldn't even attempt it. You'd push, because that would be the only way to interact with that particular piece of hardware, and the door would open. Through thoughtful design, your life was made ever so slightly easier.

If this sort of design thinking gets you excited, I warmly recommend The Design of Everyday Things. Published in 1988, it is still as relevant today as it was then. Written by cognitive scientist and usability engineer Donald Norman, it's one of those books that completely changes how you see the world around you. It's well worth a read.

Great interaction design results in products that are extremely easy to use. For simple devices, you won't need a manual, because it can only really be operated in one way. For example, it is difficult to hold an axe by the wrong end. It is also true for more advanced devices. Think about it this way: the remote control for an Apple TV has a small handful of buttons, and our TV remote probably has dozens of buttons. Which one of them is easier to use? The difference is all in the design of the user interface and the devices you interact with to access that user interface.

I once had a conversation with someone who designed the user interface for banking ATMs. Apparently her company spent 18 months of experimentation to find out where the keypad should go, how high the screen should be and what the display should look like. Another thing worth considering: when you take money out of the machine, should you be given your money or your card back first? Her team did a lot of work on this, and discovered that the answer was about people's intent. If you want people to take both their card and their money at the end of the transaction, give them their card back first. Why? Because, as the scientists discovered, if they are able to take their money and run off, leaving their card in the machine, they just might. It is a fair assumption that people are at the machine to get cash. That is what the machine is for, after all. As such, they will not walk off before they have received their money.

You will run into examples of great (and terrible) design every day of your life. Invest a little bit of your time into paying attention to design, and it will make you a far better product creator, too.

Products that are easy to use makes us feel good. We feel smarter because we somehow instinctively knew how to use the products. We are able to accomplish the tasks we want to accomplish, which results in a small release of dopamine. If you've ever walked into a hotel room that is poorly designed, you know what I mean. Having to search around for the light switch is frustrating and unnecessary. In a well-designed room, you see a light mounted on the wall, and you should instinctively be able to determine where the light switch should be.

Why am I going on and on about light switches and door handles? Because great design is an area where startups often get things wrong. If they had to choose, your customers would probably pick an ugly product that was easy to use over a beautiful product that was difficult to use. The thing is, your customers rarely have to choose. If your product confuses them, they'll close your app and never look at it again. If the product looks like it was put together by amateurs, it doesn't matter how good it is under the hood. As consumers, we are comprehensively spoiled by great design all around us. Your users will know the difference between good and bad design. Don't scare them away by falling on the "bad" side of that equation.

It's important to be careful here; yes, both interaction design and creating good user experiences are important. You also need products that look good and are dependable. I know that can sound at odds with being as fast as possible, but remember that you need to clearly identify what it is you are testing. When you are in the MVP or rapid prototyping stage, don't worry about making things look pretty. In fact, you should go the other way. Do your user interface testing with simple wireframes to prevent the people you test with from getting hung up on graphic design. More importantly: wireframes are super cheap to build and quick to change, so you can iterate much faster than by having to change and deploy code ahead of another test.

If how pretty the interface looks is irrelevant to the thing you are testing, then don't do any graphic design on it. It will take a little bit of time to explain to your test audience that the design phase is still to come, but at least people won't get distracted by half-finished designs. A lot of testing can be done with wireframes, where the functionality is abstracted away from how the app looks.

There are a few other types of design to be aware of as well, often on the technical side. Systems, database, process and logistics design are all design functions usually performed by your operational or development teams, not by the people you would traditionally think of as "designers."

The point I am trying to make is that your company is its design. Your products, too, are design. Your team is design. How can I be so certain? Nothing you do in a startup is done by accident. Everything that happens is the result of a decision at some level, either by your founding team or by your wider team. You've chosen who to accept money from, you've decided what your logo looks like, you've picked a name that reflects what you stand for and where you are based. Because all of these things are part of your overall vision for the company, that vision has to be based on something. If you have a powerful vision that permeates throughout your company, that is a function of your design for your company. Because of this, I always encourage young companies to spend a fair bit of time thinking consciously about what the message is they are projecting into the world. Design the mission for your company carefully, because it will set the tone for everything you do.

It is not urgently necessary at the beginning of your company, but at some point you're going to want to spend some time thinking about a design language, which is the way that you communicate consistently with your customers. This is often an aspect of design overlooked even by pretty big companies, but I think it is getting more and more important. Think about it this way: when you see Apple packaging, most Apple products, the Apple store, Apple's website and most of Apple's apps, they all have something in common. It might be tricky to put your finger on it, but it's there, infused in everything Apple does; something about the way things are designed makes them "feel" like Apple. In other words, Apple has been able to make a design language that is strong enough that something feels like an Apple product without even having an Apple logo on it. Car companies also tend to do this really well. Occasionally, you'll see a car you've never seen before. "That's a strange-looking Mercedes," you might think, and you will probably be correct about who manufactured the car. Why? Because Mercedes has been successful in creating a very distinct style for everything it does.

I should mention that Apple and Mercedes have probably spent billions of dollars on building up their respective brands to the point that their logos are almost superfluous, but there are a few far smaller companies that do very well on this front, too. Mailchimp is a great example. Let's face it, nobody is going to get excited about the deliverability and ease of use of email newsletters, and yet, that is precisely what Mailchimp has been able to build its business around. A slightly silly brand and a goofy logo helped it stand out early on, and it is continuing to help with its brand recognition. Today, it is the market leader in newsletters, which is extremely impressive. What is more impressive to me, however, is that you can read almost any piece of text on their website, and it is obvious that it's Mailchimp. The company realized that the distribution of language is at its heart. A strong brand and design language reinforces everything it does whenever it communicates with its customers.

To help identify what you should focus on, ask the question, "What is my thing?" Zappos and Virgin chose insanely good customer service as their "thing," and both have built a comprehensive brand and design language around that. IKEA has a similarly powerful brand, built all around value-for-money. Go into an IKEA store and count the ways it reinforces that particular message, up to and including selling subsidized food in its cafe. IKEA is so desperate to tell you what a fantastic deal you are getting that it has designed its entire existence around its price tags. Guess what? It's working.

A quick word of warning: you can't fake design, or add it as a thin veneer to make your products seem like something they are not. Adding leather seats and a coat of red paint to a Hyundai does not make it look like a Ferrari. The design decisions that resulted in a Hyundai Sonata were made many years before the designers picked the final colors for the car.

In other words, the design of your products need to come from within. One last example of what not to do: In the US, Volkswagen had an advertising campaign hunting on the slogan "Fahrvergnügen"—a German word meaning the joy of driving. That campaign can only be successful if everything about the brand reinforces the message. This includes the design of the dealerships, the literature with information about the car, the website, the car's instruction manuals and, of course, the cars themselves. The reason the campaign eventually failed was pretty obvious. For one thing, nobody was able to pronounce that word, but more importantly, while I'm sure that Volkswagen makes perfectly acceptable cars, they were never a brand that made me think, "Oh, wow, the joy of driving." The cars, with the exception of the very high-end models, are too sensible for that. Compare that with a

BMW M3, Porsche 911 or Tesla Model S. Those three are cars with a lot more joy-of-driving, but they built up those reputations based on actions, not words.

Chapter 20

User Experience 101

You **may have had a** friend at school who had "that" car. "Of course you can borrow my car," they'd say. "It works great! Except when you want to fill the gas, you have to push this panel, then give that part a kick and use a screwdriver to open the filler cap." To your fellow student, the gas cap works. Anyone else would scratch their head and conclude that it's broken. The interaction between your hand, foot, a screw driver and the gas cap is complicated, inelegant user experience design (UX).

If you spent any time around engineers, you soon learn that many of them are fantastic at coming up with incredibly innovative solutions to a problem. They see connections where most people don't. They're able to create features and functionality out of thin air. They're able to create software and hardware that works... for some definition of "works." Much like the gas cap example above, software cannot just "work." Today, when customers have a tremendous number of choices to solve every one of their problems, you can't have a product that is configured via the text command line interface. Your customers don't want to edit preference text files. Your users will simply leave if the first step of a "Mac compatible" piece of software is "Use Boot Camp and install Windows." You laugh, but I've seen all of these examples. The founders were baffled why nobody wanted to use their software.

I don't want to belittle the entire field of engineering here. By and large, I couldn't do what they do. But it is definitely true that sometimes, something that "works" for the engineer that built it doesn't work for anybody else. By paying close attention to UX, you can sidestep a lot of these challenges.

I've already quote Jef Raskin previously, but it is worth repeating, "As far as the customer is concerned, the experience is the product." That is so true that I encourage you to read that sentence out loud a few times. Let it sink in. Make it your mantra.

As we discussed back in Chapter 4, few things are as annoying as feeling stupid or "old" when you are using a product that is meant to solve a problem. Once you've rage-quit an app a few times, are you likely to go back for more punishment? Of course not.

At the risk of sounding like a fanboy, one example of a company that has taken UX to the next level is Apple. They often get a lot of criticism for removing features from their products. When the iPod first launched, for example, it was missing a number of features that were found on contemporary players. Apple correctly identified the real problem with its MP3-playing peers: it was too difficult to obtain music and load it into your MP3 player. Instead of just launching a pretty MP3 player, the company took a deeper dive into the problem. It already had its popular iTunes music player. By adding a hardware player and a music store to the mix, it was onto a winner.

I'm not saying that if you are planning to launch a portable music player, you also need to invest billions of dollars in negotiating record company contracts, of course. What is important, however, is seeing the end-to-end use case for your customers from their point of view.

Take 3D printing, for example. This is an area where I often see pitches along the lines of, "There are 60 million normal printers in the US, but only one million 3D printers. That means there is a huge opportunity here." There is a profound fallacy there, mostly around user experience. Anyone who can type an email can create something that can be printed on a home printer. The same is not at all true for 3D printing, so far.

There is no shortage of 3D printers being offered, but there are still relatively few people who own them. I think I know the reason. It isn't that 3D printers themselves are that much harder to use than, say, a laser printer. The problem is that that designing objects in three dimensions is a genuinely hard skill to learn. Open up Microsoft Word for the first time and you can probably figure out how to type and print a letter. Open up AutoCAD for the first time, and... well, good luck. If you have $1,000, you can buy a 3D printer. The learning curve that comes with having to create things to print, however, is astonishing, and is creating some interesting challenges for the home use market. I'm seeing a lot of changes coming down the pipeline, however, and this could finally be in the process of changing.

And maybe it is OK that it's comparatively difficult to design in 3D. There is still a space in the market for 3D printers. Their existence has completely revolutionized product design, for example. But the key here is that 3D printers have revolutionized the work life of people who were already working in 3D, not for people who haven't had to figure out what the Z axis is for.

The two takeaways from this are that if you are looking to start a business in the 3D space, don't create another printer. Create a way to make it easier for laypeople to use a 3D printer. The other point is that user experience is crucial enough that failing to pay attention to it has wing-clipped the entire 3D printing industry.

Okay, now that I have explained why great UX is crucial, how can you apply these lessons to your own company?

GOLOMB

Creating Great User Personas

The statement "Make a better television" is absurd without considering why you are making a better television. The first thing to consider is who your users are. Many businesses do this by creating a set of user personas for their potential customers. A persona is a caricature that stereotypes a particular type or class of customer. Eventually, you get to know these personas really well, as if they are real people. This is important, because it helps focus design decisions on particular user segment. Most products will need four or five user personas that are quite different, with a number of various needs, wants and limitations.

You might have Harry, the 43 year old architect who is red/green colorblind and slightly dyslexic. You may have Britney, the 19 year old honor-roll student who refuses to read anything on screen and who has a two-minute attention span. You may have Anna, who is a software engineer at a large bank in Sweden; she is cash rich but time poor, only ever uses the web on mobile and doesn't speak English very well. And there's Terry, a 76 year old retiree who used to work at a competitor's company, but now runs a successful blog focusing on your exact subject matter. I make no secret of loving user personas. I always recommend creating them as part of a team exercise; this adds color. Add seemingly irrelevant details: "Harry drives a silver Ford Mustang. Anna collects staplers. Terry used to be an Olympic marksman." This is meant to be a lot of fun. The more memorable your personas are, the more useful they become as a tool. I suggest having posters designed of your personas and hanging them on the wall, along with a photo or illustration of them.

The details of each individual persona don't really matter that much, as long as they are memorable. Fun fact: I cannot hear the name "Sigourney" without thinking of one of the personas we created for a business I advised. The individual personas need to be different from each other. Different ages, genders, life experiences, income, physical limitations, technology skills, etc. The reason for this is when the time comes to design your user experience, you can go through a particular interaction several different times. It means it becomes easy to say things like, "Hey, we are relying on color in this design, and Harry wouldn't be able to use it properly. Can we do that differently? How about shapes?" or "Why does our interface rely on language? Could we also use icons? That would make it a little easier for Anna and Britney."

Be Clear and Unambiguous

Personas are a great tool to remind you of certain types of users, but the basic theory that underpins all of this is to put your customers first. You need to think about the contexts in which they use your app. If your product is designed for desktop use, remember that it's hard to drag and drop things on a mobile app. If you expect customers to control a piece of hardware via an app, what happens if the phone's battery is dead? Can you still adjust, or at least turn off, the hardware?

The principle here is dangerously close to Murphy's Law: anything that can go wrong, will go wrong. As a designer, then, your job is to ensure that the customer has as few opportunities to screw up as possible. Some software developers "solve" this by having a comprehensive first-run (or "onboarding") experience to help point out anything a customer needs to know when the software is first run. That can work, but has downsides, too. It's also not something you'd expect to see in, say, an Apple app. For Apple, the design philosophy appears to be, "If we have to explain it to customers, we shouldn't have it at all." That massively reduces the number of features you can put in a product. On the other hand, it does make the products much easier to use. It makes the products fun to use. It makes customers feel good about themselves. Good design means that form should never get in the way of function.

Which, in fact, does bring us back to the first point I made in this chapter. To serve your customers, you need to know them. You need to understand them. You cannot hope to make something that makes someone happy without understanding what drives them. There is no way of knowing whether your customers are happy without asking them. The key to great UX design is to create a tight feedback loop. Before you let a single line of code be written, find out who you are solving a problem for. Come up with an idea for how you would solve the problem, and then test it on your users. Wireframes or simple whiteboard sketches are the cheapest and easiest way of doing that—don't get too fancy. Once you have the user flow (which is the actions a user takes in your product) ready, pass it to design. Here, you are making the functional design prettier. Test it again. If it still works, it's time to start coding it and releasing it to your customers. The final step is to measure what happens. Do customers achieve their goals more frequently? Do people come back to the app more often? Ask them if they're happy, why they're happy (or not happy) and what they would change.

Measuring, in particular, is a key part of UX. You may be able to ask a couple of dozen people what they think of something, but there is a problem with just asking people: they don't always know what they want. Or if they do, they might be terribly poor at putting it into words. People telling you what they think about a product or feature is helpful, but their feedback will, to a degree, be tainted by their own experiences and worldview. If you are able to measure exactly what people are doing exactly, you can see the effects of a change in design. For example, imagine that your goal is for users to sign up for a newsletter. If, after a change, the sign up rate drops from 3.1% to 2.8%, roll it back and try something else.

If all of that sounds work intensive, you are correct. It is. But the crucial thing to keep in mind is that you are working on a tight budget and an even tighter deadline. It is so much cheaper to get feedback early and often than releasing a product that doesn't do what your customers were expecting. You can catch around 85% of user experience problems by testing with just five different users. The real question isn't whether you can afford to. It is if you can afford not to.

Chapter 21

Naming, Branding and Psychographics

f you've made it this far into the book, chances are you have already picked a name for your next venture. However, I still think we should take a closer look at the importance of names, branding and the psychological impact of your communication to your target audience.

In the long run, I believe that what your company is named has very little impact on your success, but when the company is new, it makes a difference. In Forrest Gump, there's a scene where Forrest admits he never has to worry about money again, because he has invested his money in "some kind of fruit company." The joke is that the Apple Computers logo very briefly flashes up on screen. The underlying gag isn't a joke: Apple is such a well-known company that very few would even think about fruit anymore when they think "Apple." Same with Cisco. Today, it is synonymous with network hardware, but when it was founded, the name was an inside joke. The company was based in San Francisco, and the company named itself after the city. The logo is the biggest hint; the arch is meant to depict the towers of the Golden Gate Bridge.

Have you ever played the game where you say a word over and over and over again until it starts sounding weird? Try it. Say "sofa" or "knife" or "road" many times for a few minutes. At some point, you stop being sure whether you're saying the word right; it just loses its meaning. That's what has happened to Cisco, Apple, Uber, Amazon and many others. There are a ton of companies out there whose names basically don't make sense, but they don't really need to. You know what Audi makes. If you are a DIY fan, you know what a Dremel is. If you are on the pulse with tech, you know that Fitbit makes fitness trackers.

The great thing about choosing an abstract name is that if your company pivots, your name doesn't have to change. Nokia started off making wood pulping machines, telephone cables and car tires, but because the company has an abstract name (it's named after Nokia, a town in southern Finland), it can go on to manufacture mobile phones, VR cameras and a lot of other things without any confusion about its name.

Having said that, a lot of companies have done well by being named for what the companies do. For example, Lyft sounds like lift, as in "catch a lift from a friend." A Sodastream turns your normal water into bubbly water. Microsoft originally made software for microprocessors, and KitchenAid makes equipment that helps you in your kitchen. The mental shortcut people make when trying to figure out what you do when the name of your company makes sense in relation to what your company does might make it more memorable. The memorability factor doesn't matter if you become as big as Uber or Microsoft, of course, but it might make a difference in the early years of your startup.

Don't get too specific with your naming. Especially as an early-stage startup, you're running through experiments at a rapid rate. One of them might cause you to completely change the direction of your company. RelayRides is a good example. It found that its company name was slowing down its progress, because it was confusing its potential customers. Renaming the company to Turo was a great move, but it will have cost them a lot of time, money and brand recognition in the process.

For completeness, there's a third type of name in addition to nonsensical names and names that are specific to your industry. You'll probably already have guessed: companies that are named after their founders. The Bosch company, which makes dishwashers, car parts and everything in between, is named after Robert Bosch. Maserati is named after its six founders, the Maserati brothers. Craigslist is named for Craig Newmark. Nestlé (and its sub-brand Nescafé) is named for Henri Nestlé. Pfizer, Hewlett-Packard, Reuters, Tupperware, Sennheiser, Heineken; there is no shortage of brands named after their founders. I always found this an interesting naming strategy, not least because it explicitly ties the company to its founder. In today's startup world, founders change often. Many successful founders end up starting a series of companies. I don't necessarily recommend naming the company after yourself, unless you have a particular tie to the company's industry. I might let you off the hook if your name is Rockefeller and you're starting a new company in the property development space.

The best companies are able to inspire truly awesome amounts of brand loyalty. Naming the company is the first step in an important journey. The destination is to build a powerful brand that people can trust, promote and have an emotional connection to. As such, think about the emotions and connotations a name evokes. "Jerry's Home Brewery" sounds like a friendly, small craft brewery. I'd like to have a beer there. "ChemFab Industrial Supplies" has connotations of a reliable and trustworthy company that supplies chemicals for manufacturing. "Jerry's Home Industrial Supplies" and "ChemFab Home Brewery," on the other hand, are loudly shouting exactly the wrong message.

One makes no sense, and I don't think I would drink beer from a company called ChemFab. I would predict that both of these fictitious companies would fail before they ever opened their doors.

Your brand needs to reflect the personality, values, opinions and attitudes of your target customers. Supermarkets do this very well—some people wouldn't stop at Whole Foods to pick up a pint of milk in an emergency. Others wouldn't be seen shopping anywhere else. If you ask people why they shop where they do, they will probably cite price, quality or location, all of which is true. But at least some aspect of where customers do their shopping is how doing so makes them feel. The same is even more clearly visible when you look at the type of cars people drive. If I say "Toyota Prius" or "Porsche 911" or "Jeep Wrangler," you can probably envision three completely different people who would drive those cars. That goes both ways. We choose the cars we drive based not just on whether the cars do what we need them to do. They are also status symbols. Driving a hybrid is a choice, and whatever the reason you might have for driving one, your choice is printed on the back of your car, so everybody can see that you chose to drive a hybrid car. In fact, the success of the Prius can, in part, be attributed to its unusual design. When you see one, even from a distance, you know you are looking at a hybrid.

From a branding point of view, you need to think about what your brand stands for. There are a number of exercises you can do to try to give shape to what your company projects to your customers. Are you affordable or a premium brand? Is your product for everybody or an exclusive choice? Is it high-tech or approachable? Is it aimed at consumers or businesses? Does it use formal language, or is it more conversational? If your company were a car brand, which one would it be? There is a reason why brand consultants charge an arm and a leg for their services, but at the same time, I think it's easy to overthink the name of your company. If worst comes to worst, it's annoying and expensive to have to rename a company, but it's not impossible.

I always tell people that it doesn't really matter what you name your company, as long as you don't pick a bad name. One way to pick a bad name is to pick a name that is already trademarked, or where another company has a claim to the name. You should definitely do a trademark search for your potential company name and similar spellings to avoid expensive legal costs later on. You don't want to fall in the trap of starting a restaurant chain called MacDonnie's or a light bulb manufacturer called Filip's. The McDonald's and Phillips legal teams aren't known for their sense of humor and litigation gets very expensive very quickly. Be aware that sometimes the names can be pretty different from an existing trademark and still land you in legal hot water. If you're in doubt, get some advice from a lawyer. If your company has international aspirations (and it should) don't forget to check trademarks in your first few markets, to make sure your early expansion won't get caught in a legal net, either.

Legal considerations aside, take a look at foreign languages, too. If your company name means something offensive in a language that's common in one of your target geographical markets, you might have a no-go situation. Consider checking a list of the most-spoken languages, and double-check that your chosen name doesn't evoke giggles (or worse) in, say, Spanish.

The final important consideration when it comes to picking your company name is whether the domain you want is available. If your products cater to people who are less internet literate, you'll probably want to pick a name where the .com address is available or procurable. If you are running an API company where most of your customers will be tech-savvy, a .com is less relevant. Be aware that the cost of educating your customers that you are using a .ly or .io domain can be high, and the cost of a competitor somehow getting their hands on your .com would be even higher.

Similarly, have a look whether the social media accounts for your company are available. If "widgets" is taken on Twitter, along with "getwidgets," "hellowidgets," "widgetsdotcom" and every other version you can think of for your social media name, perhaps it's a sign that "widgets" isn't a great name for your company. Back to the drawing board!

As I've already alluded to a couple of times, branding is much more than picking a name, color, logo and typeface. It is about how you communicate with your customers. Some companies choose to have only one-way communication and don't typically engage with their customers in public. Others are eager to start and maintain a conversation on social media. Some brands can get down with the millennials, use informal language and use GIFs on their social media channels; others cannot, because it would just feel too weird compared to how they usually communicate.

All of this is part of your company's brand DNA. If someone asks your company a question on Twitter, should you reply? A lot of companies are taking a stand regarding a recent terrorist attack. Should your company? Would it be appropriate for your company to tweet about the Academy Awards? Over time, you'll hopefully be able to develop a brand that is so strong that you don't have to question how to react in certain situations, because it will be obvious both to your team and to your customers what your company would do in a given situation. The important thing is to start designing a voice, a style and a personality for your company. Your name will be part of that, but so is everything else you do to communicate with your customers, investors and even your suppliers. Give it some thought, and get started today.

Putting your brand into the world and communicating as your company is a little bit like learning a new language. You may as well get started sooner rather than later, because like learning any language, it will take you a little while to become completely fluent and for your company's voice to sound "right." On the bright side, the learning and exploring what works and what doesn't is part of the fun!

Chapter 22

Technology as a Core Competency

I n the early days, your company lives on its idea and the passion of the founders. You can build a series of prototypes to test your MVPs using pretty much any technology. I've seen successful MVPs that were a web form, a YouTube video, a simple WordPress site and an in-person interview. I've even seen a fake-it-till-you-make-it approach, where founders straight up lied to their customers; under the hood, all the "technology" was done by hand. All of that is OK, as long as it gets you the answers you need.

At some point, however, your company needs to grow up and start utilizing technology to build and optimize the user experience. Having a deep understanding of the technologies that are available is invaluable, because I've seen and experienced some spectacularly expensive mistakes here.

Let me kick off with an example. One company I was advising was developing a marketing product, and they were doing pretty well. When the time came to come out of beta and start charging the customers, the company experienced a six-month delay. I was baffled. There are a number of great SaaS payment services available off the shelf, with fantastic APIs. Instead, the company decided to develop its own from scratch. When asked why, the CEO told me that the CTO had convinced him that none of the payment services did exactly what he needed, so they agreed to develop their own. I spoke with the CTO, and it turned out that there was a very small aspect of their solution that wasn't covered by the available payment services. "We would be undercharging our customers," he concluded. I sat him down, together with the CEO, and we built a spreadsheet. My suspicion was confirmed. Over the lifetime of a customer, the company stood to lose between 1.5 and 2% of revenue. "That could be worth millions of dollars," the CTO argued. I agreed, but pointed out that the six months of delay meant that the company might not survive for long enough for that to become an issue. The CTO was able to direct his team to roll out an off-the-shelf solution in just a couple of days. With the rapid growth of the company, the 2% in lost revenue due to the billing quirk was irrelevant. The six-month delay almost cost them a round of investment and the company.

I am an advocate for choosing the correct tools for your business. Choosing one accounting package over another could cost you a lot of time over the years. Choosing the right platform for your product is even more important, and I've been badly burned by choosing wrong. I made the decision to build a product on a platform that simply wasn't equipped to do the heavy lifting it required. I hired a contract team and spent six months building it, and as soon as the product launched, it imploded. It turned out that, given the particular challenges in my business and the lack of technical oversight in my company, the external agency was running at high speed, but in the wrong direction. I eventually hired a CTO, who started a full rewrite. When everything was said and done, it cost the company a year's worth of development effort.

The two examples are slightly different. In the marketing company, the problem was that the technology side of the business didn't match up with the business needs. In my company, I didn't have enough technology competency in the startup to catch that we were moving in the wrong direction. The examples have something in common, however: they show what can happen when you have inadequate technology skills on tap within the business.

As a startup, it is your job to take shortcuts and cheat wherever you can. If your CTO suggests that the company should create a new content management system (CMS) for your company blog, they are probably wrong. There are a ton of powerful CMS systems out there, and for the first version of your product, it is probably easier to adapt one of them to your needs. Building a website that is a heavily modified WordPress platform, for example, means you don't have to reinvent the wheel. If you need e-commerce to sell your products, there are a thousand solutions out there. Building your own would be a tremendous waste of time.

At the core of a technology company is the ability to develop a product vision and then design, build and iterate the solution. Though at first a founding team may be able to utilize the help of contractors and specialists, ultimately technology must become a core competency that runs deep in every aspect of the business.

Twilio, an API company that enables coders to use SMS and telephone services programmatically, solves this challenge by making all of its employees create and demonstrate an app built using Twilio technology. Everyone, including human resources, facilities staff, legal and operational staff, have to create an account and create some code that interacts with the company's product. Doing so doesn't turn everybody into coders, of course, but it does help ensure that there is an understanding of the technology the company creates.

Part VI—Questions to Ask Yourself

In Part VI, we've examined design from various angles. Understanding what makes a product easy or hard to use is a crucial skill for everyone working at a startup.

As an exercise to train your mind to think in the right paths, make a habit of noticing poor design choices around you, and simple improvements on how to make it better. For example, if you commute by rail, can you tell where the train doors are going to be when the train stops? If not, could a design change to the platform improve that? With few exceptions, online banks are notoriously poor at UX. Try logging in to your own bank, and write a list of the immediate improvements that spring to mind. How would you make it easier and more frictionless to use? Try the same on a competitor's product. What makes it good to use? What would you change about it? What would it mean to your business if your competitor somehow implemented the UX changes you've come up with?

If your company or product doesn't have a name yet, run through a naming workshop with your team. Try to come up with two categories of names: ones that describe or hint at what you do and ones that don't. Names should be coming thick and fast once you get started; don't stop until you have at least a couple of hundred names up on a whiteboard or on sticky notes. As a team, rank them in both categories. Discard everything except the top ten and the bottom ten, then discuss in detail what makes the bad names bad. Figure out why the good names appeal to you, and then start doing additional research on your top ten. Start with trademark searches and check whether you can get the domains you need, and throw away all the names you can't use. With a bit of luck, you're down to one or two great names that can be used and are readily available. If not, don't worry. Naming a company or product is a lot harder than it sounds. I have faith in you; just repeat the exercise and get more creative.

The other exercise that I recommend you do with your team is to create a set of solid user personas of your potential customers. Think about users in the broadest possible sense. Are they all experiencing the same problems, or are there variants of the problem that your company solves? What are your personas' personal circumstances? What quirks do they have that impact the product development and UX of your product? If nobody on your team has done a user personas workshop before, see if you can get a bit of help from a mentor or a friend who has. Persona workshops aren't hard to do, but it helps to have someone who can give helpful suggestions along the way, especially to help ensure your personas are as varied and representatives as your real users will no doubt be.

Part VII

Managing Time

Money is a renewable resource. Time isn't. That is true in life, but it's a cold, hard and inescapable fact in startup land. More than anything else, your startup experience is going to be a marathon against the inevitable clock. The clock is a lot of things: your investor money running out, your own opportunity cost of being part of a founding team and competitors breathing down your neck.

We all have 24 hours in a day and there is no reason to let time ticking away stress you out. But there is also no reason to waste time. The best founding teams and companies work hard, of course, but whether they are able to work efficiently is a far better indicator as to whether the businesses are going to be successful.

In this part of the book, I'm going to spend a bit of time on techniques that can help you get more productivity out of yourself and your team. We'll be talking about how you can prioritize your workload to get more out of the day. I'll dwell on the advantages of agile development and methodologies you can use to reduce waste as much as possible. I'll also discuss some of the tools that will come in handy to keep you on track, and the best ways of gathering customer feedback to avoid spending time developing things your customers don't want or need.

Time's precious, let's get to it!

Chapter 23

Busy Work vs. Important Work

Ask an entrepreneur about the number one thing they wish they had more of, and they will always say "time." The to-do list to get a new company off the ground is absolutely daunting, without a doubt. It is stressful. The problem with that as a funny side-effect of the stress, for me at least, the skill of prioritization goes out the window first. When I get even just a little bit overwhelmed, everything that lands on my to-do list feels as if it's vitally important and has to be done now. This leads to a vicious cycle: without prioritization, your to-do list grows as quickly as you can check things off, which leads to falling behind and more stress.

In my experience, many startup founders simply aren't very good at figuring out what's important. It is understandable, because especially if this is your first startup, it's hard to know how much focus to place on the various parts of the business. Many founders end up so focused on being "busy" that they forget it doesn't matter. Being busy just means you're not sitting around doing nothing; it doesn't mean that you're being productive.

As a startup founder, there are temptations all around you. There are hundreds of conferences beckoning. There are tons of networking events. There are meetups. There are pretty graphs to be made. You have to post on LinkedIn and Facebook about how well your business is going. And yet, how many of those things are helping you accomplish your ultimate goals?

When I've advised companies, I've occasionally sat a founding team down and asked them how they were getting on with a particular thing they were worried about the last time we met. "Oh, yeah, we didn't get around to it yet," comes the answer, invariably. Not because it isn't important, but because something came up. Believe me, at a startup, something always comes up. It is very easy to lie to yourself and say that everything you do is helping your company accomplish its goals. Take my word for it: unless you've carefully groomed your to-do list, at least half of everything on your list is not important.

In a 1954 speech, then-President Dwight D. Eisenhower said, "I have two kinds of problems: the urgent and the important. The urgent are not important, and the important are never urgent." This way of looking at your to-do list is sometimes referred to as the "Eisenhower Principle," and is extremely useful in a startup context. It is so tempting to focus on urgent things (A tweet! It came in 23 minutes ago!) that aren't important, or important things (I have to file our taxes correctly when they are due in 3 months!) that aren't urgent. At the very least, add two columns to your to-do list. One column is for "urgent," the other is for "important". Then do the tasks in this order: Urgent and Important, Important but Not Urgent, Urgent but Not Important, Neither Important Nor Urgent. Even just making this tiny adjustment can help whip your to-do list into some shape. Over time, you will probably realize that items that go to the "Neither Important Nor Urgent" pile aren't worth doing at all. People around you might insist they get done, but delegate them if you can, or just turn them down. As a startup founder, you can work as many hours as the day will give you and still get nowhere near the bottom of your to-do list. Only through systematic culling can you hope to stay on top of things.

The single biggest thing you can do to help prioritize what you do is to figure out what the goals for your company are. I recommend having specific long term (three years), medium term (six months), and short term (two weeks) goals. If the to-do item you're about to start on doesn't get you closer to the goals, then why are you doing them? All of your company goals and metrics will probably be related to growth. If they are not, you should have a very good explanation for why you're prioritizing anything other than growth.

One of the biggest killers of time are meetings. Running efficient meetings is a hard-earned skill, but one that is supremely helpful. Meetings typically becomes a problem in large companies, and I believe that the lack of meetings is one of the big ways that startups are able to be more efficient than bigger corporations. In some startups, however, meetings are a more common occurrence, particularly if you are working with outsourced development teams, you are working closely with partners or you need to take meetings to make sales.

Meetings aren't automatically evil, by the way. There are many ways of having productive meetings, but there is nothing worse than being stuck in a session for 90 minutes when you realized 5 minutes into the meeting that your input isn't needed or (worse) is being ignored. To make meetings more efficient, try to keep them on a tight schedule. A meeting needs to have a clear objective. "We need a decision on whether we should perform additional user testing or go ahead and build that new feature" is a great meeting outcome. So is, "The objective of this meeting is to have a marketing plan for Q4." Vague objectives, like "Status update from all teams," are a lot less useful.

Make sure each meeting sticks to the scheduled time slot. The vast majority of meetings go on for far too long. Meetings should not be for catching up with people. People have things to do; if you want to catch up with them, grab a coffee or walk to work together. Finally, when the meeting is complete, the person who called it should send out a summary of decisions that were made. It helps keep track of things, and if someone who was absent from the meeting needs to be looped in, it's a lot easier to dig out an email than to try to remember what was said by whom.

If meetings are a big time sink, meetups and conferences can be an industrial-sized version of the same thing. It can often feel really important to stay on the pulse of the ecosystem in your city, especially when you're in a cycle of raising money. "How will the investors know I'm raising money," the thinking goes, "if I'm not out there shouting about my company?" We'll be talking about fundraising more in Part VIII, but for now, suffice to say that meetups rarely are the most useful places to meet potential investors.

Staying true to your goals is tricky, especially when it feels like you're overwhelmed with things you could be getting on with. I find that the best way of ensuring you stay focused is to bookend your day with a quick reminder of your goals. First thing in the morning, take a look at what you're meant to be doing. Pause for a second to reflect on those goals and compare them to your to-do list. At the end of the work day, do the same. Be honest with yourself about the time you've invested in activities that weren't strictly on target. This isn't an exercise in punishing yourself for making bad decision; it's meant as a way to train yourself to spot situations where you're letting time slip away. Staying focused is a learnable super-power. Only by working on it consistently can you master it.

When you are working as part of a team, try to encourage the whole team to stay focused, too. Don't hesitate to have a regular reminder session with your team. Some companies have a quick stand-up meeting each morning where the goals and tasks are discussed briefly.

I do mean briefly—standups should be five minutes maximum. To enforce brevity, I know of one company that has "pull-ups meetings," where you're only allowed to speak while doing pull-ups from a bar they installed in the office. I don't necessarily recommend that (it isn't fair to those who aren't in great shape) but they certainly succeeded in keeping their early morning meetings short and to the point. The idea of stating your goals for the day at the beginning has a couple of benefits. For one thing, in order to state your goals you have to consciously set them. In addition, it's harder to commit time to things that aren't helping further the company's goals if you have to stand up in front of your peers and explain what you're going to do that day in order to take the company further.

Once your company gets a little bit of success, you will start getting invitations to speak at events. These days, I spend a fair amount of my time speaking about startups, but as a VC, I see that as part of my job. When you're in the eye of your own startup storm, there are definitely benefits to being seen in the startup community, but I'd urge some caution. It's easy to get swept into the speaking circuit and lose sight of what the mission is as a startup. Speaking at events can make you feel successful, but unless it also has a positive effect on your startup's metrics, it's not helpful.

A propos metrics: I will cover them in more detail later on in Part IX, but since we're talking about time management, let me mention them here, too. There are a lot of vanity metrics out there, including press coverage, number of Twitter followers and number of likes on Facebook. Making those numbers go up can make your company seem important and makes the team feel good. You might even be able to convince some people that these are valuable metrics; getting press coverage is a great way to boost traffic to your site, and if those visitors convert into valuable customers, then that is great. The truth is, though, that many of the startups I advise get very excited about being featured on TechCrunch, Forbes or the New York Times, but the coverage is basically without value. Yes, you get a spike in number of people congratulating you, but you'll often find that the bump in new users is modest. Given how much time it takes to get press coverage, pushing for it may not be a sensible return on your time and money invested.

So, pick some metrics that definitely track how well your business is doing. By all means, do a lot of crazy experiments to see what has a positive effect on those metrics, but be disciplined about where you commit your time. After all, time is your only non-renewable resource. Spend it wisely.

Chapter 24

Agile Development

f you've had the misfortune of working in software development for larger companies, you might have been subjected to a specification document. These tomes, which are usually hundreds of pages long, are meant to describe every little detail of how a piece of software works. It describes how data is stored, where all the buttons go and what happens when a user clicks any button on the screen. If that sounds like undiluted insanity, then you're already ahead of me on this.

The problem with working in this way (known as "waterfall" delivery) is many-fold. For one thing, you don't have a "finished" piece of software until you launch it to your customers. The other problem is that you have to come up with every eventuality at the beginning of the project. That is at odds with a lot of the principles I've already discussed in this book, not least the one about testing with your customers early and often, and the tenet of failing fast.

There are some cases where waterfall-based project management is unavoidable. One example where this might be the case is in heavily regulated industries, where the specifications need to be approved before any coding takes place. On hardware projects, you are able to be agile up to a point, but once you go into the mass manufacturing phase of your project, you're in effect in a waterfall phase. It usually becomes very expensive to make even small changes to the hardware side of your product once you're making the products in batches of thousands or more.

If your product is software-based, agile software development is where it's at. The core idea of agile project management (also known as "agile management" or simply "agile") is to break down a project into much smaller parts, and at any given time have the project "launch ready." The idea is, instead of building a product that has all the bells and whistles, to build just enough to launch.

For example, if you want to build a Software as a Service (SaaS) product that helps people book appointments at a hairdresser, you might start with just the customer-facing part of the website. You would dump all the data into a spreadsheet, and then process it manually. Launch it. Next, you might implement a proper back-end, so the hairdressers could see their upcoming appointments. Launch that. Next, you implement a payment service, or a recurring scheduling service, or a mobile app interface, or... anything. The point is that because the service is already live, you're able to get feedback from your customers. If it turns out at this point that your product is failing miserably, maybe you need to change something about your marketing, or pivot the business to be for barbers rather than hairdressers. The point is that because you're launching a series of what are essentially MVP products, you are able to stay agile, and make changes as you get feedback from your users.

It is easy to see why this is a better way of working than writing up a 300-page spec document, building the entire service, and then discovering that what you were doing had a fatal flaw. Agile is closely interlinked with the philosophy of failing as quickly as possible: get what you are doing in front of customers, get feedback, adapt and launch constantly.

Some companies work in two week sprints, followed by one week of user testing, then one week of integration testing and a go-live phase. For very large companies, "go live" means test the software on a subsection of your users to ensure that there are no unexpected performance degradations. If it all seems to work fine, roll it out to more users, until everyone eventually has the new features. If you have multiple teams, you can stagger the rollout process, so you always have a new set of features being developed, tested and rolled out to customers. It's also possible to test new releases on two sets of customers, and see if the release has the intended effect. This is often known as A/B testing (if you are testing two things against each other) or multivariate testing, for more complex setups.

Other companies go even more hardcore, releasing tiny incremental updates to their users several times per day. Etsy reportedly releases code to its live servers 50 times per day. Amazon takes it even further, with a code change every 12 seconds on average. When you get to these levels, we're usually talking about "continuous delivery"—whenever a piece of code is ready, it gets pushed to the live servers for testing on real users. I don't advocate changing the code on your site several times per minute when you have a couple of hundred users, but once your user base starts growing and you are able to embrace multivariate testing and a robust agile methodology, things change. Having a rapid release-test-rollback schedule in case of unintended consequences can speed up your development dramatically. Compare those speeds with the typical release cycle of waterfall projects, which is measured in months (sometimes years) and the advantages become obvious.

Working in short, tight cycles helps reduce a lot of the things that are risky about software projects. It also helps keep your developers curious and interested. Nothing is as demotivating as working on a project for months on end without ever seeing any feedback from users along the way.

There are a few different agile methodologies in use, the most popular of which is Scrum. Within Scrum, there are three roles played by the team. The Product Owner is analogous to a product manager; this is the person on the team who is outward facing, gathering information from the world outside the team. This might include user interviews, user testing, gathering requirements from the rest of the company, etc. The product owner is also in charge of the backlog, which is the long list of features or ideas for the product that could be developed at some point in the future. When the CEO has an idea for a new feature for the product, he or she talks to the Product Owner. Together, they clarify exactly what the user benefit is, what the user wants to accomplish and what the criteria for success are.

Another role on a Scrum team is the Scrum Master, which is an inward-facing role. This person's job is to remove impediments that get in the way of the team. For example, the Scrum Master might liaise with translators (who are crucial to the product, but not usually part of the Scrum team), ensure that the developers and designers have all the tools and information they need and more. At the beginning of a "sprint", which is the name for a two-week block of time, the Scrum Master is meant to reject any requirements that aren't clear. Once a two-week sprint is filled with tasks and objectives, the team will do everything they can to deliver those tasks.

The final role in the Scrum team are Team Members, who are the designers, developers and others involved in the production of the product. In theory, the Team Members should never be disturbed by anybody except the Scrum Master. This is a reflection of how developers and designers typically ideally work: uninterrupted for hours at the time, in a productive flow state where they can stay focused at the challenges at hand.

Scrum has a couple of huge benefits over other ways of working, but for it to work, it needs buy-in from the whole company. The biggest benefit from Scrum is that the team is able to work, heads-down while a sprint is in progress. In exchange for agreeing to give it their all to deliver a particular feature for the product, the rest of the company agrees to leave them alone while they're being productive. The upshot is that at the end of a two-week sprint, the team should have a launch-ready iteration of the product ready to go.

At the end of each sprint, the Scrum team does a retrospective. The idea is to, over time, adjust the velocity of the team (that is, how much work is accepted into each sprint) and to have a bi-weekly feedback loop back to the rest of the company to ensure that the team works as efficiently as possible.

Agile in general, and Scrum in particular, is a fantastically efficient way of working. For the companies I've seen that are able to run Scrum, they get two to three times more productivity out of their development teams. That means they get two to three times more code shipped and that they are running at a 100-200% faster speed than potential competitors.

The agile movement has a manifesto that is worth a read, too (try searching on the internet for Agile Manifesto), as it helps bring home the idea behind agile and why it is worth doing. The gist is that agile puts customer satisfaction first, despite rapidly changing requirements, through rapid delivery of sprints. It unites the business and development functions towards a common goal and stresses that "working software" is the measure of progress.

As awesome as agile is, it is worth keeping in mind that agile is something that needs to be learned. Many developers find it to be a natural and productive way of working. In my experience, design and development teams often embrace Scrum with open arms; they find it makes their job both more productive and more fun. Adoption of agile can be harder for the rest of the company, however. In sales-driven companies, for example, it's common that the sales floor can be a pretty rowdy place, with phone calls, side conversations and people tapping each other on the shoulder to ask questions. That's pretty much the exact opposite of how a Scrum team works. I've seen a Scrum master unplug all the phones in the room with the engineering team to make sure they can focus on work as the first order of business.

In other words, it takes a bit of education across the business to make agile development methodologies work, but ultimately, getting a productivity boost from your team is invaluable.

The most successful adaptations I've seen of Scrum involved getting all the teams some training; get the Scrum masters and Product Owners trained and certified first, then make sure the team members are fully on board too. For established teams just introducing Scrum, consider whether using a Scrum coach a couple of days per month is worth the money. Changing established habits is hard, and I've seen too many teams adopting just the standup meeting component of the process and thinking they are agile now, without actually getting the full benefits. It is possible to start working "agile-fall" by accident. That's the worst of both worlds; none of the accountability of waterfall, and none of the rapid iteration benefits of working agile.

Chapter 25

Tools of the Trade

Ask a carpenter what the difference is between a peen hammer and a claw hammer and you've tipped your hand—you know nothing about carpentry. In the startup world, picking the right tools for the job is equally crucial. Choosing the wrong piece of software, the wrong cloud provider or the wrong programming language can turn out to be an expensive, company-killing mistake. Just like with the carpentry example, it can signal to your potential investors that you don't know what's what.

As mentioned in Chapter 23, you should only ever spend time and resources on developing things that are unique to the problem you are trying to solve. There are a ton of services and open-source frameworks out there. Use them. The fact that all of these tools exist is the precise reason why it is easier to create a startup anywhere in the world now then it was in Silicon Valley in 1999.

When you are a startup trying to run at speed, cheat whenever you can. Don't write your own payment processing software; Stripe,

Square and PayPal all exist for a reason. In fact, for a lot of businesses, there is no reason to work directly with those APIs either. If you are selling products, use a full eCommerce solution that already has a payment processor built in. If you're charging recurring payments, use a recurring payments provider. Got a SaaS business? Whatever you do, don't roll your own payment solution. There are simply too many edge cases. If someone has already gone out of their way to solve all of the problems related to payment processing, why should you?

As an early-stage business, your job is to focus exclusively on what you do best. Unless you are going into the hosting game (and frankly, you'd probably be insane to), don't build your own server farms. Amazon Web Services (AWS), Google Cloud Platform and Microsoft Azure all have more processing power and storage than you could possibly need. Let them deal with power surges, hard drives failing and capacity problems. It's all distractions to what you're meant to be doing.

Even very large businesses do this, by the way. Netflix (which, last I heard, represents almost a third of all traffic on the internet in the US in peak hours) runs off Amazon's AWS platform. Uber sends a godawful number of text messages every day, which is crucial to its business. The company didn't set up their own servers to deliver messages, however; that doesn't align with the company's goal of rapid growth. Instead, they used a third-party API to help deal with the telephony side of things. They're spending a fortune, I'm sure, but it's still cheaper than having to divert engineering staff to figure out how to deal with telephone networks in more than seventy different countries.

Similarly, if you are doing anything with embedded computers, whatever you do, don't start creating your own circuit board. For prototyping, Raspberry Pi, Texas Instruments' Launchpad, the Teensy platform and Arduino boards will get you most of the way there, most of the time. Hell, you may even find that a Raspberry Pi will make your product slightly bigger, but because they can be bought in bulk, they greatly reduces your risk. If the goal is to find a product/market fit, then use existing platforms for your first 10,000 customers if you can. After you see if you can make a product work based on an established platform, then maybe see if you can cut costs by creating your own boards from scratch.

Measuring how well your business is doing is another crucial part of being a startup. Unless you know how software changes are impacting your users, you have no way of guiding future development. There's often a temptation to implement your own reporting and analytics here. Don't. Just don't. There are dozens of powerful analytics platforms out there. They are under active development, with elegant APIs and beautiful dashboards for you to use. You'll have to spend a little bit of time to integrate with the services, of course, but the amount of functionality you get "for free" once you're integrated means it's rarely worth writing a metrics suite yourself.

You would be amazed by how much you can find online in terms of services. This will make the tech-inclined among you shudder, but I know of several largish hardware manufacturers whose websites are running on Squarespace. To the right business, having a simple website with limited possibilities for customizations is perfect. Again: if your website isn't part of your product, then why would you waste your limited resources building it?

This is true for every aspect of the business. You're not building a full software suite as much as you are trying to find elegant ways of combining services, APIs and open source software in ways that help you deliver a solution to your customers as quickly as possible.

Some of the services you'll be using cost money, and some might even cost you more money than you're willing to spend. Resist the temptation to write your own solutions unless it is absolutely core to the business. It might make sense to write integrations or even full pieces of software further down the road, but for now, embrace what is out there, limitations and all.

Occasionally, you might hear from an advisor or investor that they want a particular data point, or a way of reporting that your chosen cobbled-together set of solutions doesn't support. Don't be shy about explaining to them that what they're asking for is a lot more time consuming (and therefore expensive) than they might realize. Most investors wouldn't derail your inertia just to get an additional or slightly different data point. Alternatively, they might manage to convince you that the data they are asking for is crucial to the success of your business and that you should spend the time it takes to implement it.

The vast number of services, APIs and off-the-shelf solutions that are available today go far. Microsoft is offering computer vision APIs that could save you months of development, Google's Translate API will translate any text for you and Amazon's Mechanical Turk API enables you to get real humans to do tasks for your business where other machine-learning algorithms are failing. A lot of businesses use existing APIs to prove the business need for the problems they are trying to solve before they develop their own, better suited technology.

Microsoft's Azure, Amazon's AWS and the other players in this space know that startups are their bread and butter. They will often give huge amounts of free credits to help you get off the ground. This is fantastic business on their part: once you've chosen to go with a platform, the switching cost becomes significant, and you'll probably gladly pay for their services once everything is running smoothly. Accelerators typically have fantastic deals with the AWS's of the world as a perk of being part of the accelerator. Even if you aren't accepted into, or aren't ready for, an accelerator yet, you'll often find Microsoft and Amazon representatives at startup events. If all else fails, do a quick Google search for "Amazon AWS startup offer" or "Microsoft Azure for Startups," and you're on your way to saving thousands of dollars. The same goes for payment processors such as Stripe or PayPal, who will not charge fees for the first period of time while your startup gets on its feet.

Be aware that a lot of companies—and especially SaaS businesses—are desperate to get you to sign up. They know you will turn into a valuable customer over time, which means that their cost of acquisition (COA) can be quite high. Your suppliers will probably offer a free trial with certain limitations; if you contact support, you can usually get these limitations removed from your account, or you can try to get the trial extended to far beyond the 30 or 60 days they commonly offer. Ask; the worst that can happen is that they tell you "no."

The fantastic thing about being in a ecosystem is that you're able to stand on the shoulders of everyone who comes before you. Imagine if you were trying to build a business in the first dot-com boom, before Amazon AWS was available. You would be wasting time buying and building servers, installing operating systems and configuring, installing and maintaining actual servers. Open source basically didn't exist, so your developers would be reinventing the proverbial wheel continuously. But nowadays, you're able spin up a new company and be productive so much faster than anyone in the history of startups. Not taking advantage of that is the worst sin in your startup journey: a waste of time.

It is difficult to recommend specific tools for your business without knowing about your business in more detail, and the products and services landscape changes incredibly quickly. I encourage you to spend a bit of time researching the tools and services that are available and appropriate for your business. The market leader isn't always the best tool for the job, and sometimes it's better to pay for a service than to use a free solution. Don't rush into making decisions; remember that for every well-chosen service you use, you are shaving months and months of development time off your product, so you can afford to be picky and evaluate your options properly.

Chapter 26

Gathering Customer Feedback as Early as Possible

've already covered agile development at length in Chapter 24. As you'll recall, the point of using agile methodologies (as opposed to the waterfall methodologies also discussed) is to keep as close a feedback loop as possible with your customers. The crucial advantage is that by putting your product in front of (beta) customers early, you can start getting your customers' impressions as soon as possible and improve your product.

Some of the feedback you receive is going to be minor. Customers might find little bugs, such as the "save" and "cancel" buttons swapping places throughout a process. They might get confused by why they have to press a "save" button in the first place. Or they might point out that an important function of your application is hidden in a less-than-obvious location. All of that feedback is useful, but it isn't really going to move the needle on whether or not your company is successful. Any problem that can be resolved in an afternoon or, in some cases, a few minutes isn't going to sink you.

The rubber really hits the road where the issues are fundamental to the business.

Many years ago, I mentored a company who launched its product. As soon as they did, the early customers they had lined up reacted with something along the lines of "Oh. That isn't the problem we thought you were solving, we use Excel for that, and it works fine. We wouldn't be willing to pay for that to save our admin 20 minutes of work per month." That is a problem of an altogether different magnitude. Unless you are able to solve the problem the customer thought you were solving, or find a different market for the solution you came up with, your business is going to face a very difficult time. This sort of thing used to happen worryingly often in the startup world. It still happens to startups occasionally. The worst thing about this is that it's completely, 100% avoidable, by talking to your customers much earlier than you might think you need to.

"If you're not embarrassed by the first version of your product, you've launched too late," said Reid Hoffman, the founder of LinkedIn and a well-respected venture capitalist. I agree, but would like to point out that not all embarrassment is made of the same stuff. It is understandable that you're embarrassed when you show off a product that isn't the best you can do because you launched it early. But that's the kind of embarrassment you can chip away at by making your product better. A much worse type of embarrassment is when you launch your product, then spend the next six months of your life discovering you are solving a problem nobody is experiencing. You'll desperately try to find a market to fit your product. You're likely going to fail.

It's worth suffering the embarrassment of launching an unpolished product to avoid the embarrassment of building a product nobody wants. Getting early feedback is vital. The process of doing so is often referred to as Customer Development, and is a cornerstone of Steve Blank and Eric Ries' work. If you haven't read Lean Startup yet, it is definitely worth adding to your list.

There are many ways of gathering early feedback, and you may need to get creative to come up with ways to get answers to your questions as early as possible. The piece of advice I often give my mentee companies is to not worry about building things that scale. I hasten to point out that I'm not the only person who suggests that. Y Combinator's Paul Graham makes an emphatic plea to the accelerator's companies, too. In the early stages of a startup, the biggest problem isn't scaling. It's getting the company off the ground in the first place.

Getting the founding team involved in signing up your first customers is extremely helpful for several reasons. The most important reason is that when having conversations with customers, it becomes very clear quickly where the challenges are. When you first start your company, you probably have a pretty well-defined idea of which parts of your product are easy for your customers to understand and which they may have problems with. Trying to make a sale in person, however, will invariably refine that impression significantly. For example, you may get more or less pushback on price than you anticipated. Product features that you thought were important are shrugged off, whereas features you didn't realize were important to your target audience are deal-breakers. If you outsource the sales to a sales team, it is hard to gauge the feedback. Is your sales team just being lazy, or are they bringing up genuine concerns from your customers?

A lot of founders believe having one-on-one interactions with their potential customers is a waste of time, but I think it is a very worthwhile investment. A good way to think of it is as follows: Why are you starting the company? Your answer should include, "To make your customers' lives easier or better." Because that's part of your mission, you should talk to your customers at the very least.

So, talk to your customers early. Talk to them often. And ensure you show them work in progress. Before you have a working version of your product, find a way to get feedback anyway. A 3D render of a physical product can help get an early indication of whether the product is designed the way your target audience expects. Wireframes, or simple click-through prototypes of software, are a great tool to help your customers interact with the future product.

It is worth highlighting that you are interacting with your customers on several different levels. If you're trying to make a sale, you might be trying to get your customer from a 'no' to a 'maybe' or from a 'maybe' to a 'yes.' That isn't necessarily helpful to get the best feedback from your customers, however. I'm not saying you need to hire a full-on usability testing lab complete with one-way mirrors so you can observe your customers, but it is definitely useful to be able to see what your customers do with the software without your prompting.

Take the previous example of a "save" button. Most modern web-based software is constantly saving whatever a customer has typed in, and customers who are accustomed to working in Google's suite of products wouldn't even think to look for a save button. If you keep prompting the customer, "Now hit save, and we can go back to the product menu," the customer might dutifully do so, and there appears to be no problems with your product. That may not be accurate, because that's not how your users will be interacting with your products. They won't have the company's CEO sitting next to them telling them what to do, and so the information you get from that experiment isn't as good as it could be.

The best way to do user testing, even if you don't have fully functioning software yet, is to give specific tasks to customers. "Create a new order," or "Assign a different tax bracket," or "Create a new user profile for a colleague" are great examples. They shouldn't take long to complete, but they will give a far better impression of whether your software is intuitively designed. If customers get stuck along the way, don't guide them; take a note of what happened, and put the confusion as a challenge to your designers. As I have mentioned before, it's rarely the user's fault that they can't use the software; it's your job to design a product that cannot be used the wrong way.

Throughout this book, I talk a lot about how you can test your product on your customers, but remember that you don't need a product to get some useful feedback. In fact, you don't need anything at all in order to get real value from potential customers. A well-executed interview can be invaluable to get a deeper understanding of who your customers are. Keep in mind that you are not selling, here; you are trying to find out more about the problem you are trying to fix.

I've conducted many of these interviews in the past. In my experience, the most valuable information comes from questions that involve the buying process. Invite your customers to explain the problems they are facing in their own words, and how they are currently solving these problems. Find out what their current solutions are, how much they are paying for them and who made the decision about spending that money. Find out whether they believe their competitors and similar companies are facing similar issues, or whether there is something unique to their company that means that they are the only ones who have this particular problem. Ask them how much it would be worth to them to have their problem completely resolved. Ask them what a perfect solution would look like. Once you have answers to all of those questions, try to explain what your product will do for them, and how it will resolve some of this particular pain point.

It is undeniable that interviews like these take a very long time. The interview itself might take an hour to 90 minutes, but you should also factor in the time it will take you to write up the findings in a way that will be useful to the business. Crucially, you can't make decisions based on a single interview, so plan to do several interviews throughout the development process.

For user testing early prototypes, it is often said that only five or six sessions of user testing can identify more than 80% of usability issues. It really isn't that hard, and you simply can't afford not to add this to your process. Find some customers and put user testing in your development schedule.

Let me finish this chapter with an anecdote. I have a friend who has been running a company for almost five years. It's extremely successful in its space, it is growing rapidly and it has several hundred team members. My friend challenges his customer support team to find him people to go have coffee with every week, like he has been doing since the start, back when he was doing the customer support himself. The perfect conversation, he tells me, is with a customer who had a problem, contacted customer service and had a two- to three-star experience. He looks for customers who were disappointed in what the product was able to do, customers who contacted the company to cancel their subscription or customers who were let down in some way. He spends an hour per week with a customer, buying them a coffee and sitting down to learn more about their business, their problems and how his company is (or isn't) helping solve their problems. He says that over the years, he has invested thousands of dollars and more than two hundred hours on going for coffee with customers, but he still says it's the most valuable thing he does every week. Every week, he writes up a "learnings of the week," which are just a couple of observations in the form of bullet points on the company's internal communication platform, so the whole company can draw the benefit from the session.

Taking customers for coffee for an informal chat may not work for you or your business, but there is an important lesson to learn here. However you do customer development, it remains important that you keep a finger on the pulse on what your customers are doing and how they interact with your products. If you don't, trust me, your competitors will be.

Part VII—Questions to Ask Yourself

Losing a customer is painful and making a bad decision and losing money is annoying, but ultimately there are always more customers out there, and a great company can always raise more money if it needs to. The one thing you can never claw back is time, so managing it carefully is crucial.

There are two easy ways of ensuring you make the most of your time. Don't do things you don't need to do, and do everything else as efficiently as possible.

The first exercise is related to what you actually need to do in a day. In Chapter 23 I explained the Urgent/Important matrix and in this exercise, I'm going to encourage you to put that into action, but with a twist. If you have a cofounder, make sure both/all of you keep track of what you do on a daily basis for a couple of weeks. At the end of the period, put the tasks into the matrix. The catch: you have to defend your decisions to your cofounders. This is important for two reasons. The first is that it is much easier to lie to yourself in isolation than if you need to defend your choices to other people. The other advantage is a bigger-picture analysis: becoming more aware of what you and your cofounders do all day makes it easier to ensure that you're all pulling in the same direction. Who knows, perhaps you find that you have been doing things that everyone else in the company feels is busy work, and you may save yourself some time in the process.

The second piece of homework is to map out some of the core processes in your business. For example: How does a feature go from an idea to being launched to your customers? Map this process out on a piece of paper, and try to include all the steps that you feel should be part of the process. This could include idea, design, user testing, front end development, back end development, integration testing, unit testing, translation, submission to the app store, and app approval process. You get the idea; every step. Next, get your team together and see if there are steps that are taking too long or that can be skipped, outsourced or amended to be more efficient. By being conscious about how you do something, you are often able to make tremendous savings in time; something that makes sense on a day-to-day basis might look completely ridiculous on paper. Fixing the processes can help save a ton of time. Best of all, once you've fixed the way you do things, you also have the process charts, which can serve as documentation for when you're onboarding new staff, having conversations with mentors or trying to improve your internal processes going forward.

Part VIII

Raising Money

Part VIII

Let's be honest: no entrepreneur likes raising money. It takes a lot of time we'd rather spend on finding customers or improving the product. However, it's a necessary evil for most startups. You need some money in the coffers to prove that your market is huge, the problem you are solving is real and the customers who are willing to pay for your product are out there.

In Part VIII, I'll take you through the process of fundraising. We'll talk about the different sources of money and how to put together a pitch that will get investors excited about your company.

The CEO has two main jobs: hire the best people possible for each role and make sure the company never runs out of money. What makes startups different from small businesses is the concept of staged financing: hit progressive milestones and raise progressive rounds of funding, usually in progressively higher amounts. The milestones for each company are different and you have to figure out yours. This is usually done by measuring certain success metrics (which will be covered in Part IX). For example, you may think that the milestone for you being able to raise a Series A investment is hitting 1,000 paying customers. The first thing you do is figure out what resources you need in order to hit that milestone. What will it cost to hire the right people, develop the right technology and attract the right customers between now and that milestone? That, plus a bit of extra time to raise your next round, plus a safety buffer, is how much money you'll need to raise.

Fundraising is pretty intense, but it is also incredibly exciting. Let's put that pitch deck together and get started...

Chapter 27

Venture Capital and Angel Investors 101

You may already have raised a small amount of money from Friends, Family and Fools, as we talked about in Chapter 14. Once you start getting a little bit of traction, it's likely that you'll need another injection of cash to take your company to the next level. In this chapter, we'll take a closer look at the two most common ways of doing that: by raising funding from angels and VCs.

Angel investors tend to invest their own money. In Silicon Valley and other startup ecosystems, the source of their money is often from exits in their own startups, which means that angels are a fantastic source of much more than just cold, hard cash. Many angel investors have a number of battle scars from when they were building their own companies. Even if they don't act as formal advisors or mentors to your company, you'll often find that your angel investors have a very broad set of experience. This is important, especially if your angel investors have experience that is relevant to your specific business. Angels who add value beyond the money they invest are often referred to as "smart money."

There are, of course, also angel investors who see startups as part the high-risk-high-return portion of their diversified investment portfolio, but who don't have startup experience themselves. Sports stars and celebrities are worth highlighting here. Your favorite movie star or basketball player might not be able to offer in-depth advice about the advantages of PHP or Ruby, but that doesn't mean they wouldn't be useful to your business, especially on the marketing side. Basically, anybody who has a large pile of cash could be an angel investor.

Angels often invest in order to make a return, of course, but many angels like investing as a hobby. They might want to keep a finger on the startup pulse or keep a close eye on an industry they've worked in or are interested in. Some angels invest as a social activity in angel groups or investment clubs.

Angel investors usually invest modest sums of money alongside other angels. An "Angel round" or a "Seed round" can vary in size based on where you are geographically and the industry you are in. Some seed rounds are a couple of hundred thousand dollars, whereas others can be a couple of million dollars in size.

More than the dollar amounts, what separates a seed round from a Series A round is the status of the business. If you don't have a clear product/market fit or you don't have a relatively mature product, you're probably raising seed funding from angel investors. Angels tend to be willing to accept much higher risk than VCs, often investing much earlier in the process.

I feel I also need to mention angel syndicates here. This is a hybrid angel/VC construct, where a number of angels pool their money together. One of the angels brings an investment to the syndicate, and if the group thinks it's a good investment, they participate in the round. If an investment pays off, the spoils are split proportionally with the other participating investors in the syndicate. Some angel syndicates are led by only a small number of angel investors who make the decisions on behalf of the syndicate; this is often the case with very successful angel investors who use the money of the other angels to help amplify their own investment strategies. Angel syndicates are a big part of the AngelList (angel.co) platform, but even if you aren't looking for syndicates specifically, ensuring that your company is included on AngelList, CrunchBase and Mattermark is a very good idea.

Venture capitalists (VCs) are a different type of investor. The most important difference is that VCs are professional investors, managing money that is, in turn, invested into their funds. The VCs have to raise their funds much like a startup raises money from VCs. Venture capital typically comes from investors that have very large pools of money in their portfolio. That might include pension funds, investment banks, high net worth individuals, family offices (that is, professional investors investing on behalf of a wealthy family), government funds and similar.

Like any investor, a VC firm is trying to get a return on its investment. Understanding where the money comes from is useful, but ultimately it's most important to understand what the purpose of the fund is. Depending on where the money came from, a fund might focus on a particular type of technology. For example, a large oil company might invest into a VC fund that focuses on green technology. Such an investment makes the oil company look good ("Look how much we care about the environment!"), but it also means that the company gets a return if one of the green-tech technologies they invested in ends up striking it big. It is also done as a hedge, knowing that new technologies eventually replace the previous generation.

There's a separate class of VCs worth being aware of, in the form of Corporate VCs. These are VC offices that invest in ventures on behalf of a larger company. Most of the big tech companies and brands you can think of have their own VC arms, and typically invest in companies that augment the space they are in. For example, a large publisher might have a VC arm that invests in advertising, education and media technologies.

At HP Tech Ventures, where I lead corporate investments, we focus on 3D printing, IoT, immersive computing and smart machines. These are not business categories you think of immediately when you hear the name HP. However, the company is 76 years old (as of this writing) and has gone through several generational transitions: from audio oscillators and Disney as the first customer in the 1930s and 40s to calculators in the 50s and 60s to personal computers in the 70s, etc. The job of the corporate venture arm is to look to the future and scout for what's coming next. We invest for financial returns, but even more so for strategic fit, which can be characterized into market segment expansion (trying to get more of the business we are already in), market expansion (helping the general market where we sell product grow) and new category development (future businesses where we are considering launching new products and services).

Both angel and VC investing is about learning as much as possible about the teams, the market and the products that are being invested in, before making a number of bets. The difference is in the breakdown of how likely those bets are to play out.

In the world of angel investments, you'd expect around 90% of the companies to fail. 8% of the companies will return the investment to the investors. 1% will give a 2-3x exit, and a final 1% will be a 10x exit. An entry ticket to this particular gamble can cost as little as $1,000 if you're investing as a syndicate. At the high end, you do occasionally hear of angels investing huge sums of money, but $50,000-$100,000 tends to be a pretty common upper limit.

Because of the nature of angel investing, angels might be willing to take a bet on a company even if the angel is unlikely to make a lot of money on a successful investment. On the VC side of things, the numbers change quite a bit, as does the risk profile. For the risk equation to make sense for VCs, the typical VC firm won't look at investments that don't have the potential to have a 20x return on investment. In other words, if the VC is looking to invest $5 million for a 20% stake of the company, the company would potentially need to be able to exit at a valuation of $500 million. If your company doesn't have a chance at selling at least half a billion dollars, you'll find it's tricky to raise from these types of investors.

As an aside, the very basic math above is often the difference between whether a company is VC investible or not. If the problem your company is solving is too small, if an exit is unlikely or if you're unable to sell the opportunity in your pitch, it becomes very hard for VC investors to make the money side of things work out. Incidentally, this is why Uber is such an interesting company. Uber's mission is basically to replace personal car ownership altogether, which means that the company can continue to scale until every single car is operated by Uber; this, combined with a strong track record, is what is driving the value of the company up, up, up.

Not all VC firms are the same, either. Some firms focus specifically on very early-stage startups, investing instead of (or alongside) angel investors. Other firms invest much later in the history of a company and won't even take a meeting unless the investment round is $20 million or above. Most VCs fall somewhere in between. You should do your research on the angel investors you are pitching, but for angels, it's more a game of who you know. The same approach doesn't work with VCs; there are a great number of VC funds out there, and doing solid research before you put a pitch deck together and start visiting every firm up and down Sandhill Road is crucial. Pitching the wrong industry at the wrong valuation with the wrong exit strategies to the wrong VC firm is a waste of their time, and your own.

Having said all of that, in the venture capital world, you'll always find a number of exceptions. A firm that "only" invests in software startups might invest in Fitbit. A firm that focuses on late-stage investments might do a 180 and suddenly make a $500k investment in an early-stage company because they believe in the founding team and the market. From an efficiency point of view, I caution against assuming that you're going to be an exception. Most of the investments that are made against the typical grain of a fund have a story behind them that might not always be obvious from the outside. Do your research, and focus your efforts on the VC firms that are most likely to be a good fit.

Understanding what makes angel investors tick and how that is different from VCs is going to be really important to whether or not you're able to raise money successfully. To take but a simple example: a pitch deck that is successful in raising angel investment is unlikely to work when you kick off your VC road tour, and vice versa.

Chapter 28

Making the First Impression

It **might feel weird to** make a dating analogy when you're hunting for money, but it isn't as farfetched as you might think. The working relationship you have with your investors is, in many ways, like a marriage. You'll need trust in each other. You'll need to be able to rely on one another. And occasionally, you'll disagree and find a way to make it work anyway. There is another similarity between raising money and relationships. You only get one opportunity to make a first impression, and that part is important enough that I want to dedicate a chapter in this book to it.

The first impression is so important because successful angels and VCs get thousands and thousands of pitches every week. They have to filter their attention somehow, and that's exactly what I mean by a first impression. One example: if you start your email with "I noticed you recently invested in Company X," you'd better double check that that investment actually took place. If not, the email goes in the trash and you'll never even know why. Similarly, be careful about starting with "Mr. X said I should get in touch with you." If the investor has a strained relationship with Mr. X, or (worse) if they can't immediately remember who Mr. X is, you're wasting everybody's time.

The best way to make a perfect first impression is by remembering what the investors want. They want to know that you are a strong team, with a unique approach to solving a major problem in a growing market. They want to know what you're looking to do, and that you won't waste their time in the process.

In this chapter, we'll delve a bit deeper into the personal relationships that make the startup ecosystem go around. Remember that, especially as an early-stage startup, when your product is in the idea stage and you don't have metrics to back up your track record, the investors are essentially investing on blind faith in the team. To do that, it's all about trust. Make sure you make a great first impression and that the introduction creates inherent trust.

As doubtful as I am about business schools in general (I always say that startup accelerators are the new business school), they do get one thing right: the Executive Summary. For decades, business schools taught that the Executive Summary was just the introduction to a business plan. That might have been true in the past, but these days, this snapshot of your company should provide just the right amount of information for a savvy investor to make a decision. Not enough information to invest, but to actually open a dialogue.

An interesting thing happens in investments. There is a point you need to reach in the process. Up to that point, the investor will do anything they can to throw your pitch in the trash; the attitude is very much one of "Give me any excuse to turn you down." Misspell the investor's name, have a calculation error or give a hint that you haven't done your research on your competitors, and it's game over. Once you get past the point, the attitude of the investors change. Instead of looking for a reason to throw out your pitch, they'll start looking for reasons to take things forward. Once you get to that point, you've won half the battle, and your investors will start to take you seriously. They might even take the time to correct any mistakes or errors they find, or point out additional competitors that you might consider, instead of using those very same things as excuses to turn you down. That point I'm talking about here is one of trust and mutual respect. Most startups don't make it that far, but for the ones that do, I'm absolutely certain that the first impression had an important role to play.

Before you pinpoint who to pitch to, you should get a clear picture of your business's investment profile. What is the stage of the business, on a scale from pre-seed (idea stage), prototype stage (usually no public product), pre-revenue, revenue generating and profitable? Some investors only invest in one or two stages of the business.

The next thing you need to figure out is which current categories or themes your business falls into. Some investors only invest in a particular sector. Are you doing hardware, software or both? Are you focusing on health, education, entertainment or something else altogether? How much funding are you looking to raise? Where are you based geographically? Where are your customers? All of these things will factor into whether or not an investor is interested in talking to you, so draw up a clear and concise profile of your business to aid your research into which investors you should be approaching.

Oh, and if an investor has invested in a direct competitor, strike them off the list, too. They might want to hear you out, but ultimately you don't want to show your hand to competitors because they'll be fiercely loyal to their portfolio companies. Most investors are professional enough to not share a pitch deck with a competing company, but remember that there's money on the line. If your company is completely going to upend the market of one of the investors' portfolio companies, the temptation to leak your pitch deck or share some salient details might prove too strong. Trust me, this happens much more often than people will admit.

You may already have guessed: the best way to open a dialogue with an investor isn't by sending an email to businessplans@a16z.com. I mean, you can; that's a working email address. But it is extremely rare that anything comes of this. This business isn't powered by cold calls; it is fueled by warm introductions and glowing recommendations. The way to get these introductions is to work your network. An obvious place to start is the people who are already in your address book. I'm talking about your team, your advisors, your early-stage investors and potentially even your customers, depending on the type of business you're running.

There is a pecking order in how good an introduction is. If you've already successfully raised money from a particular VC with a previous venture, and that venture went on to do a huge exit that made the VCs a lot of money, you probably don't even need the introduction (but, then again, you probably don't need this book, either). If that is the ideal introduction, it's easy to guess what the second-best introduction is. If you have someone in your network who is a successful founder, and especially if they've already worked with an investor you've identified as a good fit, ask him or her to make the intro. An angel investor who has co-invested or referred good investments to the VC in the past would make a great introduction as well.

From here, the introduction quality drops off rapidly, and eventually becomes counter-productive. Imagine if you receive an introduction from person A trying to introduce you to person B. If you can't remember who person A is, it's worse than receiving a cold email; the entrepreneur obviously hasn't done the research. On the other hand, don't forget to look to your industry service providers, too. Your lawyers, accountants and banking connections know your business pretty well. If they have connections in common with the investors you are trying to reach, that might be an efficient introduction.

Because you've been doing a lot of networking anyway, you probably have a pretty well-stocked list of connections on LinkedIn. It's a great tool for scoping out who knows whom and how you can get a solid introduction. Be careful, though; it is possible to fall into a trap here. An acquaintance who might want to impress you with how well-connected he or she is could say, "Yeah, I totally know Mark Zuckerberg. Send me your deck and I'll do an intro." Which is lovely, unless the acquaintance is overstating how well he or she knows Facebook's founder. As I mentioned, the introduction is important and you don't want someone to make a bad first impression on your behalf. It might be awkward, but don't be afraid to clarify with your friends how well they know the potential investors. They will understand.

If none of these things work, you're going to need some new friends to help you make an introduction. It's time to get creative. Events and pitch competitions (more about those in Chapter 31) can help you get started. Realistically, if you don't have a way of getting a message to a potential investor, maybe it's time to face a harsh truth: you aren't really ready to start a company.

So, now that you know how to get the attention of an investor, what should be in that message? Consider what the intended outcome of your message is. You aren't expecting investors to write you a check off the back of your introduction email. There will be a number of meetings before you get close to that goal. The mission you've set yourself at this point is just to be invited to a meeting. Some investors prefer an informal, 15-minute coffee in order to gauge how serious you and your business are. Others might schedule in a longer slot where you get a chance to pitch to them properly. Either way, the intended outcome of your first interaction is a meeting or at least a screening phone call. You need to give investors enough information to decide they want that meeting to find out more.

The message should definitely be as short as possible. See it as a micro-pitch. Include a couple of sentences about who the customer is and what the problem is. Include the size of the market, or at least make it obvious that it's a market that's too big to ignore. Include a sentence about what traction you have to date; give the investor a reason to believe that it's worth placing a bet on who you are and what you've done so far. Finally, summarize how much money you are raising, what you'll spend the money on and what milestone you are expecting to reach with that money. If your round is already in progress, it's also worth mentioning who is already participating and how much you've already raised.

An example email I would gladly forward may read something like this: "I want to introduce you to my good friend Jane. She is one of the best rounded entrepreneurs I know and sold a computer vision company to Microsoft. She is now doing something that I think may be up your alley. Nextco is working on the cross-border shopping experience problem - late deliveries, unexpected fees, lost packages, inferior quality and difficult returns - by using artificial intelligence and deep learning to expedite international delivery, eliminate fees, automate returns and create highly personalized shopping experiences that increase conversion and order frequency. The founders have built the largest fashion logistics centers in Asia - delivering 500k orders and processing 100k returns daily, scaled ecommerce operations for luxury retailers in Europe, headed up a leading 3PL acquired by Bigco and lead product at the computer vision company that was acquired by Microsoft. Nextco is based in San Francisco with offices in Guangzhou and Kyiv and is now raising Series A."

So, now that you have your list of investors, the people who are willing to introduce you and your micro-pitch, there's only one thing left to do: make the introductions! The people introducing you probably know how already, and everyone has a slightly different style. I like to keep things simple, with something like, "A, please meet founder B from company C. I've worked with them before as an advisor at Accelerator D, and I think they're well positioned to disrupt the X market with their product, they are showing some great traction in solving problem Y. I'll leave you guys to talk..."

It's short, sweet, and to the point, adding a tiny bit of context for why I am willing to invest my personal social capital in introducing this startup to an investor. If everything goes to plan, the investor will contact you and the next thing you know, you'll be on your way to a meeting. Fingers crossed.

Chapter 29

Crowdfunding

When someone says "crowdfunding," many people immediately think Kickstarter and Indiegogo. That's fair. Product-driven crowdfunding platforms get a lot of press and can be quite powerful as validation for startups.

Crowdfunding goes far beyond movies, gadgets and games, however. There have been a series of changes in the laws in US and a few other countries recently that make turning to the crowd a viable option for other types of funding. This type of crowdfunding is often referred to as equity crowdfunding, to differentiate itself from its product-focused siblings. It offers some powerful new options for startups.

A lot of the advice I have regarding equity crowdfunding and product crowdfunding is similar, but there are some important differences, so I've split this chapter in two.

Equity Crowdfunding

To understand why crowdfunding might be an interesting prospect for investors, we need to go back to the math in Chapter 27. As I showed, the vast majority of companies fail, a few make the investor some money, and a small number will bring big wins. The problem is that, from the perspective of an early angel investor, it is hard to identify which is which, so in order to make a decent return, you have to invest in a broad portfolio of startups. Crowdfunding is emerging as an efficient way of doing exactly that, which enables smaller investors to invest smaller sums of money into a larger number of companies.

Unlike many other types of investing, crowdfunding is happening in semi-public. Anybody who has a reasonably-sized bank account can be accredited as an investor, and in so doing gets access to the offerings on the various equity crowdfunding sites.

Pitching for investment on equity crowdfunding sites is not dissimilar from pitching more traditional investors. We'll talk more about pitching in Chapter 30, but for now, the main thing to keep in mind is that because of the public nature of equity crowdfunding, consider what you are sharing with the investors. This is in itself a challenge, of course. You want to tell a complete story to help your investors make the decision to write you a check, but at the same time, a lot of entrepreneurs worry about how much sensitive data they put out into the world.

Product crowdfunding is useful for marketing purposes, but equity crowdfunding is, too. As the popularity of equity crowdfunding increases, more and more large, institutional investors are paying attention to what is capturing the hearts and minds of investors on those platforms.

Equity crowdfunding is still in its infancy, and we haven't really seen many companies have exits. That's likely to be the case for the next few years, so it's hard to fully ascertain what the impacts will be. One obvious effect on the company is that instead of having two or three angels on the cap table, there could now be several hundred. The effect this has on the company's network is hard to understate; at the very least, your company now has at least a couple of hundred individuals who are cheering you on and are available to get advice from. Of course, how useful each investor is to you beyond the money they invested will vary greatly, but chances are that at least some of them can offer advice or connections. There are a number of companies who have raised follow-on funding, both from the crowd and from VCs, and anecdotal evidence suggests that the crowd can be a benefit both in terms of the number of connections and proof of early traction.

If you are considering doing an equity crowdfunding campaign, don't start with a completely blank slate in terms of investors. Tap into your network of angel investors, friends and family, and ensure that you have at least a few thousand dollars committed before you launch the campaign. This is more important for crowdfunding than for other types of investment. Crowdfunding literally has the word "crowd" in it, after all, and herd mentality is particularly visible in these campaigns. My rule of thumb is that if you can't get around 10% of the campaign committed from your personal network, you probably aren't ready to do a campaign, but you should probably aim for closer to 25%, if possible. Most equity crowdfunding platforms let you have a "private" period before the campaign becomes public. The private period is a window where you ask your own network to invest, so when the campaign goes live to the public, the pump is primed and you are able to convince other investors that your startup is worth a closer look.

Product Crowdfunding

Some industry experts argue that crowdfunding is a marketing exercise above anything. I can see the reasoning behind that. Kickstarter and Indiegogo campaigns have been embraced by companies for two key reasons: validation and money. The money part is easiest to understand: accepting pre-orders for a product that costs a lot to manufacture is a great way to smooth out the cash flow challenges of getting a product to market. The validation side of things is worth dwelling on, too; from a company's point of view, a big question is, "Does anybody want this?" Part IV of this book discussed various ways of testing that, but there is no truer test than asking people to pay cold hard cash for what you are offering. It may not answer all the questions you have about your market or your audience, but if your Kickstarter campaign sells $500,000 worth of pre-orders, that's a strong indicator that you're doing something right.

I don't know how you found out about the book you're holding in your hands right now, but crowdfunding played a role in its existence. I wrote a couple of chapters and created a crowdfunding campaign for it to gauge whether people were interested. I decided that if at least 250 people were interested in reading the book, perhaps it would be worth writing. This, in turn, is an example of failing fast. Imagine if I spent all this time writing this book, only to discover that nobody wanted it! Writing a book takes up a lot of time. This is time that might be better spent writing a different book, starting another company, researching companies to invest in or playing with my kids. I was delighted to get 282 pre-orders for the book. I had a feeling that people would be interested in Accelerated Startup, and set out to test that hypothesis. The Publishizer campaign was a way for me to do that and here I am, typing on my keyboard.

It's easy to understand how a product crowdfunding campaign is helpful in getting the word for your product out there. Don't fall into the trap of thinking that the work is done once you hit the publish button on your Kickstarter campaign, though. Crowdfunding is a tool for marketing; it doesn't replace the marketing itself. You still have to find customers any way you can and convince them that they are experiencing the problem you are solving, before selling them the solution. The great thing is that the goal for a crowdfunding campaign is obvious and unambiguous: you either succeed in making a pre-sale, or you do not. It avoids the "maybe if..." answers that you often get with other types of validation research. Perhaps the biggest advantage is that once you make it to the end of the campaign itself, you have a number of users who have already given you money. When you ask them for advice about aspects of your solution, they are likely to fill in surveys, reply to emails or pick up the phone. Their incentives are aligned with yours; they want the best possible solution for the problem they are experiencing.

One final note on product crowdfunding: Kickstarter and Indiegogo are the two biggest players in this space, but there are dozens of others, too, some of which offer specific benefits. I already mentioned the 500 Startups-backed Publishizer, which focuses on books and publishing. Other sites focus on charitable fundraising, artistic endeavors, video games, etc. The market is changing rapidly, with new sites popping up and unsuccessful ones folding all the time, so I'm hesitant to offer specific recommendations for which sites to look to.

There are a lot of specific guides out there for how you can create a great crowdfunding campaign. Going into too much detail is out of scope for this book, but there is one topic I would like to highlight. It is more important than anything else you will do. Whether you are trying to pre-sell your products or raise equity investment from the crowd, the way you tell your story is the single most important factor to your success. I've looked at a lot of crowdfunding campaigns in the last few years. The thing a lot of people get wrong is thinking that they are telling the story of their company. That makes perfect sense; if you're shedding blood, sweat and tears for your startup, it can be difficult to understand that others don't care as passionately about your startup as you do. The magic of really good storytelling, however, is to make it relatable to the person who is watching or reading the story. Put bluntly: your personal story doesn't matter.

What does matter is how your story affects the person who is watching it. The story you are telling has a goal: for those consuming it to potentially spend their hard-earned money on a product that doesn't exist yet, or to buy shares in a company that hasn't yet proven itself. The key is to tell the story of your company in a way that appeals to your audience; how you do that depends on what you are trying to accomplish. If you are doing a product campaign, you don't sell the product on how many megabytes of something or other it has. You sell it on how well it solves your customer's problems. The same is true for equity campaigns. It doesn't matter that you overcame problems in getting where you are today; that is true for everybody. What matters is how much your investors believe that you and your company are able to make them money. Tell that story. Include everything that bolsters their faith in what you're doing and help them make the case for themselves to invest in your company. It isn't easy, but again, advisors and people who aren't as closely involved with the business as you are will be invaluable here.

Chapter 30

The Art of the Pitch

f you've ever seen me speak at an event, you have probably noticed that I get very excited and passionate about pitching. There's an excellent reason for that. I believe that a great pitch is useful in so many walks of business. As the CEO of a company, you'll be pitching your startup morning, noon and night. Short, 90-second elevator pitches. Three- to six-minute pitches as part of a demo day or a pitch competition. And finally, the Holy Grail: in a VC's office, for a 30- to 60-minute explanation of what the future looks like, if you have anything to do about it. Becoming a truly great pitch artist takes a lot of practice, which I encourage you to invest time in. But that doesn't mean that there's any excuse for having a downright poor pitch.

First things first, what is a pitch? In my mind, it's a narrative that ends in a specific call to action. You're pitching because you want something from someone. Maybe you want their advice, their business or (in the context we'll be focusing on here) their investment. Whatever you'll be pitching for in the future, know that you've done many pitches for your business already. You probably pitched your friends, family and significant other to convince them that this crazy startup thing you're about to embark on was a good idea. Maybe you pitched your old boss to let you work part time, or when you told him or her you were considering quitting your job.

The "call to action" part of the pitch is extremely important. If you're including stuff in your pitch that doesn't help build the case for your call to action, you should absolutely scrub it from the script. For example, a 90-second elevator pitch has the same purpose as the introductions we talked about in Chapter 28. The idea is to get a meeting. You don't get a meeting by speaking extra fast and loading tons and tons of information into your pitch. You're not trying to explain everything; you're trying to share enough information to pique their curiosity and make them want to learn more.

Most pitches take place on a stage, of sorts. Not always a literal stage, but a stage nonetheless. Like everything delivered from a stage, your pitch is a performance. If your business is the most innovative thing on stage that day but you're staring at your shoes, mumbling and reading from the slides... guess who won't be getting a phone call.

As your company grows and evolves, you'll probably get to do a number of three-minute pitches, as part of accelerator demo days, pitch competitions, and so on. The goal here is the same: get that meeting. But there are also a couple of other objectives. If you are part of a large, well-known accelerator, you're probably a great startup, but you have a problem: you will be pitching alongside dozens, if not a hundred, other startups. They've all been prepped well. They all need to raise money. That means your goal changes: out of the hundreds of pitches your audience will sit through, you need to stand out enough that you're remembered. When the investors go home at the end of the day, their notepads will have a ton of notes scribbled down on them. Your goal is to ensure that there's a circle around your company's name, and a dollar sign in the margin.

Think of every pitch you do as a competition. You're pitching to win the grand prize in a competitive field. That means you need to be rehearsed, prepared, well rested and ready for battle. The prize, by the way? Yeah, that's that meeting we were talking about. It is a little bit like winning a hot-dog eating competition, only to learn that the prize is a jumbo-sized hot dog, but trust me: it's worth it. The meeting will include another pitch, this time about 20 minutes in length. If they like what they're hearing and if there's a good back-and-forth happening, the meeting will stretch to an hour.

So, what goes into the pitch, any pitch? First of all, you need to capture your audience's attention. They have their phones in their hand, and they are probably checking Twitter and reading emails as they watch your pitch. If they hear something interesting halfway through your pitch and decide to start paying attention, they won't have heard anything up to that point. That sucks for you, but it's the reality of things. So, you need to lead with the one thing that will get their attention. The single most important part of your presentation: traction. How well is your company doing? How many users do you have? How fast are you growing? How much revenue are you generating? If your numbers are good, chances are that the investors will pay attention, even if they're not immediately interested in your space. If someone is pitching something that is consistently growing at 50 percent per week, I'm reaching for my checkbook, and you can explain to me what it is later. It's that simple.

The next part of your pitch is what your company is about. Who is your customer, and what is the problem you are solving? This is important because if I don't know those two things, I don't have any context for evaluating the company. As I discussed in Chapter 20, it's much easier to start with a very focused customer. Make them obsessed about the product, and expand from there. In other words: it is a far better story to say that a third of people in San Francisco use your product and that you have a plan for scaling it to the rest of the world, rather than saying that 200,000 people use your product worldwide. The absolute numbers might be the same, but the implication and the story are vastly different. There is no shame to limiting your user base geographically, or to a more narrowly focused market, but make sure you explain that as part of your presentation.

Okay, we've now checked off your traction and the market, and explained why the problem is important to the users. Next, consider exploring how the problem is currently being solved. It is unlikely that you came along and found a completely new market. Uber didn't invent transportation; they just looked at the taxi industry and thought, "You know what? That's terrible, we can do better." In explaining how customers are currently solving these problem, you are helping illustrate that it is worth solving. If nobody is experiencing the problem you have a solution for, I have some bad news for you: you don't have a business. The same goes for competitors, by the way. If you don't have any, it means there is no problem, there's no market and you don't have a business.

If your presentation has gone well up to this point, the audience is at the edge of their seats. They know the market, they feel the problem and now they are eager to hear how you're going to solve this problem. Explain how your solution is perfect for the task at hand. I like to compare painkillers to vitamins: if your solution is something that's nice to have that people can't be bothered restocking when they run out, you are facing a challenge. Conversely, when my Advil bottle is half empty, you'd better believe I'll be stopping at a pharmacy on my way home. Be Advil, not vitamins, and make sure that your audience knows it.

Trust me, everything I've explained above can be done in 90 seconds. For presentations where you have more than just a quick elevator ride worth of time, hit the audience with the how. If you have 20 minutes, it's time for a live demo. If the clock is running out, a few screen shots do the trick. Either way, the investors want to know exactly how you're going to deliver on your promises.

For something to be a VC-investable proposition, the next part of your pitch is going to be all about the market. It had better be huge. It needs to be, because otherwise the VCs aren't interested in placing a bet on you. Explain how big the market is, and how quickly it is growing. In fact, the speed of growth of a market is even more important than its current size. If you are coming into a big market that's stagnant, you'll have to take each customer from a competitor with a bigger name, more money and more trust. On the other hand, if you become a leading player in a market growing 100% per year, you will grow that fast by just playing the game.

Next, it's time to explain what your business model is. How are you going to attract new customers and how is your company going to make money? How will you find new customers, how much does it cost and how long does it take? How soon will you break even on them? How much revenue will they bring your company over their lifetime? And now that we understand the total market size and your business model, provide some summary financials. How much money will you be making in three years? How big will your team need to be then?

Something your investors will definitely want to learn more about is your management team. As investors, they are about to place a sizable bet on your company. They need to be convinced that the people in the company know what they are doing and have the capacity to deliver. If you and your team have built companies and exited them before, brag about it. If you used to work at Budweiser, and you're about to launch a product that makes selling more beer easier, make that clear. If you are the foremost expert in the world on something and you have a doctorate to prove it, shout it from the rooftops. I wouldn't spend too much time on this in short pitches, but if you have a little bit more time, do so. Remember, your company's chance of success will be guesstimated based on your traction and your team. Ideas are cheap, execution is everything. This part of your pitch is where you explain to your audience that you have the right team to execute your idea. If there's even the slightest doubt in your mind that you have the right team, then stop pitching and start hiring.

Right. That's it for your pitch, except the most important part: closing the deal. A great way to end your pitch is to restate why you're there. "We have some really smart tech that will change the way you order groceries, and the best, most experienced team in the business. We are raising $2 million. My details are on the screen, please email me to find out more." Perfect, clean and to-the-point.

For the pitching itself, I want to briefly talk about body language. I strongly recommend getting some one-to-one training with a pitch coach. This is part of the package in an accelerator, but even if you haven't gone through an accelerator program (yet), try to find someone who can see you in action and give you some pointers. Exuding confidence, planting your feet solidly on the ground, projecting your voice well and working on having eye contact with your audience is crucial and not that difficult to master. All it takes is some practice.

A few investors will ask you to send them your slides before you pitch to them, which is a little bit awkward. If you've ever seen a very good presentation, you realize that the slides are there to help set the pace and to illustrate what the presenter is saying. It doesn't tell the full story. If you send the slide deck to your investors, they probably won't understand what the deal is, so I typically recommending saving it for the meeting. One way around this issue (worth considering especially if you are based geographically far away from potential investors) is to prepare two slide decks. One is your normal deck for presenting, the other is an executive summary designed for reading and getting a feel for what you're about to present.

Albert Einstein once said, "If you can't explain it simply, you don't understand it well enough." Bear that in mind; if you can't explain your company to a room full of investors who may not be experts on your market segment, go back to the drawing board.

Chapter 31

Conferences and Pitch Competitions

'**ve met with quite a** few founders who believe conferences are a waste of time, and try to avoid them as much as possible. Typically, these founders are from a corporate background and have had to suffer though some yawn-filled corporate conference on the socio-economic impact of green energy. The problem isn't that the topics are boring, but that corporate conferences often are lifeless, soul-sucking events. Startup conferences are frequently the exact opposite, for a few reasons. Remember that only a small part of a conference is what happens on stage. Sure, speakers can inspire you to do great things. They can teach you new skills or offer a new way of seeing things. But the real magic at conferences happens by what looks like luck. It isn't luck. It is, in fact, the exact opposite of luck.

To me, the best thing about conferences is that they attract a number of people who aren't usually in the same geographic space, with a mindset of communicating, sharing, learning and doing business. As a startup on the funding path, you'll probably find that conferences and pitch events are going to be up there with your most valuable experiences.

I always say that striking up a conversation is like throwing a pair of dice. If you throw two sixes, your conversation will result in something awesome: a potential early hire, an investment, a sale made, or an exchange of knowledge that means that your company is better off. You don't have to be a genius to know how to throw 12 on a pair of dice. There is, in fact, a way to guarantee that will happen: throw the dice. A lot. Instead of having eight conversations, have a hundred. Instead of spending several hours speaking with someone that you've already convinced to be a customer, go find some new ones. Being good at networking efficiently is a hard-earned skill, but I think it's worth working on.

At conferences, you'll find two potential audiences who are of interest: potential customers and the people in the startup echo chamber. They'll both exist at the same conferences, but in different ratios. Depending on what you are looking at for your startup, you can optimize your conversations and the conferences you choose to attend in order to maximize the outcomes.

When I say "echo chamber," I mean the type of events where you have startups talking about startups to other startups. These events can be helpful to your startup. You're surrounded by people who are on the same path as you, so it's a great place to get advice or to do some recruiting for your own company. The other group of people you'll run into these events are investors who are scouting for companies to invest in next.

The other type of conference is trade shows and conferences focused on specific parts of your business model. There are SaaS-specific conferences, marketing conferences and sales conferences that might be interesting. More importantly, perhaps, is that there are conferences focusing on your content vertical. If you are starting an education business, you'll want to be at the education trade shows.

It's a great way to get to know your peers, learn more about what competitors are up to and find customers for your business, and if you pick the right show, it's a great opportunity for doing a lot of early customer development.

The challenge with trade shows is that the big ones are usually annual. Unless your timing happens to be fortunate, it can be a long time for the next one to roll around. 11 months to wait for the next one is a literal eternity in startup years. Exhibiting at trade shows can be horrendously expensive, too, so think carefully. There may be better ways to deploy your limited resources.

Once you have your product-to-market fit nailed down and you enter the selling/growth stage of your startup, trade shows start to become a lot more interesting. If you are attending a business to consumer show, consider the people who come around to trade shows. At a photography show, for example, you're not going to find a casual photographer. Instead, you'll get all the gear-heads and the people who care about the technology for technology's sake. If you have a company in the photography space, then that means you have a large, self-selected audience for your products. Great—all you need to do is grab anyone who walks by your booth and sell your heart out.

As your company starts doing better and the ecosystem around you becomes more aware of you, you might be invited onto the stage as a speaker or panelist. It's an amazing ego-boost, but be cognizant of the divide between busy work and important work. It is easy to get sucked into the speaking circuit but, in my experience, having the CEO on stage is rarely meaningful to the long-term success of a startup. Spend your time carefully.

It's also important to pick the conferences you go to carefully. When my friend Matthew Prince had to choose a venue to launch his little startup, Cloudflare, he was trying to choose between DEMO or TechCrunch Disrupt. He chose the latter, knowing that a lot of investors are paying close attention to TechCrunch Battlefield. I think it was the right decision; it's unlikely you've even heard of the DEMO conference at this point. Cloudflare? It's a unicorn now.

When attending a conference, have a clear picture of what you want to accomplish, then design your activities around your goal. If you are there to meet investors, for example, spending your entire day at the stage watching people speak isn't going to help. Conversely, if you want to learn from some of the speakers, getting caught up in conversations of dubious value elsewhere in the venue isn't helpful. Time flies at conferences, so be ruthless with where you invest yours. Plan as many meetings and events as you can in advance, but keep them short and to the point.

You probably figured this one out already, but just in case: yes, you will be pitching your startup. You probably won't have the ability to use your pitch deck, but every conversation you have will include some version of the pitch you use to explain what your startup is all about. Make sure you have your narrative straight before you head to the event. One of the great thing about conferences is that you get very direct feedback on your pitch. If a particular section doesn't work with your audience, change it up on the fly. Pitching your startup fifty times per day for a week is the best way to perfect the script. Keep your enthusiasm up throughout—remember that even though you've already rattled through this introduction 35 times that morning, whoever you're pitching to now doesn't know about you. They deserve every bit of enthusiasm you've given every other pitch.

Preparation is key for great conferences beyond just polishing your pitch to perfection. Look into who is going to be there, and make sure you recognize the speakers as they are milling around. It's often far easier to have a quick chat with a speaker before they've taken the stage. Do your research, find out who you want to speak to and simply make it happen.

Remember that, just like you, the people you speak to will meet dozens, if not hundreds, of people at a conference. See these new encounters as the beginning of a relationship rather than as ships passing in the night. Follow up with people you've met by email as soon as you can. Refer to something you spoke about with them, or include a link if you mentioned something in particular you would send through (or if they mentioned something they were interested in). And, again, just like with any other pitch, make sure that your email has an ask, or a specific outcome you are gunning for, such as a meeting, a coffee or a piece of information. Always ask for something or offer an actionable item, because it means you're opening a conversation. Just emailing "Nice to meet you, stay in touch" is guaranteed to go nowhere.

Depending on your audience, don't forget about social media. Using social media to engage with other people at the event is easy. There will probably be other attendees tweeting with the event hashtag. Keep an eye on it; if someone pops up who seems like they are particularly worth seeking out, engage them on social media and arrange a quick coffee, for example. It doesn't take much, but it means you have pre-qualified the people you're speaking to and it means you increase your chances for achieving your goals.

As your team grows, you'll probably stop sending every single team member to every event, but of course, the team members that do go will be learning things. I encourage teams to do a knowledge transfer at the end of a conference. Write a blog post for the company blog or intranet about what you learned. Even a short "Five things we learned, and five things that surprised us" email message to the whole company is useful. Conferences aren't cheap, so anything you can do to maximize the value for the company is helpful.

Pitch competitions are often an element of startup conferences. They can be a great way to get introduced to investors, and pitching well from a stage can do wonders for your confidence. Of course, whether or not pitch competitions are worth it often comes down to the conference itself. If you've been successful in hustling your way to be invited to pitch at Founders Forum or TechCrunch Disrupt, you'd be crazy not to. If you get yourself in an accelerator program, the demo day pitch is going to be fantastically valuable, too. Either way, make a cost/benefit calculation as to which pitch events you attend. At some point, it will stop making sense. Even though pitching can be tremendous fun, if the value isn't there, stop.

Sometimes, you get startups going on stage speaking about their metrics and how successful they are, but without having a clear ask from the pitch. Don't do that. Unless you have an idea of the intended goal of taking the stage, it's a waste. If you're not raising money or you don't have a product to launch, you probably have better things to do than spending days rehearsing for a performance that will go nowhere.

Ultimately, trade shows and conferences are intensely hard work. To get the most out of the event, you need to prepare in advance. Part of that preparation is making sure that the part of the team that isn't participating in the event aren't left hanging; you will need to be fully, 100% present at the conference to make the most of it, so make sure your team knows who makes decisions in your absence, or that they have enough to work on while you're out. During the event, you'll be on your feet most of the day, striking up conversations, networking and getting feedback on what you're up to. In the evenings there's chances for more networking and you need to try to carve out the time to contact anyone you spoke to that day. After the event, recapping it all to your team and doing a retrospective to find out what worked and what you would change for the next event is important.

Whatever you do, bear in mind that your company is not about the products and services it sells. It is about the people it solves those problems for. It's about your team, your investors, your advisors and your customers. All of this is about people, and the better you get at convincing people that your business has a fiercely bright future ahead of it, the more benefit you will get from networking events. It's a virtuous circle: keep working on your networking skills and always work on improving your pitch. You never know who you'll meet in the next coffee queue.

Part VIII—Questions to Ask Yourself

Fundraising is one of my favorite topics. A lot of the speaking I do is about how to put together and deliver a great pitch. As a venture capitalist, a lot of my interactions with startups are in the context of raising money. And as an advisor, I know how important it is to keep your eyes on the prize, ensuring your company is always moving in the right direction. Nowhere do all of these things come together as when a startup is raising a round, so getting things right is crucial to your sustained success.

First off, I strongly encourage you to build a three-year metrics roadmap. Of course, you're building an agile business, so things may change, but having a good plan in place is a crucial first step towards figuring out how much money you need to raise. The roadmap shouldn't be as much about the product as it is about the metrics you track in your business, and where you expect them to be.

Once you have your metrics road map, overlay that with a product and sales road map. To achieve the goals you set in your metrics roadmap, what products do you need? How many customers do you need to find, and how are you going to reach them? What is your marketing strategy to deliver on your metrics?

Armed with your product-and-metrics roadmap, it's time to start plotting out how much all of this will cost. Create a resource plan that shows how many staff members you need. Figure out how much money you'll be spending on sales and marketing, and what impact this will have on your number of users. A lot of this will be pretty heavy spreadsheet shuffling, but it is important; only by having a clear picture of your road map will you know how much money you need to raise. I would add another 50% on top as contingency, and, as I mentioned in the introduction of this section, tack on an extra six months for the series A fundraising, just to be sure.

The outcome of all of the above is really just a dollar sign and a number. The number represents everything you need to raise in order to build your company. Perfect; now put together the other 9-10 slides of your slide deck. Remember to build a compelling narrative, and once you have your pitch deck together, find some of your entrepreneurial friends and pitch your company to them. Ask them to be brutal with their feedback. No matter how harsh your peers are, investors will be even more critical, and they won't give you the slightest hint on what you're doing wrong.

Part IX

Growth

Starting your company was hard. Finding the product market fit was hard. Raising money was hard. But as you reach your growth phase, it's time to really prove what you and your company are all about. Whether you're optimizing for dollars, eyeballs or other metrics of success, reaching the growth phase of your company means it's time to grow, rapidly, at any cost.

Starting to scale and grow your business is where you'll really find out if you were right about having a replicable business model. There aren't really any ways to cheat here, either. Before you start scaling, you might be able to step over the odd hole in the ground or duck under the tripwires, but that doesn't work when your company starts accelerating. If anything about your smooth-running machine isn't as well-oiled as you thought it was, trust me when I say that this is when you will find out.

The truth is, most companies fail after they've secured their first few customers, not before. Growing too fast is a pretty common mode of failure, too. Software scales infinitely, but the operational side of your business might not.

The inability to build scalable marketing and sales models becomes the Achilles heel of many entrepreneurs. In Part IX, I will discuss how to build a business model, explore today's marketing mix, figure out how to create a scalable sales process, and go after major customers and ways of working with partners.

Chapter 32

Measure Everything

The first idea for your company came to you in a wave of gut-feel guided inspiration. That works for the very early days of a startup, but as soon as you move out of the starting blocks, a more scientific approach is useful.

There are a few reasons why startups have opportunities that businesses a few decades ago didn't have. We live in an always-on, always-connected world. More and more software is moving from the desktop into the cloud. This book is an excellent example. When I speak to successful authors, even pretty technologically savvy and experienced ones, they talk about sending Microsoft Word documents to and from editors and collaborators. Microsoft Word! I'm sure Microsoft's flagship word processing tool is the right tool for some people, but in a collaborative world, we have much better tools. Sharing and working collaboratively on the same document is a lot easier on a cloud-based solution such as Google Docs. Sure, it doesn't have all the desktop publishing tools of Microsoft Word, but working on a document together is far easier, and it doesn't matter which version of Word your collaborators use or which computer OS they are on. Combine the ease of use with the price (Docs is free), and choosing the tools for writing Accelerated Startups became easy.

Forgive the aside on word processing. The thing I want to highlight is that, as an independent user, I don't pay for using Google Docs, so how does it make sense for Google to build and maintain such a big product? To be fair, some companies do pay for Google Docs, but I'd hazard a guess that the metrics and data Google gets from these services are far more important than the cash they generate. Millions of people write emails in Gmail and documents in Google Docs, and Google can use use machine learning to learn more about the English language, and many other languages as well. That alone gives them a tremendous competitive advantage over other companies who need a huge sample for natural language processing or AI.

The point I am making is about the value of data. Facebook is valuable to advertisers because it knows more about its users than the vast majority of other sites. Uber is building a huge database of how people move in cities. A company like Mailchimp knows more about what makes a successful email campaign than most other companies; it can use the findings as marketing to attract even more customers. The value of the data collected by these companies is crucial to advertising, future products and marketing, respectively. The sooner you can start collecting data on your own customers and progress, the better.

Ask yourself a question: "How do I measure success in my business?" The answer will depend on the industry you are in, but there will be some metric that encapsulates how fast your company is growing. If you are creating a free-to-use app, your monthly active users number (MAU) is going to be your weather vane for knowing how things are going. If you are running a SaaS business, your recurring revenue is your guiding star, often expressed as a monthly (MRR) or annual recurring revenue (ARR) metric. If you are running a marketplace business, metrics like number of sellers, number of buyers, average time until a product is sold on your platform, number of items for sale, average value of item, total commissions and a ton of other metrics spring to mind; any one of them could be representative of how you build and grow your business.

In order to really get down and dirty with the numbers, however, you need to measure a lot of different data points. I encourage you to measure everything that's measurable from the start. Even if you don't report or dig deep into every aspect of your business, it's helpful to have data you can go back through to find causality or correlations between different aspects of your business.

I'm a big fan of the so-called "Pirate Metrics," as explored by Dave McClure. The name is a joke; the metrics in question are Acquisition, Activation, Retention, Revenue and Referral. With an acronym like AARRR, of course they would be called Pirate Metrics! The idea is to find metrics that reflect each of these five stages of customer engagement, and then focus your attention on the part of the customer journey where you are losing the most conversions.

Imagine your sales funnel is a giant leaky bucket. Everyone who ever hears about your company goes into the bucket, but there are some areas where you lose people. By measuring everything about your business, you can determine where you're losing customers and come up with a plan for how to patch the bucket. Start measuring your process as it currently stands, and then gradually improve your metrics to improve your conversion rate. Most importantly, once you have a large amount of data, you can start getting help from people. Your advisors might comment that your activation rate is extraordinarily high, but your number of paying customers is low, and they might be able to suggest ways of improving that ratio.

Imagine you have a software as a service accounting software package such as Freshbooks, Xero or Quickbooks. Your service is starting to get a little bit of press, and you have been out there pitching your startup at various conferences. Every time someone hits your website for more information, he or she should be tracked as an acquisition, ideally with the source captured as well. Traffic from social media, from news sites or from other sources can and should be separated (more about why in just a moment).

Once you have your customers on your site, you have to interact with them somehow; some people will never be converted, but if you're able to capture some data about them, you're on your way to modeling your business. Imagine you spend $1 on Google Adwords for each customer who visits your site. Out of them, 10% sign up for a free trial. That means that $10 bought you 10 visits to the site, and one new customer. In other words, if those numbers hold true over a larger number of customers, your average Cost of Acquisition (CAC) is $10 per customer.

Once someone has signed up for a trial, you need to convince him or her to "activate." For the accounting software example, you might want them to connect the software to a bank account or integrate with Dropbox for capturing receipts. Or maybe you want them to enter their payment details, as this tends to be a strong indicator that the customer wants to continue to work with your solution. However you define an activation, measure it. This is something you'll be working hard on optimizing later.

Next, you're going to want to figure out how much it actually costs you to service a customer. If you have a self-service model, the marginal cost per customer is probably next to nothing, but if you are sending out physical products, or you need to dedicate staff time to each customer, it does incur a cost. Add all of these costs up, and you know your Cost of Goods Sold (COGS).

The next metric you'll be looking at is revenue per customer. Some customers may be worth more money than others. If you find a group of customers who are worth a lot more than others, you can trace them up through your metrics, find out where they came from and how you were able to convert them, and focus more of your marketing there. It's not rocket science to conclude that it makes sense to spend $1,000 to acquire a customer that will make you $50,000 in Lifetime Value (LTV).

On the other hand, you may find that you have a large number of customers who aren't as valuable. They might only use the free version of your product, or maybe they only sign up for the newsletter. They are not without value, as a portion of them will eventually convert, or they might be useful for referrals further down the line. It doesn't make sense to spend $1,000 on someone to only sign them up for the newsletter, however.

Once you have an active customer, your challenge becomes to keep him or her as a customer. This is what "retention" means. Especially in companies that charge a recurring fee, such as a SaaS business or subscription-based businesses, retention is the lifeblood of the company. The cost per month multiplied by the average time your customers stay around becomes your customer Lifetime Value (LTV).

Now, you can start bringing the numbers to life. As long as your COGS plus CAC is less than a customer's LTV, you are running a profit on your product. In theory, this means you are ready to start scaling rapidly. As soon as you're ready to pour $10 million into marketing and create $15 million of revenue, you've achieved the gold standard for a startup.

The final moving piece of the Pirate Metrics model is referrals. Are you able to incentivize your customers to become your champions? Uber and Lyft do this by offering both you and your friend $25 worth of fares for making a referral, which makes sense on two levels. Giving you $25 is a great way to incentivize you to promote Uber. Giving your friend five $5 rides is a great way of trying to get them to change their habits. In order to get full benefit from the promotion, they have to use Uber 10 times. Uber's bet is that in those ten rides, the customer will be convinced that Uber is a great way for getting around town, and the hope is that your friend will continue to use the service even when the free rides run out.

There are many, many more things you can and should keep an eye on. Measure things that are specific to your industry and to your company. Measure every interaction your customers have in your product; it might help identify different behaviors that are strong indicators (or contra-indicators) of future behavior. You might discover that people who stopped putting receipts into the accounting software for six weeks are at an 80% chance of "churning," or cancelling their subscription. If that is the case for your business, you can put a plan in place for when someone hits four weeks. Offer them help with entering receipts or send a reminder that putting receipts in regularly is a better way of staying on top of your accounts. You could even incentivize them by saying, "If you enter three more receipts, you can get the next month's fees at 30% off." Use any creative solution you can come up with to re-engage your customers.

Once you have all your metrics in place, start graphing them over time and pay attention to trends. I find it extremely helpful to focus on one metric at the time. For example, if only 2% of your customers are sharing your product, set a goal of 10% and brainstorm with your technical and marketing teams to see how that goal might be reached. Once you get close enough, move to another goal. Perhaps you want to increase the average spend of a customer from $30 to $35 per month, for example. Come up with potential reasons for your customers to spend more money with you, and see if you can convince them to do so. Continually revising, improving and optimizing your sales funnel is the best way to gradually grow your business.

The other thing you find once the metrics are growing at a healthy clip is that the different metrics affect on each other. If you get customers to refer new customers, your average cost of acquisition might go down. If you are able to increase the average time your customers stick around from 12 to 18 months, it'll increase your LTV by 50%, which in turn means you can afford to spend more money acquiring each customer. If you're able to do A/B testing on your website to find out how to activate a higher proportion of customers, the cost of acquisition might drop sharply, which again has a knock-on effect on all other parts of the business.

As an investor, I only take companies who have instrumented their business and know their numbers seriously. It shows me how well the company is doing, of course, but more importantly, it shows that the founders understand what it takes to build a business. Measuring everything you can think to measure is the first step.

Chapter 33

The First 10,000 Users

How do you measure success when your product is free? For free-to-play games, applications and web-based software, the metric that matters is your number of users. However, the exact definition across all business models can vary wildly.

The metric that I think makes the most sense for most companies is Monthly Active Users (MAU). This particular metric is defined slightly differently from product to product. Some apps consider users "active" if they open the app. That makes sense for products where users don't really need to interact to get the benefit out of the product (such as an app that simply reports the weather). If users open the app, it's fair to assume they've looked at it, even if they did nothing else. In other categories, just opening the app does not make for an active user. For example, if you create an app that is for adding receipts to an expense report, you'd expect the user to add a receipt to qualify as an active user.

The distinction is important, because many founders tend to

gravitate towards vanity metrics in the absence of true product traction with their chosen audience. One company I was advising was covered on Good Morning America. The company saw a 9,000% rise in traffic on that day, which sounds amazing, right? It turns out, however, that the conversion rate went through the floor, and overall the company only saw a 1% bump in revenue that month. A lot of founders will argue until they are blue in the face that a 9,000% rise in traffic for a day is valuable. "Think of the long term brand awareness," they will say. Maybe, but unless traffic has inherent value (for example, if you sell advertising on your website), traffic in itself is meaningless. The founders were understandably excited about having been featured on television, but I wanted to grab them by the shoulders and shake some sense into them. A 1% bump isn't worth the amount of time that's wasted to get a television appearance.

Another way to see your route to the first 10,000 users is to consider whether the metrics you are tracking are actionable. If they aren't, they probably aren't really worth paying attention to. Think of the long-term goal of your company. You know who your customers are, what their problem is and what your solution is. The metrics you use as tools to help make decisions need to reflect those goals. If you are able to increase a particular metric 15% week over week, does it help you reach your goal? 10,000 users might seem like an arbitrary number. It is arbitrary to a degree, but there is some logic behind aiming for that particular figure. It's a critical milestone that proves that your product solves a valuable customer problem or is otherwise interesting enough to a substantial audience. Those initial sign-ups or downloads rarely come fast for most startups and require a combination of built-in product sharing features (or virality, if you like), publicity and advertising.

Growth can come from any number of sources and as your business starts picking up speed, don't write off any of them. I've heard of apps that have had great success in sending direct mail to customers' mailboxes. Whenever you order something from certain online retailers, you also get a small stack of promotional flyers and money-off coupons for their partners. Whenever you get food delivered, you're likely to get a flyer for another complementary service. It all makes sense. If you are selling car insurance, making sure your brochure is available in a car dealership is prudent. If you sell new, high-tech flip-flops, sending a 10% off coupon to everyone who books a flight to Hawaii might be a great way to capture people when they're in the right buying mood. As with all marketing, creativity and catching the customer at the right time are crucial.

For most companies who measure their success by the number of times their app is downloaded, you'll find that the hockey stick growth will probably come from a few tried and tested marketing channels. These include advertising, affiliate marketing and attempts at making the app go viral. Remember that your customer acquisition strategy will likely consist of a number of different channels, each with their own idiosyncrasies.

For example, encouraging your existing customers to tell their friends is a way of amplifying "word of mouth" marketing. This will probably be one of your cheapest ways of getting new customers, but the problem is that it doesn't scale very well in many cases. This will be related to your viral coefficient. You may have heard the phrase "going viral," which is the Holy Grail for this type of marketing. It is defined as having a viral coefficient of more than one. In other words: every customer who signs up will cause more than one other customer to sign up, on average. It takes hard work, careful design and a little bit of luck, but it's obvious why this is so attractive; going viral means that your company will go through a phase of explosive growth.

Even if your company or product doesn't go fully viral, remember that any word-of-mouth growth is good for your company. If every two customers you add to the product, on average, recruit another customer, that's a viral coefficient of 0.5. Not "viral," but still extremely valuable. See it as an amplification effect. The result is that every $1 you spend on advertising gives you 50% more value per customer signed up. Designing incentives into your product workflow and asking your customers to tell their friends is always a good idea.

Especially in their early days, a lot of startups have scaling challenges. In the beginning, it is fine to do things that don't scale fully. That might mean that you're still doing part of the process by hand, or that there are inefficiencies in your processes. Leverage that; quite a few startups have very effectively added a road block for themselves, by having a waiting list for customers. It certainly worked for Gmail's early popularity. As a result, Google was able to scale the service slowly enough to avoid running into capacity problems. Growing this way has several advantages. You can collect information about customers early on, and you can encourage people to "get bumped to the top of the list" by sharing your service with others. However, this doesn't work well for many business models. One reason this may work well is the psychological effect of scarcity. If you see everyone rushing to a product in a store, you might get interested. If you see the product running low, you might buy faster. All these people can't be wrong! Of course, it's absurd to have scarcity for software, but it still works extremely well as a marketing tactic.

When you're growing your early user base, remember that you are not necessarily looking for the customers that cost the least to acquire. They might not actually be representative examples of scalable growth. Ideally, you will find a marketing channel that is elastic, which means that you can pour as much money into it as you're able to afford, and therefore grow as fast as you can handle. The key is to always ensure that you have a high enough ROI that every dollar you spend returns more than one dollar in long-term value. The only way to know whether a particular marketing channel is worth pursuing is to ensure that everything is measured, tracked and analyzed, and that you are making changes based on the things you are learning about your customers' behavior.

Having accurate metrics is how you can reliably grow your company, especially if you're in a position to start spending money on customer acquisition. Online advertising is not only one of the likeliest methods of driving signups, downloads or sales today, but can also be very helpful in shaping the product itself. It is important to build a solution customers can instantly recognize as something useful to them. Testing advertising messages for click-through and conversion, measured through ratios of signups, downloads or sales, is something that any successful startup does with a high level of sophistication.

If you're selling physical objects, trying to sell 10,000 of them is a straightforward goal. In most cases, however, you're trying to get consumer engagement of some sort. Your milestone probably isn't the number of users who signed up at some point, but the number of customers who are active on the platform. This could be a number of paying subscribers, or another metric that more accurately reflects how well your customers engage with your company or product.

Whether you are building a subscription-based SaaS or a company that relies on a high number of free users, keeping your hard-won customers around is the key. Your most important growth metrics will probably be based around retention, rather than just getting the customers in the first place. To analyze why and how people are leaving your service, you're going to have to look at your churn rate. It's no good signing up 300 new customers one month if 250 of the ones you signed up the month before stop using your service. Your net growth is only 50 customers at that point, and trying to find out why your customers are leaving, and preventing that from happening, might be a more productive use of your time than figuring out how to bring new customers on board. The number one reason most startups fail is trying to scale prematurely. If your churn is still high, the last thing you should be doing is throwing your limited ad money down the drain. Patch that hole in the bucket as quickly as possible.

Some degree of churn is natural. Some customers will discover that the service you are offering is slightly different than they expected. Others might need your services for a while, but then eventually just lose interest and leave. For others, their situation might change. For example, if you offer payment services, but your customer changes its business model from a paid-for app to an advertising-driven model, there's not a lot you can do to retain them. Figuring out why your customers are leaving, however, is still an important thing to keep an eye on, especially in businesses where engagement is paramount. Even just reducing your churn rate from 6% to 5% will have a tremendous long-term effect on the business, and will bring your 10,000 active users goal in range significantly faster.

Fine-tuning your marketing activities in your existing marketing channels is a given. But even if you've found something that works, don't stop looking. A lot of startups are quite formulaic in their marketing, which means that some marketing channels are extremely crowded. In Chapter 34, we'll talk about media coverage, which works great for some startups. For other companies, engaging with potential customers on social media works very well. Try meetups, arranging your own events, or going to trade shows. Don't leave any stone unturned. Creative, high-energy marketing is hard to get right, but when you do, it's a licence to print money.

Some people like to refer to metrics-driven marketing efforts as "growth hacking," especially if the marketers also have decent coding skills. In reality, marketers have been using metrics in their efforts for as long as marketing (and metrics) have been available. I'm not a huge fan of the term, but if you're looking to hire someone specifically to help with this aspect of your growth effort, the title growth hacker might come in handy to attract someone with the right combination of technical and marketing skills.

In the process of working on your new startup, you also increase your domain expertise dramatically. This is valuable to your startup, of course, but don't forget that it may have value beyond your own company too. Having a company blog where you share findings and news about your industry can be a tremendously valuable resource. When done right, company blogs can go viral and have a serious trickle-down effect on sign-ups and sales. There are a lot of reasons why blogging and creating great content for your site is generally a good game plan. Optimizing for search engines (SEO) is particularly important; visitors that come to your site because they are searching for relevant information in Google and other search engines are in effect "free," meaning that a good content strategy can result in a very high return on investment.

All in all, there are many marketing channels and tactics available to you today. To create long-term, sustainable growth you'll need to set sales or usage goals and utilize all of the tools at your disposal to go from a startup experiment to a real company. The metric confirming that your product or service has product-to-market fit may or may not end up being exactly 10,000 users. Whatever that number is, it has to show that you've figured out how to consistently and profitably find customers. There is nothing more existential to your business than this.

Chapter 34

Journalism in the Digital Age:
A Blogger's Perspective

John Biggs is a serial entrepreneur and an editor at TechCrunch, the most read technology news source online. I've known John for years and we've shared many stages and pints around the world. Getting press can be a huge boost to your company and I couldn't think of a better person to tell you how to do it in this guest chapter.

Without further ado... ladies and gentlemen, John Biggs.

* * *

I've been taking PR calls for 15 years. In the beginning, when everything was new and the world was bright, I cheerfully answered all comers and actually said nice things. Now, 15 years into the game, I've garnered a reputation as a curmudgeon who hangs up as quickly a possible. I'm a difficult journalist and I make a PR person's life harder. Except I'm not really. I've just come out the other side of the looking glass.

Here's the problem: you have no news but you deserve coverage. Anything you tell me is immediately suspect but it is part of my job to cover you. Your ideas are small, unimportant and boring, yet you could change the world. So we're kind of stuck. In addition, you sent a PR person after me, which is a bad move. It shows that you're too busy to tell your own story, and no one is too busy to do that unless you have millions of dollars to throw at a real, solid PR person. Your $8,000 a month hack won't cut it.

It's a dilemma. How do you tell your important story in the right way? The first step is to figure out what your story really is. But first let's talk about blogging. I used to tell people that blogging was journalism on a tight deadline, but I've since learned that I was wrong. Blogging is journalism and it's only one part of the strange, interconnected world of media. In fact, I'm now the old man at the barricades yelling that listicles, viral videos and social media aren't true sources of news. I'm wrong, of course, but I do enjoy yelling and I've gotten a lot better at social media since I gave up my prejudices. In short, everything I wrote is at once correct and incorrect. I was correct in assuming blogging would be the future, but I did not understand the overall intensity of the media as a global phenomenon.

Want another prediction? Pretty soon PR people are going to be extinct. Soon brands will connect directly to consumers in an unmediated stream. We will not be able to tell the difference between "content" and "advertising" and programmatic tools will allow brands to target consumers on autopilot, a process that will track users from item to item and, ultimately, put both us journalists and PR people out of a job.

So this is important for both of us. I believe journalism—whether it is focused on fashion, art, world politics or tech—is a worthy endeavor. And I know it doesn't exist in a vacuum. A good PR person is a journalist's counterpoint. There are multiple ways to build a band. The journalist is the bassist—forgettable but important—and the PR person is the drummer, the one who keeps driving things forward. You are the lead singer. We backing players exist primarily because unmediated brand-to-consumer connectivity is far too imbalanced to maintain a free and open society. When consumers are bought and sold like pork bellies, we all lose.

The thing is, I don't like you very much. It's not personal, but let me tell you what I think about you. You seek attention in the same way a toddler takes it: repetitively, with no subtlety and with no grace. If you think that your job is hard because you have to cold call me and try to game the system with sad-sack techniques, you are mistaken. Your job is actually hard because you make it hard. A good marketing person's work is effortless. It is a process of storytelling, active thinking and strategy. It isn't pressing "Send All" in MailChump and then waiting for the coverage to roll in.

Again, I'm jaded. I don't want to hear from you over and over. If you've gotten past my surprisingly simple gatekeeping system, then you're probably in anyway and shouldn't worry too much. If you haven't and want to know why you're failing, I'll tell you in this chapter. I want all of us to succeed. End of story. Like one of those parasites that replaces a fish's tongue with itself, I expect you to be as close to me as you can. It is by doing this you make both of our jobs easier. PR is about relationships. It's called Public Relations for a reason. These relations are gold.

For us to get along well, though, you need to have real "news," so let's start there. Let's try something. See if you can find the "newsworthy" stories in this list of sample press release headlines: "Wanglo Hires Noted Ebay Engineer As Head Of Product," "Flarpo Adds iPad Support To Its SaaS Cat Walking Platform," "Boof, The App For Boxes, Is Now Android Watch-Ready!", "Krablr Launches New Stores In Scranton And Austin," "Goopo Acquires Fish Scale Measuring Company Flippo," "Bob's Hot Sauce Changes Its Label."

If you are the CEO of Flarpo, Boof, Krablr, Goopo, Flippo, or Wanglo (or you're Bob) you care about these headlines implicitly. These things are all "newsworthy" because they signal a milestone in your business, a change in the status quo and a massive improvement to the world in the form of a launch, an acquisition, an update or a hire. But none of these are news. Not to me. Not to most of the tech press.

Yes, in the fish scaling and hot sauce rags you've got some news here. And that is where the press releases need to go. If Bob knows the folks at Hot Sauce Monthly, then he can pick up the phone and tell them he has changed his label. It's a big deal for the editors of Hot Sauce Monthly. But if Bob—or any of these folks—hired a PR person to blast this news, they've wasted their money.

Why do we want to send out press releases? To tell the world about our projects and to sell more product. That's all. It's seen as an opportunity for free advertising. But everyone else has the same idea. Want to know how effective those press releases will be? Want to know how much upside you'll get? Here's a little exercise: instead of writing a press release and hiring someone to disseminate it, write the press release yourself. Take your time. Take a week. Show it to lawyers. Get sign-off from all the investors and partners. Hire an editor to make it great. Spend some money. Worry about it all week. Do nothing else. When you are done, please drag the press release into the trash can and delete it. Erase it from everywhere you have it stored. Never talk about it again. Then, instead of hiring a PR person, take about $8,000 (which is maybe $2,000 less than an entry-level PR person will cost you to reflect potential sales) and burn it. Take it out into the parking lot, put it into a bucket and light it on fire. Then go inside and do it again and again and again. Write a dozen more press releases and thrown them away. Burn more money. When you try traditional PR, that's what you get: zero. Bupkus. Nothing.

That's the value of PR in a crowded world. When everything is said, then nothing is said. The world is too busy for your milestone. You need to grab it by the scruff of the neck and force the issue.

When you pitch a story, your mission is to tell a universal story. It must be a human story that resonates throughout media, from top to bottom. The story must resonate with Hot Sauce Monthly and the Columbus Dispatch. It should work well on CNN and on local news. It must be a mirror of society as a whole. Anything less is piffle.

I'm going to give you an example of how this works. Let's say Bob is fighting depression. He's been dealing with it for decades. So if Bob took my advice, the next obvious move would be for Bob to release a press release that says "Bob's Hot Sauce Changes Label To Support The Fight Against Teen Suicide." It's human, it's friendly and it touches on a problem we all face. But it's wrong. Bob's efforts are good-hearted but they are not newsworthy. They resonate in a few places: potentially a partner he's working with on the project, potentially Hot Sauce Monthly, potentially the folks who eat and like his hot sauce. But what's the real story here?

Bob is fighting depression. He is so dedicated to helping people that he is doing the only thing he knows how to do. He's making great hot sauce and, while doing it, he's getting the word out about depression. He's serious about this. He's realistic. And he will be successful. The true story, the true piece of "news" is this: Bob is a real person fighting a real problem and he needs your help. Please write about his hot sauce. Please tell his story with him. Hot sauce sales might go up but that's not what he wants. He wants help. Authentic stories will beat milestones every day. It is hard to find an authentic story. In some cases it's impossible. And that's fine. Don't use PR. Don't send out releases. Sell your product, buy ads and keep at it. But you must be a boring person indeed if you can't find something that will interest the world about your business. The best stories are stories about tradition, dedication, adversity, pain, fear, redemption.

If you don't have a good story, then make my job easier. This is my go-to list of questions for startups. They apply in every situation and they're valuable at all times. Use them when you send opening emails to journalists and you'll never go wrong.

Who are the founders and what is their background? What is your funding? How much traction do you have? (Real numbers: monthly or daily active users, not downloads or registered or transaction volume.) What are the key differentiators between you and other players? Describe the genesis of the project. Describe the project in your own words.

Don't just answer these questions in order. Answer them in two paragraphs.

Joe Smith founded Zombo.com to help his daughter with her zombie costume. The company has raised no money and is self-funded with 5,000 customers daily. We have sold 20,000 zombie costumes so far. We are different because we only sell zombie costumes - all kinds. Need a Walking Dead costume? We got it. Need a zombie with no head? No problem.

Joe created Zombo.com when he realized zombie costumes weren't realistic enough. He made his first costumes out of rubber at home and then began mass producing them in Detroit, where he lives. In short, Zombo.com is the worlds only zombie costume outlet.

Pretty cool, right? Easy? That's all you need to do.

You've probably heard something about embargos. Forget everything you know: the embargo is dead. Or, rather, the embargo for the embargo's sake is dead. But what is an embargo? And why does it exist? The first embargoes were designed primarily to put everyone on a level playing field. News, in the old days, was spread via snail mail from PR people to journalists and then published on paper. This took time. Press releases are still sometimes sent in the mail, but only by the most eccentric PR professionals to the most eccentric journalists, and it's only a matter of time before these two groups keel over their postal scales forever. Press releases sent in this manner took days to arrive. Therefore, so the Scranton paper could be on the same footing as the New York papers, the PR person set an embargo. This gave the Scranton folks a little more time to write while New York got special treatment thanks to a deskside visit (a term of art that journalists hate to hear these days) or a fancy cocktail party. Scranton got the news but New York got the love.

This system has remained in place since those days simply because it gives the PR person a modicum of power. By assigning a time frame to news (a process that is literally called a "Time Frame" by negotiation experts and is a way to exert pressure without seeming to) the PR person makes the biggest splash and makes it seem like the news is important.

We all know that having a story go up at the same time all over the world is a big deal. This allows maximum exposure for minimal cost. But when every single news story from "Osama Bin Laden is Dead" to "Porktron Introduces New Grade of Inedible Pork Byproduct Classifications" is embargoed, then there is no value in the embargo.

Even a few years ago the embargo still worked. Getting the word out about the Sony W23XRZZ99 Transistor Radio was a hard job, to be sure, and telling everyone on the world about it at once made a lot of sense. But that was when Sony and many more companies released hundreds of products a year. Now, in the consumer electronics market, Apple reigns and there are multiple tentpole launches per year, but not so many that you flood the market with news. Therefore overexposing a particular product is a bad idea. Having one day full of reviews of a product and then no follow-on coverage is a waste of time for both the client and the reporter.

Ultimately the embargo makes the client feel better. It makes everyone excited for, quite literally, a single day and then helps the product sink into obscurity. The scoop, as it has always existed, is gone. There is no value in being first for journalists in 2016 primarily because they have been burned time and time again by embargoes. Good journalists will overshoot an embargo by a few hours or even a few days, and only stupid journalists line up to take an embargoed story. I haven't acted on a piece of news from an embargoed story in years. It's not worth my time, and there are many journalists in the same boat. The blogger's publishing schedule is such that it makes no sense to drop everything and write about something that is launching a few days hence. News happens during a single day. There is no time or value in dropping today's news to focus on tomorrow's. This is a reflection of the current always-on news cycle. Again, when news broke in the morning and afternoon papers, an embargo and general media bombing was a solid strategy. Today it is not.

So where does that leave you? It leaves you in the enviable position of working directly with a journalist on something special they can have for their own publication. Instead of an embargo, let's call it a "unique." The timeline should be this: a week before, reach out personally to your favorite journalists and tell them the story. Say you will send the press release in a week and tell them that the website (a key portion of any online story) is offline right now and will be turned on in a week. They can see it early and you can even send screenshots. Three days before, send out a mass email about "an exciting piece of news we are about to announce. Look out for it." One day before, remind the journalist you're about to send news. Ask if they can work on a special story related to it. This requires that you understand the journalist and the journalist's beat. This isn't an exclusive, it's a unique. Work with the journalist to frame a story that will be of interest. On the day, release the news. Let the blogs pick it up, as they inevitably will. You already allowed bigger guys to pre-write their uniques—even if the uniques just include different quotes—and the little guys simply scavenged through the press release. Everyone feels like they got a heads up, the news gets out, and you get coverage over a 24-hour period rather than a 1-hour window.

Uniques aren't difficult nor are they much different from embargoes. However, by using embargoes you are essentially saying "You are unimportant enough in our eyes to get special treatment but you are important enough to our marketing plan to be part of our massive roll out." If you want to be a PR professional in the 21st century, one-on-one connection is key. Anything less is failure.

The exclusive comes at us in a similar vein. By offering exclusives you intrinsically exclude everyone else from covering your product. But remember: it's not an exclusive if no one cares. Like the proverbial tree in the forest, if your exclusive is handed over to a big organization and is lost, then you're essentially burning relationships instead of getting news out. Exclusives are stupid unless the product is truly revolutionary, and it never is.

You need to understand that in a world of exclusive, exciting news nuggets it is insanely difficult to get above the noise. The only recourse, then, is to create an authentic relationship with your target journalists. They have to look forward to hearing from you. This doesn't mean you have to send them cookies at Christmas and organize bar crawls for their birthday. Instead you take them out for a coffee and tell them about your clients. Be sure you are well aware what they are writing about (there is nothing worse than pitching car stories to booze writers or fashion stories to power tool bloggers) and while it would be helpful for your journalist friend to expand his or her mental reach, you're not the person who will do it.

The Bottom Line is that as a journalist, I would love for you to be a friend or as close to friendly as possible. I don't need any more

PR people in my life. I want founders, creators, makers. Reach out to journalists you admire and tell them this. I know the lawyers will warn you not to and expensive PR people will tell you that you need them (and, if they're good, you will need them once you get too big). But in the end it's just like Notting Hill: you're just a founder, standing in front of a journalist, asking him or her to love you.

Chapter 35

The Sales Funnel, Elephant Hunting and Partnerships

As you might expect, your route to making a sale will differ depending on your business model. The higher-value the product or service, the more complex its sales process typically becomes. The process is important to success, not because it is how you start getting revenue into the business, but because the repeatability of your sales process is the number one indicator of how well you'll be able to grow.

The complexity of the sales funnel depends largely on how much your average customer is likely to spend with you. If you have a free app, you probably can't spend too much per customer, because the customer's lifetime value (LTV) is low. If you are selling enterprise solutions that are worth millions of dollars per quarter, you can obviously spend more to acquire a new customer.

On the enterprise side of things, sales cycles are often slow. If you're looking to sell your fancy new drone solution to the US Army, expect years of vetting, background checks and meetings just to be added to the approved suppliers list. From there, you still have to do the actual selling. On the other hand, the military tend to be a reliable customer that has very different requirements than most others, which can make those contracts a lot more lucrative than in the private sector.

One approach is to outsource the sales of your product to channel partners. For example, if you're a huge hotel chain, your most valuable customers are the ones who go directly to your website or call in to the front desk of the hotel to make a booking. No middlemen, no commissions, just profits. However, most of us don't book hotels that way. In the hotel industry, channel partners like Expedia, TripAdvisor, Orbitz and the thousands of travel agencies out there drive traffic to the hotels.

If you're reading this, it's unlikely that you're starting a hotel chain, but that doesn't mean channel partners are irrelevant to you. Dropbox is a great example; it was doing perfectly fine growing off word of mouth, but the install base for Dropbox users had a huge, sharp increase as soon as the company negotiated a deal where it was pre-installed on Samsung devices.

Similarly, think about the world of search. Google makes most of its money from advertising that is relevant to the searches you make at Google.com, but what happens when traffic starts shifting from the desktop to mobile? As Apple's iPhones became more popular, Google was facing a conundrum. The company needed to be the default search engine on Apple's devices in order to continue driving traffic. Back in 2014, Apple threatened to make Yahoo! search the default, but Google ended up paying the phone manufacturer a billion dollars to stay the default. In fact, there has been some speculation that Google's eagerness to get involved with Android was in part to control a slice of the mobile phone market, ensuring that the company's search and native apps stayed installed.

If you create car accessories, convincing car manufacturers to include your accessories as standard might be prudent. If you're an app creator, being preinstalled on devices as they ship from the factory is the Holy Grail of app install numbers.

Remember that the first question any potential buyer will ask you is, "What is in it for me?" That is doubly true for partnerships, and the secret to crafting successful partnerships is ensuring that the arrangement is beneficial to both your company and the business you're teaming up with. Looking at the Apple/Google partnership again for a moment, it's easy to see how that's a symbiotic relationship. Yes, there are other search engines out there, but none of them are as good as Google, so defaulting to Yahoo! or Bing would create a poor experience for Apple's customers. By letting Google take over default search, Google generates revenue from Apple's customers, while Apple's customers, in turn, enjoy a better user experience. And, of course, Apple can generate revenue from Google.

A great partnership starts the same way as an investor relationship. Much like raising money, you're going to need to hunt down the right person on the right team to get the ball rolling, and a warm introduction is the best way to go. Work your networks, leverage your strengths and sell the partnership on what your partner stands to gain.

This is going to sound obvious, but it's important: to make a $100 million per year business, you can either make 100 $1 million sales or a million $100 sales. Or, more realistically, anything in between. The biggest thing that changes between the different models is how you find, reach and sell to your customers. What works great for a customer looking to buy a $100 per year service probably won't work for your $1 million customers, and vice versa. You might be willing to get on an airplane to get a $1 million contract across the finish line, but that won't be the case for someone who wants to buy a $0.99 in-app purchase in a game. You need to adapt your sales and marketing strategies accordingly.

In the world of enterprise business, huge sales are where it's at.

To be successful in this market, bear in mind that you probably can't outgun Microsoft, IBM or Oracle for marketing spend at their own game. But there was a reason you started your company in the first place: you are offering your customers something that nobody else can. The trick is to make that an advantage and convince the world that you are the best company to offer that particular solution. That was true when you were fundraising and putting your team together, and it continues to be true when it comes to selling your products to your potential customers.

It's almost certain that somebody on the buying side will be taking a chance on doing business with you. There's a reason why the phrase "Nobody ever got fired for choosing IBM" exists. If the solution works out well, it's a win. If it doesn't, you went with the market leader, so whoever ultimately made the decision has someone to blame. That is less true for a large corporate taking a bet on a startup, so you should factor that into your pitch. To take an example: there's a pretty good chance that IBM, Microsoft and Oracle will still be around ten years from now. Unless everything goes to plan, your company won't be. Most startups fail or are acquired long before that amount of time rolls by. Convincing a company to take a chance on your solutions despite this is part of the challenge.

While startups do face a few sales challenges that more established companies don't have, the deck is not completely stacked against you. As an agile startup, you're able to move faster, adapt more quickly and integrate far faster than more established players. I once sat in on a meeting where a startup pitched to do a particular task for $700,000. The large multi-national consultancy firm who was also in the meeting laughed at the startup, saying that they would need six months and around $1 million just to scope the project. They wouldn't commit to the final cost of the project, but later confided in me that it would be in the tens of millions of dollars. This, to me, is the perfect example of how startups are able to turn the process on its head. The consultancy firm would possibly be a more accepted choice for the large company in question, but it's extremely hard to ignore a price tag that is an order of magnitude lower.

Similarly, when I ran my web development company, we beat a well-known and well-respected design powerhouse on a bid to redesign Namco's (home of PacMan) website. We cut the price by a factor of three, and got the contract as a result. A lot of the subsequent success we had as an agency stemmed from this crucial point in our history.

I am not saying that you should compete on price. Anybody who has ever worked as a freelancer or as part of an agency knows that trying to undercut the competition is a long-term losing game. Pricing work done as a one-off is an art in itself. Even if you offer enterprise API or software solutions that are mostly off the shelf, remember that there is invariably some integration work that needs to be done to make your solution work for very big clients. Keep this in mind when you price your solutions, and remember that exceptional solutions command exceptional prices. Even if you have free and cheap self-serve tiers on your platform, there is usually a space for a top-level tier in your business model.

That doesn't mean that when you sell 10,000 software licenses you should automatically give a steep discount, by the way; your customers are coming to you because you are solving a pain point. Yes, it is fantastic that you'll be able to fill 10,000 seats, but your business model will change here. The usage patterns for your 10,000-seat customer will be different than a customer who uses 20-30 licenses. It may prove technically cheaper to serve the large customer, but they might have higher customer service requirements and different security, integration or data collection/reporting requirements. Because each of these huge accounts will have unique challenges, you should treat each of them as a different sale, with a different negotiation on price.

One interesting example is the UK Government. The Gov.uk Government Digital Service (GDS) covers almost every aspect of UK government. Most governments would probably have created their own ticketing system to deal with customer support for their digital portal, but in this instance, the government decided to go another way, choosing Zendesk for its digital help-desk. A huge scoop for Zendesk, of course, but you don't have to look far to see why this makes sense for the GDS, too. Instead of having to dedicate resources to developing, maintaining and supporting a piece of software, it can spend that time helping customers. When the GDS bosses looked at Zendesk, they concluded that it had the best cost/benefit ratio of all the options available to them. For our purposes, there are two things worth noting. For one, it's really exciting that a relatively young startup like Zendesk is able to make a sale to the government of the country that ranks number five in the world by GDP. Secondly, you can bet that GDS has a very different contract in place with Zendesk than what you or I would be offered if we signed up for Zendesk via the website.

When selling to large organizations, it becomes crucial to play to your strengths. There will be aspects where you can't compete, so make the most of the parts where you can. Personal customer service, price and the passion you have for solving your customers' problems are very hard to replicate for large businesses, so use those as selling points in your pitch.

Because sales cycles to large businesses tend to be slow, it's a good idea to focus on making local sales first. You will probably have a lot of meetings to iron out the details, and having to jump on a plane or drive for long distances to seal deals will probably be a challenge. This is one of the considerations when you are deciding where to locate your company.

Because large companies have a lot of staff, it's a good idea to get creative about how to get on the company's radar. Imagine you are selling a new type of ergonomic chair; who would you approach? The HR department seems obvious, but that's the route every other salesperson also has taken. Think creatively: who gets the most value from an ergonomic chair? The people who sit the most. Who are they? The developers, perhaps? If so, maybe a different approach would be to sell your products on their benefit (less back pain, more productivity) to the company's CTO. If you get through to the CTO, rest assured that he or she will understand the problem and the solution you are offering. As a result, you will be able to leverage the CTO's influence in the organization to hear you out. In the end, it will probably still be the HR department who places the order, but they're a lot more likely to listen to an email from their CTO than from someone who comes and knocks on the door. Break or bend the "rules" of the game if you have to, as long as you get the results you need.

The API company Twilio springs to mind. The company kicked open the back-door to enterprise sales in a fantastic way. In the months leading up to the company's IPO, it had a billboard along the highway coming into San Francisco. It had the company's logo, and the phrase "Ask your developer." Genius, because it worked as a sneaky introduction to a lot of the company's potential customers. Managers who didn't know what Twilio was might take the billboard up on its advice, and ask their developers. Developers who saw the billboard and didn't know what Twilio was, would look into the company's products and services. After all, imagine how embarrassing it would be otherwise if your boss came in and asked you about Twilio, and you didn't know?

Again, your network is going to be the most efficient way in. Use your knowledge of the industry and the people in it to get warm introductions to the people you need to reach.

Chapter 36

Dialing For Dollars

Few things are as important as getting early customer feedback on your products and how well you are solving their problems. Inexplicably, many founders prefer to send emails or use other indirect communication media. There seems to be a notion that if your emails are good enough and if your automated sales and marketing approach is thorough enough, you will be successful. That might work for some, but I believe that strategy puts most founders at a tremendous disadvantage.

Being good on the phone is a skill that can be learned. There are a lot of tips on how to be a great salesperson (and I'll talk about some of them in this chapter), but the single most important aspect of being a great salesman is enthusiasm. You started your company because you believe that you have a problem that is worth solving. You love your customers. You want to help them. Picking up the phone to ensure that you're helping them is the least you should do. You might learn a few things and make a few extra sales in the process, too.

Remember that you're a founder. To get here, you've probably already proven yourself to be a pretty successful salesperson. You've pitched your company to investors, cofounders and staff. You've done short elevator pitches and longer pitch presentations. Selling is more of the same, but with a slightly different angle: instead of raising funding or hiring a staff member, you're selling a product to a potential customer.

All founders need to get very comfortable with sales techniques and selling their products. There is no one who is more passionate about the product than the founder. Magical rainmaker sales people exist only in fiction. Sales and getting early feedback are very similar in this respect. Both take a lot of hard work, but the payoff is tremendous. Don't outsource early sales; as the founder, you are very well positioned to sell your product. Just go and do it.

In Chapter 32, we talked about the marketing funnel in the context of measuring things. The funnel exists in a less abstract way in sales, too. You need to find a number of people who can be sold to. This is sometimes called lead generation or prospecting. The goal at this stage is to find customers for you to talk to. Collecting business cards at a conference works, as does working your network or doing research via LinkedIn or other platforms. In the end, the only thing that matters is that you want a list of a hundred or so companies or target customers to talk to. At this stage, you'll also want to consider the types of potential customers who would be willing to buy a product or service from a startup in the first place. In reality, only a small proportion of potential customers will be future-oriented and innovative enough to do business with you. Don't let that deter you; yes, you may have to sift through a lot of stick-in-the-mud customers who aren't willing to take a chance on you, but the ones who are willing will give you huge insights into the problems you're solving and the solutions you're offering. The best customers at this stage will not just be willing to pay you for your products; they'll also offer you some of your best feedback. In short: do whatever you can to get the first contact and schedule a phone call as soon as you can.

Part of getting this first call is all about research. The very least you need to do is to understand the business your customer is in. If they have competitors (trick question—everybody has competitors), know who they are, and ideally how the companies differ. Remember that sales is about solving a problem, of course, but it is even more about having a connection with the person you are selling to. Think about it this way: would you rather buy a very good solution from a lovely salesperson, or the perfect solution from someone who was rushed and didn't really seem to care about your challenges? In the cold hard light of day, and reading it on this page, you would probably argue that you'd take the better solution. But if you were being honest, wouldn't you agree that there are some phone calls you look forward to, and others you really don't? The same is true for your potential customers. If they look forward to your calls, you're a few steps ahead of the game already.

Once you have your potential customer on the phone, the really hard work begins. And by really hard work, I mean shutting the hell up. In a perfect sales call, you give a short introduction to the problem you are trying to solve, but ideally, the person you are speaking to will be eager enough to have the problem solved that he or she will take the reins. Perfect—this gives you have a great opportunity to hear how your potential customer actually describes the problems he or she is facing. Sometimes, it turns out that your product doesn't solve the exact problem, but in my experience, that is valuable, too. I've seen more than a few businesses who, in the process of talking to their customers, adjusted the product to fit customer needs at this point, and built fantastically successful companies as a result.

There's an old saying: you have two ears and one mouth, because you should listen twice as much as you speak. In sales calls, that's definitely true. The key to enabling that to happen is to ask a lot of open-ended questions. "What is the biggest problem facing your business right now?" "What is preventing you from growing faster?" "What are the challenges you have with your customer service solution?" "What would your perfect solution look like?" You may not always get the answers you want here, but that's fine. The key is to listen, take notes and learn.

When you do ask questions or make comments, remember that the conversation isn't about you. You are probably going to be very excited about the features you just launched and the innovations your company has introduced into this market. Great, but irrelevant; your customers want to know what's in it for them. Make sure you understand the problems they are trying to solve, and then feel free to explain how your product is the perfect solution. Resist the temptation to explain too early.

After you've had a call, whether for sales or for customer development purposes, be rigorous about following up. Realize that everyone who has the authority to make a purchase from you is probably a busy person. That means that unless you somehow end up on their (no doubt very long) to-do list, that next step is never going to get made. As a startup, there will always be many reasons not to do business with you. That's fine, but that's also a problem: it's easy to delete an email. Being relentless in your followups and making sure that no email goes unanswered is key here. There are a few tools you can use, but the cheapest and simplest I've found is Boomerang. It's a browser plugin that works with Gmail. The main feature is to remind you when you haven't received a reply to an email, which is a crucial aspect of effective sales. I urge you to never give up until you get a "yes" (either a sale or feedback) or a "no" out of somebody.

The mantra for a good salesperson is ABC: Always Be Closing. If you're making big sales, that probably means that at some point you will be talking about contracts with your customers. If that's the case, my top tip is to not sweat the small stuff. When writing contracts with corporates, the legal department will invariably get involved, and you'll get your contract back covered in red pen. That's OK—that's their legal team doing their work. Work with your own lawyers to ensure that you know which parts of the contract are crucial, and which ones you are willing to let slide in a negotiation. Especially for early deals, it doesn't make sense to lose a deal over details. It's better to have one customer with a slightly wonky contract than no customers at all. It's better to have eight customers on slightly different contracts than two on the same contract. If your company is successful, these things won't matter in the long run, and if your company fails... well, it doesn't matter either.

You're now in the growth stage of your company, so chances are you've heard your fair share of soft "no"s already. An investor who tells you they might want to invest once you hit a certain milestone, or a potential hire who says they'll get involved when you have ten staff. They aren't setting you a goal, they're saying no. Or at least almost no. This happens in sales a lot, too. Many of the people you try to sell to will tell you that they would buy your product if it just had one little extra feature. Or that they'd sign up for your conference if someone else is going to be there, too. Or maybe they'll introduce you to a key potential client, but only if you do something for them first. As founders, our first instinct is to leap on the opportunity. We'll code up the feature, we'll try to get that one speaker to the conference. We'll just jump through that one final hoop. Understandable, but be aware: if your company is a successful painkiller, your customers won't care that there's a side effect or two. They won't mind that your product doesn't remove 100% of the pain, as long as it helps significantly. If a potential customer quibbles over little things, they're not quibbling: they are saying "no." Move on, and focus your attentions elsewhere. If you want, follow up six months down the line, but in my experience, these sales pitches just don't go anywhere. Regroup, and go for the next customer.

After you've successfully made the first 20-30 sales, it's time to think about scaling the operation. Don't make the mistake of hiring a senior sales person right off the bat; hire two hard-working juniors instead. They'll be able to take what you've learned about what works and what doesn't, and polish it further. Once they start adding their own twists to the sales processes, they can start learning from each other, and you can take half a step back into more of a manager position. For the next step of growth, hire a VP of sales. His or her job isn't going to be to sell the product, but to hire more sales reps to further scale growth.

Chapter 37

Building a Community

The best companies evoke passion and excitement from their customers. For some companies, it happens organically, but for most, building a community around customers is something that needs to be done consciously. The seeds for a powerful community are sown from the beginning. The community depends on how you communicate with your customers, and how they're able to communicate with you in return.

Building a community isn't just a nice-to-have these days. A strong community has a number of advantages to your startup, and the sooner you can start building it, the better. Your community can help beta-test early versions of software. They often help each other come up with creative ways of using your product, and will be some of your most ferocious champions. I've come across examples where members of the community ended up being worth tens of thousands of dollars in sales, just because they kept referring more and more customers to a business.

Think about that for a moment. Why would someone be willing to put their social capital at stake to recommend a product? The answer is that people start feeling a sense of ownership. It's like people who love sports; when "their" team wins, they feel personal pride, happiness and accomplishment. When you're a young business, playing the underdog card and making your customers feel valued can build a strong tribe around your brand or your product. These are people who will leap to your defense when someone says something bad about your brand. They will jump into the comments on news stories about competitors to make sure that readers know about you. And they will amplify your message at trade shows, online and offline.

The question is, how do you go about encouraging such behavior? In my experience, the best communities are created when the company already has an open communications policy. Moreover, some of the most fanatical cheerleaders I've ever seen for startups are converted from customer service channels. When customers have a bad experience, don't think, "Ugh, how are we going to deal with this guy?" Think, "Yes! Someone who reached out to us for a solution rather than giving up on us! We can delight them!" People are far easier to delight if they expect mediocre service but are met with enthusiastic, pull-out-all-the-stops customer service.

As an example, I know the CEO of a hardware startup who became aware of a customer whose product had died in the hands of FedEx on the way to their house. In looking up the customer's information, the CEO realized that the customer was only a 20-minute motorbike ride away, and since it was a nice day, he decided to jump on the bike and hand-deliver a new product to them. Can you imagine? Of course, this doesn't scale, and it doesn't work for all products. In this particular case, the customer was blown away. It turned a negative experience into a hugely positive one, and this customer turned out to have a lot of sway in the educational ecosystem. Soon, orders for the product started flowing in from universities all over the country. Would that have happened anyway? Maybe. In taking 45 minutes out of his day, this particular CEO sparked a sequence of events that generated tens of thousands of dollars worth of sales.

Community building isn't entirely dissimilar to networking in general. Just like with networking, you'll have a large number of more or less nice conversations that don't end up being worth your time. The ones who turn out to be worth it are the 10x customers who can amplify your message and brand far beyond your own networks.

Facilitating a community means participation. Many companies do this by starting and maintaining their own forums or discussion boards, but others have been successful in creating an "official" Reddit forum (called a "subreddit") for the company. Don't ignore the other obvious places discussions take place. If you run a crowdfunding campaign, be active in the comments. If you have a Flickr pool or an Instagram presence, make sure you participate in the conversations that happen there. And, of course, be active on your company's Facebook page and on Twitter as well.

Some of the conversations will come to you; participating in those is table stakes in today's busy and noisy social media market. It is also possible to bring your community to people, however. The king of this is probably Gary Vaynerchuk (whose book Jab, Jab, Jab, Right Hook is worth reading). He took over his father's wine business. By having a passion for wine and social media, Gary started wading into people's conversations about wine. He interjected with statements such as, "I saw you tweeted about red wine X, have you tried the similar but cheaper wine Y?" without necessarily linking to his own store. By being part of the conversations, he was able to become a voice in this space, which caused the business to start growing rapidly.

There are other ways of diving into conversations as well. Think about any platform where conversations that are related to your company or your market are taking place. I already mentioned Reddit; if there is a subreddit that is relevant to what your company does, create an account and dive in with solid advice. The same goes for Quora, Stack Overflow or any number of other websites. There are a lot of topic-based discussions going on, and there's nothing wrong with injecting yourself and your company into the narrative. Do be extremely careful, however. People don't want to be marketed to at this level; offering genuinely good advice that may or may not involve your own company is important, as is gauging the tone of the discourse that is going on. In a way, you're barging into a conversation that is happening among friends in a bar. There's an appropriate way to do that ("Hey, I couldn't help but overhearing you guys talk about bourbon. I love bourbon, have you tried High West's Bourye?") and an inappropriate way ("I'mma let you finish, but we all know Bourye is the best and everything else sucks, ok I'm going now, bye.").

As your community starts to get some momentum, it's time to find ways of leveraging the community to help you out. Creating a separate mailing list for your highest-value mavens (read Malcolm Gladwell's The Tipping Point for more about mavens, how to find them and how to influence them) and simply explaining to them what your business needs goes a long way. In my experience, the people who love your company and your brand, who feel an ownership of what you're trying to accomplish, will go above and beyond what you would imagine to help out. Some communities organize meetups, others will volunteer to help create tutorials for your products, and others again would be delighted to write guest posts for your company blog about your product, how they use it and how it makes their lives better. All you need to do is ask, and be aware that you can't always completely influence your community. It will take on a life on its own, but that's often part of the excitement. You're creating something that has become bigger than the office where the actual work is done.

If your product has a creative aspect, consider showing off the things your customers make using your product. If you are Nikon (used by professional photographers all over the world) or Adobe

Photoshop (used by all photographers around the world), it is easy to imagine what such a photo gallery might look like. Be creative, however; even businesses that aren't inherently creative might come up with great user-generated content that showcases the sort of things your customers are doing.

If you're creating a holiday app, encourage your users to submit holiday photos. If you create a dog walking app (and I hope you don't...), have a "Dog of the Week" gallery. People love feeling included in the community and are proud of being featured. Photographs are also great tools for bringing companies and products to life, so it's a win-win.

Communities built around a company are like communities everywhere else. You'll have leaders who drive the community effort forward. You'll find the odd loudmouth who is just bored and out to stir trouble. It'll have ebbs and flows of activity and interest. The bottom line is that people choose to be part of a community because they feel they get something out of their affiliation. Your least valuable community members are part of it on the off chance that you might post a 20% discount voucher from time to time. The most valuable members are active, opinionated and extremely powerful taste-makers for your product. They'll be the first ones to stick their hand up when you ask for volunteers or feedback. They might not always be right, but you're far better off with them on your side than alienating them by not listening to them.

Managing a community is important to its success, and there are different approaches on how to do that. Some companies see great success with just passively monitoring the community and occasionally stepping in when there's a question. Others hire dedicated staff as community managers who help shape the conversation, police any unwanted activity and even organize events for the community.

Remember that your community will often be an extension of your user experience and your customer support efforts, but don't be tempted to see community purely as an expense. A lot of companies see customer service and community as a burden, but with that mindset, it's unlikely that a thriving community will develop. Virgin Atlantic is a great example of this; by focusing on customer service above everything, it has built up a strong user base of people who are championing the brand. In my friend circle, whenever someone has a bad airline experience (we all travel a lot; it's not rare), someone will pipe up with, "Should have flown Virgin." These people aren't paid to say that, but they feel such a strong ownership and affinity with Branson's airline that they will wade into conversations on the brand's behalf. You can't put a monetary value on that—it is priceless.

How close you choose to get to your community depends entirely on your business model, and whether or not the community is going to have inherent value. Don't get me wrong, the choice isn't about whether or not you have a community of people talking about your brand; that is going to happen regardless. The choice is how involved you want to be in the conversation, and whether you are making a space available for these discussions to take place.

Chapter 38

Industry Events and Trade Shows

n Chapter 31 we took at look at pitch competitions and conferences in the context of your fundraising journey. In passing, I mentioned that industry events and trade shows were of limited use. That is true, when you are raising money. When you're growing, though, things change quite a bit, and suddenly trade shows become a lot more useful.

Whatever you do, the first time you go to a particular trade show, don't go as an exhibitor. All trade shows have quirks, and doing a solid reconnaissance run is a good way to make sure you don't end up with a booth that gets very low foot traffic because it's in an awkward corner. More importantly, in my experience, you can often get a lot out of trade shows by being an attendee. It's a lot cheaper than setting up your own booth, and it's a much better way to do a deep dive into your competitors and potential partners than being stuck in one place while the trade show rages around you.

Going to a show or industry event isn't that different from going to a conference, in that proper preparation prevents poor performance. Before you travel to the show, you should have an idea what you're trying to achieve. Check in with your goal throughout the show, too, because before you know it, the show will be over.

Most trade shows publish show guides as PDFs, interactive websites or apps. Read through them, and create a list of the exhibitors you really want to have a chat with. Focus on those in the first half of the show; it's easy to get distracted by other exhibitors, and nothing is as frustrating as missing out on having a conversation with someone who is in the same town as you only once per year. If there are more than one of you going from the company, coordinate your efforts to cover more of the show between you.

The other thing worth planning is what information you need from each exhibitor. Some will be very forthcoming about price, but for others, you need to work a bit to get a price indication. Some will be more than happy to talk about the underlying technology, whereas others will clam up immediately. You may not be able to get all the information you are looking for from every exhibitor, but if you don't ask the same set of questions to everyone, you lose the ability to compare them properly.

A lot of startups are doing away with business cards these days. Most of the time, that is fine; for trade shows, not so much. Having plain cards with space to write on the back is perfect; it's pretty common to jot down a quick note on the back of a card to remind you why you need to get back to someone—making that easier for people is a winning move.

Oh, and as long as we're talking logistics, don't forget to book everything as early as possible. Especially when big shows are in town, hotel and travel prices spike like you wouldn't believe. Booking early can help save some money. After booking the tickets, I find it becomes easier to carve out some time to do research and preparation, too, because the question of whether or not you're going is answered.

As you're working the show floor, remember that every single person is there because they are interested in the industry. That means that everyone around you is a potential partner, employee, competitor or mortal enemy. The only way to find out who is who is to strike up a lot of conversations. You have your pitch down pat; use it! The flipside of that is that you'll often run into people who try to sell you something that is irrelevant to what you are doing. If you have your software business in the cloud, but they are trying to sell you servers, saying a polite "No, thank you" and moving on saves your time and theirs. At trade shows, time is a valuable commodity, and the people pitching you will appreciate the quick answer.

As a final tip for shows: get the hell out of there well before it closes. Towards the end of the day people don't have as much energy and the show stops being fun, but more importantly, there's nothing as annoying as being stuck in a two-hour line for buses, taxis or whatever other transportation is available.

Exhibiting at a Trade Show

The first thing to know about exhibiting at a trade show is that all trade shows aren't created equal. There are some behemoths that everyone in the industry is drawn to, but you have to make quite the spectacle to stand out from the crowd. The shows I'm talking about are NAB if you're in film and TV, CES if you are in consumer tech or consumer electronics or SEMA if you're in the automotive space. As a startup, you're unlikely to be able to out-spend Sony, Samsung or BMW, so you have to be smart about where you deploy your time and money.

Exhibiting at trade shows can be extremely expensive, and the costs often go beyond just the space rental. I've seen trade shows that will refuse to let you install your own TV screen, for example, so you have to rent one from the venue (usually at a price similar to what you'd pay to buy the same television), and pay the union laborers to install the TV for you. The same goes for a lot of things on a booth. Booths often just come with the concrete, so you need to pay for flooring and any basic carpentry to put up anything in the booth. Anything to do with electrical will come at a cost, too. I have seen trade shows where exhibitors pay $200 for three days' worth of electricity, and only get one power outlet, to boot. Before you decide to exhibit, make sure that you get a full quote, and beware that some exhibition halls and/or shows refuse to give you a comprehensive quote. It can be a complete shake-down; make sure that whoever is in charge of arranging the booth for your company has done it before, or gets some advice from someone who has. You wouldn't be the first company to have over-stretched on the financial commitment and ended up suffering financially for quite a while afterwards.

Oh, and on the topic of the booth, here's a pro tip: don't skimp on the flooring. When you walk around a trade show, you'll find that some of the booth have soft, bouncy flooring that feels almost like there's a layer of rubber underneath the carpeting. It can feel weird at first, but trust me: that's what you want. If you are going to be standing up for ten hours per day for a week straight, a combination of good shoes and soft carpets will save your back, your legs and your will to live.

Booth design is crucially important for trade shows. You are going to need something to stand out from the hundreds of other exhibitors at the show. Find a creative way of showing off your product's benefit that visitors can understand at a single glance; that will be the difference between them shuffling past your booth or engaging you in a conversation. Remember that your booth will look differently when there is nobody standing in it and when there is a throng of people, so ensure you repeat your key messages higher up on the walls of your booth, so potential visitors can see what you are selling over the heads of other show-goers.

Don't be tempted to place tables along the outside of the booth. Psychologically, the separation isn't helping you, but it also means that your visitors have to stand in the aisle of the trade show. If your booth is successful (and it should be—you have an awesome product to sell, right?), it hinders the flow of traffic, and people will pass you by just to avoid the stoppage. Instead, put the tables near the back of the booth, and place any promotional material or flyers on the tables.

In my experience, it's often helpful to come up with a question that can qualify your customers right away. When it's quiet, stand in the hallway of the show and ask your question to people as they walk by. "Does your business send text messages?" is a great filter; if the answer is no, and your company does programmatic SMS messaging, then you can wish them well and send them on their way with as little time lost as possible. "Are you looking for ways to engage with your customers better?" or "Do you know how much money you lose every month due to fraud?" are other good ones. Be creative, and ensure that your main selling point is part of the question.

Once someone engages you in conversation, it helps to be able to walk him or her into the booth. Do your 90-second sales pitch, answer any questions, and ideally capture his or her information. Some trade shows have scanners to scan the badges of show participants. Again, these can be ludicrously expensive, but do the math. If you are able to collect a couple of thousand qualified sales leads, it may be worth investing in the rental of a badge scanner. If not, there are a lot of iPad apps that can be used for collecting customer data. If you are using Mailchimp for your emailing list management, look into the (terribly-named) Chimpadeedoo app that helps you import email addresses directly into your Mailchimp lists. At the end of every day, simply send out an email to everyone who just joined the list to keep your leads warm, and then start selling in earnest.

Trade shows can be great for building your community, getting sales leads, making actual sales, informing potential customers about what you are doing, finding distributors for your products, scouting out potential partners and much more. It's helpful to have the conversation about what your priorities are before you open the booth on the first day; there will be situations where everyone at the booth is engaged in conversations and more people are turning up. For situations like that, try to keep one person free to field short questions and hand out promotional/informational material.

A good strategy for some companies is to have a booth manager who can help direct traffic. The booth manager keeps half an ear on all the conversations that are going on; if one of them seems unproductive, a quick tap on the shoulder of one of the team mates with "Hey, Steve is here to see you" works wonders; it enables your teammates to wrap up conversations that are taking too long without being rude, and it means you are able to increase the number of people who are flowing through your booth.

Whether I'm at a trade show as an exhibitor or as a visitor, I always find them invigorating. There's something inspiring about being reminded who your customers are and how they react to your products. It's a great way to re-align the expectations from your customers too, to see what the recurring questions and objections are and to figure out whether there's anything you can change about your pitch to make it better and more efficient. If nothing else, after a week of speaking to hundreds of people back-to-back, your short pitch of what your company does will be pitch perfect!

Part IX—Questions to Ask Yourself

The growth stage of a company will always give you a lot to think about, but as we wrap up Part IX, let's pause for a moment and consider what "growth" actually entails.

As a startup, you are working towards very specific milestones that all culminate in one thing: proving traction. Even if you screw up everything else about the business, as long as you can prove that your customers want to give you money to use your product, you are onto something. Deep in the bowels of your company, there is going to be a metric that is the be-all and end-all of your company. If that metric goes up, you're doing well. If it goes down or remains stagnant, you are dying.

For some companies, a single metric does the trick. For SaaS companies, it's usually monthly recurring revenue. For free apps, it's monthly or daily active users. For your company... it's your turn now. What do you think is the single most important metric in your company?

The other consideration is that a lot of metrics are trailing metrics that prove only how well you have been doing in the past. If you are looking at monthly sales figures, for example, chances are that on the 10th of February, you're analyzing how you did in January. As a result, you are looking at data that is almost five weeks old. That works for some businesses, but ideally, your business will also have leading metrics. These are metrics that tell you something about what your future will look like. Not all businesses have access to, or are able to generate, leading metrics, but that shouldn't stop you from trying. Look outside your business at the wider industry. Is there anything you can measure or analyze to help predict the future? For example, if you double the number of sales leads in January, does that double the support burden and triple your revenue in March? If so, start using these numbers in your forecasting and planning. Leading indicators can be a red herring (that is, the correlations you find may not always hold), but anything you can do to help predict your future performance can be immensely valuable when predicting and generating future growth. Give it some thought.

Part X

From Project to Company

A startup isn't a smaller version of a large company, but what happens when your startup grows at a rate that means it is on a course to become a true enterprise? Eventually, you will have done everything possible at the startup phase. At that point, you have two options. One is that you've proven that there is no space in the market for the company to exist, and you're going to have to find a way of closing it down.

The other option is that growth continues, and at some point the organization becomes so big that the original founders barely recognize what they've created. This is a sensitive and very important part of a company's development.

Entrepreneurs who start companies and professional managers who know how to run a large business are two wildly different types of people. It's possible that a startup CEO can learn how to be the CEO of a larger company gunning for listing on a stock exchange, but more often than not, the interests of startup CEOs simply lie elsewhere. Founders often don't survive the transition from small, scrappy startup founded in someone's garage to large company, but this phase is a necessary aspect of a successful company. In Part X, we're going to discuss scaling, how to take on the international market and hiring experienced managers.

We're also going to be talking about how you stop being a startup. That can mean bringing in a layer of management and turning your startup into a company, shutting the startup down or leading the company to an exit. Either way, this is where the rubber really hits the road, so strap yourself in, the ride is about to get bumpy...

Chapter 39

Transitioning From Startup to Company

At a certain point, a startup ceases being an experiment and becomes a company. That transition is a surprise to some founders, and often an unpleasant one. In this chapter, I will take a closer look at what it means to "grow up," and help prepare you for some of the changes that might be coming your way.

Often founders get so caught up in the startup journey that changing gears becomes hard. They will continue to look for a business model or to innovate in some aspect of the business model long after they've arrived at the destination. The company has already found a repeatable business model. It is ready to scale and accelerate. It is important to acknowledge the transition process to becoming a real company and the comfort zone for each individual founder. Realizing that you're built for the scrappy startup life and you're wilting on the vine in a larger corporation is fine. You chose to found a startup for a reason, and for many founders, one of those reasons is to escape corporate life.

Waking up one day and realizing that your little company has become something else can be hard to admit.

It is possible, even easy to run a company with a relatively flat structure up to about about 25 team members. Beyond that, it starts to become daunting to be a new employee; it's hard to get to know 25 people properly. It also becomes less necessary. When there are only 15 people in the company, it would be weird if someone in sales never spoke to the designer who sits in the corner and creates the product they're pitching. When the company starts growing, however, the salesperson is more likely to speak with the product manager. There's less of a business reason to speak with the designer directly. At some point the sales manager talking directly with a junior designer becomes downright inefficient. That change starts to happen at 20 or so team members, and will definitely rear its head at 25. This coincides with when it becomes helpful to put a formal structure in place, and usually also with when a startup flips into rapid growth mode.

The truth is, as soon as you have a product-to-market fit and a repeatable, scalable business model, your entire area of authority changes. Steve Blank makes a great argument when he points out that a startup isn't a smaller version of a big company, but the corollary is also true: a successful startup isn't a small corporation. Some founders (Bill Gates, Steve Jobs, Mark Zuckerberg) take to the new roles with great gusto. Others, not so much. If you belong in the latter category, this period of change represents a huge upheaval in your business. Either you, as a founder, need to completely re-tool your skill set to match the new requirements in your business, or you have to find and hire more experienced managers to help the company grow, adapt, and thrive.

You've built the company up with hard work along with some blood, sweat and tears. Chances are that once it grows to a certain level, there will be other people who are better positioned to move the needle than you are. Think of it this way: as a founder, you probably have a significant chunk of equity in this business. Letting that equity grow in value by putting other people in the top slots of the company makes as much sense as selling off chunks of your company in exchange for investment.

This problem does occasionally show up before the founders have to take a step back. Hiring a new person above someone who's already in the company can be awkward. For example, you may have a developer named Eric who has been with you since the early days. Eric rolled out the early versions of the software and assembled your infrastructure. As you're starting to grow quickly, however, you realize that he's butting against the edges of what he can do. If he's being limited by bandwidth (that is, how much he can do), you can hire an assistant or a junior. It gets more complex as soon as you realize that he's being limited by his creativity, vision or experience.

It's a fact that you probably couldn't afford the most visionary engineers from the first day of your startup. That makes sense on several levels; you wouldn't be able to afford them, but even if you could, they probably wouldn't thrive unless they had a team working with them. In other words: hiring a VP of Engineering into a small startup isn't a great move. The best senior-level engineering managers are fantastic at creating complex systems, sketching out big-picture solutions and hiring and managing people, but they might not be the best at production-level coding. It's a different skill set. You will come across this again and again in all aspects in the business; in sales, design, operations, customer support and everywhere else. Your staff will grow and get smarter and better, but chances are that your company will need people who are better at a rate that's faster than your own staff develops.

In my experience, hiring senior staff above your existing staff is a great exercise in re-aligning what your organization is all about. It sends a strong signal to the whole company about which parts of the organization you're increasing the focus on. As long as you are aware at the time, it's also a way for you to see first-hand what it's like to be managed into a hierarchical management structure. That's helpful for you, too, should you bring in a professional manager to run business units of your company, or even the whole company itself.

There are dozens of great (and hundreds of bad) books out there about change management. There are the personal impacts, psychological impacts and organizational impacts of making drastic changes in an organization. The challenge isn't just drastic change, by the way. As humans, we are all creatures of habit. Even small changes are often resented across the company; if you don't believe me, replace the coffee machine with a different one. Half the company will love the change, the other half will mutter that the old coffee machine was better. For bigger changes, and especially decisions that go against a person's perceived value within an organization, you will have to make a bigger effort to manage the changes. Harvard Business Review published a great book called On Change Management, which includes a collection of ten articles that are extremely helpful in pointing you in the right direction.

One of the biggest challenges is what you actually do with a person whose job is affected by the new hire. If you are the company's CEO, and you are hiring a new CEO, that is a complicated situation. Of course, if you've been the de facto CMO of the company for years, and the company doesn't have a CMO, the answer is simple: you gleefully hop into your new role as CMO and you place the new hire into the CEO slot. Where it gets more tricky is if you don't have an obvious place to go.

The elephant in the room is that in a lot of companies, it will be detrimental for you to still be around after you've been replaced. Company culture dies hard, and there will be a strong temptation for you to still work with your coworkers who are now your friends. These friends will turn to you for help, advice and decisions as they have done for years. You will be tempted to give answers to the questions you know the answer to, but a shift has happened: you're no longer the right person to give those answers. The last thing you want is for someone who came to you for an answer to turn to the new CEO and say, "But the old CEO and my good friend Vitaly said..."

I have a good friend who was part of the founding team of a high-flying unicorn startup that grew to hundreds of employees and reached the limit of the CEO's abilities. The board of directors decided to replace the CEO and, after some time, hired a former division president of one of the tech giants. The old CEO gracefully handed off the reins, stepped up to Chairman and, after some time passed, left the company entirely. He did this to give the new CEO the room to implement his own management approach.

Gradually the old management team was politely shown the door one by one, and my friend was one of the last remaining original executives. All the while he confided in me about all of his disagreements and frustrations with the new CEO. I had to remind him that the the original CEO was akin to an aerobatic pilot bobbing and weaving and seeming to do impossible tricks in his little plane, while the new CEO was an airline captain flying the 747 on instruments with hundreds of passengers on board through the storm. They had different skill sets and management styles for different stages of the company. My friend subsequently quit to start his own startup where he is again in his happy place while a year later, the once unicorn had a much more focused business, turned its first profit, and is well on its way to an IPO.

There are other considerations here, too. An early hire into the company might have a larger chunk of equity, but it's possible that the person who gets hired above him or her ends up with a smaller slice of the pie. You can argue that the earlier hire took a bigger risk in joining the company, but it still potentially puts you at a disadvantage when you are negotiating the compensation package for a new hire. I'm not necessarily saying you should give the senior head of sales a more generous chunk of equity than your earlier, more junior staff, but it's a conversation you need to be ready for. Remember also that there are more people in play than just a person who has been, effectively, demoted. It is hard to swallow someone being hired above you in the hierarchy. If it is handled poorly, it can cause issues with morale and productivity both between the people who are directly affected by the shake-up, but also with the wider company, who will notice that changes are afoot.

Remember that while it might feel drastic to be ousted from the C-suite of the company you founded, a lot of VC-backed startups go through this process. About half of companies that raise a Series B investment have a new CEO within 18 months of raising that investment. This means two things: it's a pretty common occurrence, and the people who invested in you have seen this happen many times before. Yes, they invested in you because of your team, your product and the market potential, but if you feel you're not up for the job of leading this company through the next stage of growth, asking your board for advice isn't the world's worst idea. There are plenty of founder/CEOs who have been through this in their past, and most boards and investors have seen this happen, too. Don't hesitate to turn to those with experience for help and advice. It is a hard decision to make, but having the self-awareness to make it for yourself is better than turning up to a board meeting to discover that the decision has been made for you.

Remember also that you aren't immune to being asked to step down from one of the top slots at the company you founded. Steve Jobs is undeniably one of the most visionary founder/CEOs in the history of business. In 1985, he tendered his resignation from the company he founded nine years prior. Of course, Jobs also has one of the best comeback stories in modern corporate history, but that's another matter. Remember that loyalty is long dead in the professional world. The days of being at the same company for 50 years and then retiring are in the past. This is true for any level within the company: individual contributor, manager and especially at the very top. You probably have a fantastic set of skills that applies more to one stage of the business than another. Working with those skills rather than fighting against them is an important realization most founders need to make to ensure their own long-term professional satisfaction.

Chapter 40

Going International

Let's be honest: in the majority of industries out there, the US is the biggest single market in the world. There are tons of examples of companies that have done phenomenally well from a revenue point of view, and who have achieved a fantastic exit without ever worrying about what's happening outside the US borders. Thinking that the US is the only market, however, is a huge mistake.

For startups outside the US, you're probably in markets that are far smaller. A startup founded in Finland, the Netherlands or Thailand has its own challenges, but these companies do have an immediate advantage. As soon as the company is founded, the founders know that the big money exists outside of the country's borders. This has a few knock-on effects: companies founded outside the US may be faster to localize their products into different languages, may be better at adapting multiple payment systems or may have realized that credit cards are not as prominent outside the U.S. Even if you didn't found your company in California, New York or Texas, I wouldn't necessarily recommend that you immediately try to take on the US first. This country does have a few idiosyncrasies that can make an international expansion challenging. International founders usually grossly underestimate the effort and capital it takes to win the US market. They often attempt to expand to the US too early, sometimes with lackluster results. When local companies out-spend them on marketing, the attempt can put the company in an early grave. Which isn't to say that international expansion is impossible, of course.

US startups typically wait until they are the undisputed champions domestically before attempting to go international. This isn't a bad strategy, but as a result, many find themselves copied by local companies that hope to become an acquisition target of the US mothership. In Europe and Russia there are incubators, such as Rocket Internet, that operate pretty much exclusively on this model: see something cool across the Atlantic, copy it, take over the local market and wait for an exit when the US mothership starts looking at how to take over the European market.

Remember that you don't necessarily have to completely dominate the market to "go international." As we've discussed elsewhere in this book, talent is the single most important part of your company, and if you are ambitious to grow, opening a satellite office for talent acquisition is an option. Engineering talent is notoriously expensive and hard to attract in Silicon Valley. At Keen, I decided to open an office in Kyiv, Ukraine to capitalize on the relative abundance of great engineers at affordable salaries. The other way also works; I have friends who started companies outside of the US and "outsource" their sales and marketing to the US.

The first question about when to start thinking about the Big World Out There is timing. It becomes a cost/benefit calculation, like most other decisions. The cost here is about a lot more than money; it encompasses all the resources your company has available across the business.

App translations are a good example. If an app has been written in such a way that the strings used in the app can be easily translated, finding a freelancer to do the actual translations is trivial, and won't cost a lot of money. In my experience, you're looking at $300 to $1,000 per language, depending on the complexity of the app. Given the potential for growth, even the high end of that estimate is an absolute bargain. That isn't where the translation job ends, however. Every language you add adds another roadblock in the way of being able to launch a new version of an app. Say you add a new feature that adds 10 new translation strings. These need to be sent to the translators, translated, checked, integrated into the app and tested for visual bugs in the app's interface, before submitting it to the various app stores. Sounds easy, but when you're dealing with 10 different languages, that means you have to coordinate 10 different translators. The amount of work isn't high, but you still need to get it done. One company I advised had their app translated into 18 different languages. The cost was minimal, but the CTO complained that it completely ruined their ability to be agile. "From the time the coders have finished a new feature until we are ready to ship can take up to six weeks! It's ridiculous!" he said. And he was right.

These days, there are services that can speed the translation process up and that can help hire and do quality control on translations for you, but there are other challenges lurking too. Once you translate the app, users also expect that any documentation is translated, and they will certainly expect to be able to contact support in their native language. All of these are considerations you have to analyze before making the decision to add another language to your product.

Expanding internationally is about far more than just translating your product into the target languages. Yes, you may be able to sell more television sets to Japan if the interface is available in Japanese, but as you can imagine, there is a whole sales and marketing machinery that goes with an international roll-out.

Language is part of it, of course, but there are legal, cultural and market considerations, too. If you are planning a full-scale invasion of a new market, having boots on the ground is almost mandatory, at least temporarily. Staff who have intimate local knowledge is crucial to success, as is researching what the legal implications are of entering a market. Be especially aware that countries other than your own can have tremendously different employment laws and requirements for product testing, marking, buyer protection, and much more.

For US companies, it's often tempting to expand to Canada, South Africa, Australia and the United Kingdom first, because most of them are willing to accept software in US English. If you do decide to localize for those markets, it's usually much faster to replace some Z's with S's and sprinkle some U's throughout your app to keep the Brits happy. Be aware, however, that just because the language is very similar, it doesn't mean that the countries are the same culturally. Each of the other English-speaking countries will have different legal frameworks, social norms and expectations around your app. In Canada, for example, in some cases, you'll be legally required to also have a French version available. Oh, and time zones can't be ignored either; between the English-speaking countries, you're covering a tremendous number of time zones, and offering sales and support in all of them is going to be a real challenge.

In fact, language doesn't even enter into it in some industries. There are many industries now where English is the de facto operating language. In other cases, the companies you are selling to are operating in languages other than English, but are perfectly happy to use software, products or services that are in English only. Even if you are operating in a B2C industry, English is often acceptable to a large number of users. Don't rush to translate and localize your products until you have a clear message from the market that this is a requirement, or unless your expansion strategy shows that it is a necessity.

One good reason to localize your content and products is for search engine optimization. Customers who might be happy to use your app in English might start their research journey searching for solutions in their own language. If your competitor is available in, say, German, and their website comes up first, you may never even know some customers exist: they'll have chosen your competitor's services before you even appeared on their radar.

Be aware of local quirks. For example, Japan is an undeniably huge market with a very future-oriented population that is willing to spend money on technology, but opening a satellite office in Tokyo is easier said than done. You'll need a local general manager with strong ties to your industry before you'll be able to open an office, hire staff, or expect any of the local corporations to do business with you. Germany is another large and tech-savvy market, but it has very different privacy laws than you might be used to, and is one of the few western countries where almost nobody has a credit card, so you'll have to find an alternative solution for taking payments. Of course, your mileage will vary here depending on your industry, but it's just another illustration that some comprehensive research will go a long way.

If you are looking to open an office elsewhere because you need local staff, there are different ways of doing it. It's possible to have your US corporation own and run the office, you can set up a local entity or (particularly in the European Union) it's sometimes possible to incorporate in a neighboring country. There are legal and tax implications for whatever you choose, and the intricacies change based on the type of product you sell and the countries involved. All of these factors are three-dimensional chess depending on when you decide to make the move. Suffice to say that all the details are way beyond the scope of this book, and I strongly recommend you team up with accountants and lawyers who are experienced in the specifics of the business you're hoping to spark into life.

Even if you are running a business on a SaaS-based model that is largely self-serve in the US, and you expect that your operations can be run from abroad, remember that marketing, privacy laws, revenue-collection and taxes might be considerations, too. If your growth strategy includes public relations firms (and when you're getting to this size, there's an argument to be made for that it should), you're going to need to recruit a firm with local knowledge who know the local journalists. The same is true for advertising, sales, partnerships and possibly even design firms involved with designing local versions of your products.

When the time comes to open local sales offices, you're going to need a landing team. This is a group of people from your original country who can help set up the local office. Don't outsource this part. The landing team brings far more than a book of contacts; it is also the only way of exporting your company's culture and inherent values to the new location, and should therefore be closely involved with hiring the leadership in the new location. A poor culture fit is bad when you're hiring at your headquarters; it can be disastrous if it turns out further down the line that you put someone who is a poor fit in charge of a whole country or region.

There are a number of cautionary tales to look into if you're looking to start expanding internationally. Groupon, AirBnB's first attempt at international expansion and Fab all spring to mind; they all suffered from slightly different challenges, but the result was similar. The companies over-extended themselves, tried to grow into too many territories too quickly and ultimately lost a lot of money in the process.

Finally, consider doing exactly what I warned you about in the beginning of this chapter. If there is a market leader (or a strong runner-up) in the market you are looking to enter, acquiring that company might be a way to leapfrog a lot of hard work. International expansion is hard and expensive, and simply snapping up the competitor may be a money-saving shortcut in some cases.

Chapter 41

Failing Forward

There are a few industries where it's possible to build a slow-burning lifestyle business that lasts the rest of your life, or at least the rest of your career. Restaurants, shops or certain service businesses spring to mind. A very small number of startups do the same, where the founders take it from an idea and stay with the company to watch it grow into something worth hundreds of billions of dollars. In the world of startups, these scenarios are extremely rare, however. So rare, in fact, that you shouldn't even really consider them as options. One way or another, your business will transition from a startup to a company, and then from a company into something else: perhaps a corporation listed on a stock exchange, maybe an acquisition by another company. If we're looking at the statistics, however, it is likely that your company will end up as a failed endeavor that needs to shut down.

Whatever the endgame is for your company, you have to ensure that you are ready for it. You'll see an IPO coming, but an acquisition or a failure can be relatively sudden. The best way to ensure you are prepared is to make sure your business is set up in such a way that you are ready from day one.

As I discussed in Chapter 3, startups are a lot of things, but most important is how they will help you learn. Whether your company fails or succeeds, you'll learn a lot. If you are open to the learning experience the whole way through, even when the going gets tough, failure can also be a tremendous learning experience. Some of the best startups I know are run by founders who have failed many times over, but who were able to keep the clarity of mind to analyze what worked and what didn't, and then take that learning with them into the next chapter of their lives and the next startup on their resume. The biggest failure is failing to learn.

One of the most important pieces of advice I have here is crucially important both for companies that eventually succeed or fail: run a clean business. It's really important to have all the right contracts in place, keep your tax situation above board, have full and complete accounting and make sure that all the agreements you have with your team are solid. This will save you a lot of grief if the company ends up folding, but is non-negotiable in case someone comes knocking and wants to buy your business. Many a business deal has fallen apart between a letter of intent and the final sale, because the company didn't have its paperwork in order, and the due diligence process ended up taking forever.

There is also the consideration of when to sell, and that's an extremely difficult question to answer. AirBnB is a good example here. For the first years of its existence, it looked like it was going to fail. A lot of investors passed on the idea. It had a small core of enthusiastic customers, but the mass market just didn't get it. There were many opportunities for the founders to give up, leaving the company as yet another footnote in the annals of startup history. But they didn't. The team kept superhuman tenacity, and the company is today worth a tremendous amount of money. In my opinion, AirBnB is an outlier. Yes, it eventually became very successful, but the company failing to get traction for such a long time before it finally found product/market fit and a marketing message that worked is extremely rare. It illustrates one of the most difficult things about a "failing" startup, too. When should you pull the plug?

Whether you shut a company down of your own volition or because you have to, I encourage you to see if there is a way to wrap up the company gracefully. As an investor in a failed venture, there is not much I have to do other than write off the investment, but there are tax implications. It becomes far easier for me to have an official letter from the company stating that it is planning to cease operations. I fully understand that sending out letters and ensuring you close a company down with integrity won't necessarily be high on the list of things to do when it feels like the world is collapsing around you, but please consider doing it anyway. The main reason for closing a company down properly is that it is usually far faster than letting the courts do it for you, but far more importantly, your investors will remember you for it. The end of your company isn't the end of the world. You'll have other ideas in new markets, with new chances of big success. Your investors will remember how you started the company, how well you kept them in the loop throughout and how you acted when the time came to wind the company down.

If bankruptcy is looming and there doesn't seem to be any way to extend a startup's life, the decision may be made for you, but there are many other reasons why you might want to decide to wind the company down. Most startups begin with huge dreams and ambitions, and sometimes founders wake up one day to the realization that their moonshot ended up on the roof of the house instead. The company didn't fail per se, but it certainly didn't reach the heights the founders hoped. Some founders decide to continue to slave away on the company until it takes off like a rocket or crashes into the mountain side. I don't think that's a healthy way of thinking about it. Of course, you do need some resilience to get through hard times and setbacks, but there is also the matter of your personal non-refundable lifetime. When faced with the possibility of fighting for a company that doesn't seem to be going anywhere for the next five years, or starting something new that might be successful, what do you choose?

My friend Alex Fishman founded a company called Dishero. It was headed for pretty decent success, with a team of 17 and steady revenue growth. Nonetheless, the growth was too slow for them, and one day Alex came to the realization that mediocre success, to him, was worse than failure. He learned that there was a deep flaw in his business model: restaurants are really hard to sell to and not particularly business savvy. As a direct result of that, he felt that there couldn't be a situation where his company could grow exponentially. He decided to shut it down because while the revenue was growing, he didn't see the company growing into profitability, and he foresaw that he would have trouble raising another round.

There are a lot of things to keep in mind when potentially shutting down a company, but bear in mind who stands to lose the most when this decision is made. The three groups of people you obviously need to pay especially close attention to are the team, the founders and the investors. Your customers will be relying on you to a degree, and your suppliers and partners will also have a horse in the race. The decision to shut down a company can be an emotional one, but at least you were part of the decision-making process, and it's likely that this particular decision has been playing on your mind for a while. To the outside world, the announcement will come as some degree of a surprise. Managing the announcement and treating stakeholders with respect becomes important. Neither your staff nor your investors will want to read on TechCrunch that your company is on its way out. Ensuring that the people who are most affected by a closure are well informed is the bare minimum. While we are talking about staff: remember that your team relies on the company for more than just a paycheck. In the US especially, health care coverage (and how to transition to a new healthcare package) is an important consideration. In either case, offering to help your team find new employment through introductions, recommendations and references is crucial. Your staff dispersing in all directions will have their version of the story of why the company ended up shutting down, and Silicon Valley is a small place. You're going to want people to work for you or invest in your businesses in the future, so doing your utmost to keep even ex-staff and ex-investors on your side is a prudent approach.

There is always the option of selling the company to a competitor or to your senior staff. The former can be challenging, but if you just want your life back, you'd be surprised who's willing to take a meeting with you in order to take over your customers and brand. It can feel weird to put a company on the chopping block for less than you feel it's worth, but you have to balance this against your own personal opportunity cost. If you're able to get your investors their money back and get your life back so you can take a long break and then start another venture, it's definitely worth considering.

Letting your senior staff buy the company is known as a management buyout (MBO). It was particularly popular in the 1980s, but it still happens today. There are a couple of advantages to doing an MBO, not least that your senior team doesn't usually have to do very deep due diligence. After all, they already know the company's strengths and weaknesses, and maybe they feel that they'll be able to grow the company in new ways without your help. Bear in mind that your company's corporate lawyers will be obliged to act in the firm's best interest, so if you're considering an MBO, it's important to find a separate set of legal advisors to facilitate the sale from your perspective.

There's an old saying: "Companies aren't sold, they are bought." What people mean by this is that unless someone is already considering buying, doing a cold sell of a whole company is very difficult. I believe that, but I also think that most successful companies get some possible buyers sniffing around either way. There are usually competitors who are sniffing around, who have either already approached you about a potential sale or who have been asking you and your staff a lot of questions at trade shows. In either case, feeling potential buyers out is a good idea, as is creating a pitch deck. It's also possible to find a third-party broker who can help navigate the deal. A good broker or M&A banker who knows your industry very well has probably already done a number of deals working with the same companies who might potentially be acquiring you. A good way to get to the bottom of how these deals happen is to research acquisitions by your potential acquirers and work your network to speak to the founders of the other startups to see if they have any contacts, tips or advice relevant specifically to your industry and its big players.

Exiting yourself out of a company doesn't necessarily mean that you have to shut it down or sell it. Hiring a professional CEO (as we discussed in Chapter 39) can be done even if there's no imminent explosive growth phase happening. Although a CEO is definitely one of the hardest hires, this is where your investors and advisors will come in handy, not least because once you're gone, the new CEO will be their main point of contact for the company.

Part X—Questions to Ask Yourself

Hitting the rapid growth stage and watching your startup wrap itself up into a cocoon is an intense period of time. The world is going through a metamorphosis around you, and it's hard to tell whether what comes out the end will be a wonderfully vibrant butterfly, or something unexpected.

One of the best ways to prepare for this phase of your company is to revisit some of your early thinking. Reconsider what your goals are, both for the company and for you personally. What would success look like? Is there a version of success that you wouldn't be willing to accept? Making sure that your cofounders are all on the same page about your personal ambitions and those of the company can prevent some serious conflicts down the line.

Talk to your investors, mentors and advisors about why this company exists. What are the investors' expectations of the company, and how can you maximize your success? Looking deep into your own soul, you might realize at this point that what your advisors and investors see as success is a future you're not able to deliver. That is fine, but communicating that clearly is crucial. If it turns out that you need to replace yourself as the CEO, it's important to be able to elucidate clearly what you feel you are missing for the job, and what your replacement would need. Being acutely aware of your strengths, weaknesses and capacities is the key to being able to navigate this minefield. Involve your close friends and confidantes and see whether you have the capacity and desire to grow your own skill set quickly enough to be able to continue delivering value to the company you founded. If not, realizing that early and starting to consider what a transition might look like is a great investment of your time.

Part XI

Paying It Forward

A startup is a temporary state. Either you discover a way to create a repeatable business model, or you don't. Either you find customers who love the way you solve a real problem, or you fail. As an entrepreneur, you'll be throwing years of your life into a project you are passionate about. You'll learn more than you ever have before in your life. You'll make decisions about big and small things at a rate you didn't think possible.

If you are a very successful entrepreneur, you'll find yourself with a large amount of wealth, and you won't have to work again. If you don't find commercial success, chances are that other factors in your life (raising your children, spending time with your family, not having as much energy as you used to) will slow you down enough that the entrepreneurial lifestyle doesn't seem as shiny as it did before. Typical founders may have up to three or four startups in them before other life priorities take over. During those startups, however, you'll build up a wealth of contacts, knowledge and experience that has a deep inherent value.

Finding out what you do next is up to you, but even if you decide you've had enough of startups, the experience you built up still has tremendous value to other founders. In Part XI, I'll come full circle, and explain how you can take the lessons you've learned and help the next generation of startup founders find their feet.

Chapter 42

The Silicon Valley Way

started this book by talking about the magic of Silicon Valley. Part of that magic comes from the fact that almost no matter what you are hoping to do, there will be people who've done that very same thing, or something similar, before you. There's a pattern to the thinking that takes companies and turns them into actual, bona-fide magic. I like to call that the Silicon Valley Way.

As I've mentioned before, Silicon Valley isn't really a place; it's a mindset. You can't travel to it by getting on a plane or driving your car there, but you can come visit by changing how you think about problems in the world around you. The Silicon Valley Way is to be observant and analytical. You don't accept anything at face value; instead, you constantly ask, "Why?" Why does it take so many steps to make a payment? Why is it so complicated to book a taxi? Why is printing things for a small conference such a hassle? If you are thinking along the wrong ways, all of these things are annoyances.

If you embrace your inner Silicon Valley entrepreneur, all of these questions turn into opportunities.

As a startup founder, you've probably already started embracing this way of thinking. A lot of the exercises in the "Questions to Ask Yourself" sections of this book are designed to help you engage your brain in the right gear. You're asking the right questions. You're refusing the status quo. And in talking to your friends and co-workers about these questions, you're coming up with a dozen ideas for companies, products or improvements to existing solutions. When that curiosity has been awakened, you've been changed for life. You won't ever be able to see the world the same way again. The next time someone bemoans that they can't see any good business opportunities, you'll giggle. It's not spotting opportunities that's become your problem; it is figuring out how to say no to all of the ideas that are coming your way and choosing carefully where to invest your time.

There are a few things that are required to retrain your mind to work in this way. Depending on your geographical and cultural background, some of these will be harder to deal with than others. Most importantly, you have to learn to embrace failure. In many corporate jobs, there's a deep blame culture. If something goes wrong, fingers start pointing, and if enough fingers point at one person, he or she will feel the retribution one way or the other. In Silicon Valley's mindset, however, we've gone beyond that. It's a reality that we'll all make a number of mistakes. Thomas Edison was a clever man. With more than 1,000 patents to his name and inventions such as the first film camera, the photograph and the first working lightbulb, he knew a thing or two about how progress and innovation works. Edison famously said, "I have not failed, I just found 10,000 ways that don't work." That encapsulates the spirit of what we are talking about here. By finding a way that doesn't work, you're not failing. You are learning. For every failed experiment, for every metric that didn't move in the direction you were hoping, you're adding new knowledge to yourself, your company and the world.

If embracing and learning from failure is the lifeblood of Silicon Valley, networking is its heart. I can't overstate how often I've seen almost impossibly huge challenges overcome because founders built up a network they could rely on for help and advice. The only way to grow your network is to work hard on it. Exposing yourself to the startup ecosystem through events, meetups and industry functions can be daunting, but trust me: the value of your network is directly proportional to its size. Remember that for every person you add as someone you can chat with and reach out to for problem-solving, you're not just increasing your network by one. You're increasing it by one plus all the people they know. If you one day ask your friends, "Gee, I wish I knew someone at Coca-Cola for this really interesting marketing idea I have for them," chances are that someone has a connection, or can help you one step in the right direction. Cultivating and paying attention to those relationships is one of the most valuable things about Silicon Valley.

One of the poorly kept secrets of Silicon Valley is that you can't learn how to be an entrepreneur from a book or in a classroom. That doesn't mean that taking classes and reading books isn't useful. But you can't learn to be a successful entrepreneur from reading a book any more than you can become a professional boxer by reading Muhammad Ali's biography and watching his fights against George Foreman on a loop. Entrepreneurship is like a set of muscles that needs to be trained over time. Start a company. Make mistakes. Make friends. Watch it explode in a giant ball of fire. Take a break, regroup and try again. These failures are common, and they are useful. In Silicon Valley, they aren't called failures; they're experience.

There are three ways of learning from mistakes. The first is to never make them in the first place, but experience teaches us that this is unlikely even for the most hard-boiled entrepreneurs. The next way is to make your own mistakes and learn from them. Hard-won lessons are the ones that will stick with you for life, and some of them will make great stories that you can share with the community in the hope that others don't walk into the same traps you did. The best and cheapest way to learn from mistakes, however, is to learn from someone else's, and this is where the Silicon Valley mindset really shines. There are a great number of amazing blog posts, books and workshops where big mistakes and expensive failures are picked apart and analyzed. This ability and willingness to learn and grow is invaluable. The ability to share what you've learned with the bigger group is, ultimately, the true magic of startups.

If you look at a number of startups, you'll soon learn that there isn't a single cookie-cutter recipe for what makes a great startup or a great startup team. There have been successful founders who came at the challenge of starting and running a company from all sorts of angles. Sales experts, product-driven founders, operationally focused founders and big-vision thinkers all have very different ways of approaching problems, and will probably come up with vastly different ways of solving them. The most successful founders do have some things in common: they are honest, hard-working, stable under pressure and extremely supportive of their teams. The final one is especially important.

Mutual support is a cornerstone of how Silicon Valley is able to produce incredible teams climbing seemingly unscalable mountains. Investing in your team on an emotional and intellectual level is one way to supercharge your organization. Encouraging your teams to take the time to get to know each other outside of work and facilitating cross-training of your organization means that it becomes possible to draw from the collective experience of all of your team members. As a result, the team runs smoother, the company learns faster and you see results earlier. Building this social layer on a company culture that encourages and embraces failure as a learning experience is a liberating experience that will help catalyze the innovation process within your company.

Ultimately, what this is all about is that you want your company full of people to be eager to help and mentor each other. And now that I've mentioned mentoring: you're in luck, that's what the last chapter is all about.

Chapter 43

Becoming a Mentor

I **owe a lot to people** who took me under their wings: coworkers who had advice to offer, and mentors who were able to talk me through difficult problems and offer advice along the way. As I mentioned in Chapter 8, I founded Keen without a cofounder, but as a result we pivoted later, grew slower and developed in directions that we might not have if I had a constant intellectual sparring partner. If it hadn't been for the mentors I had along the way, I think things would have have gone differently, and not in a good way.

If you've never experienced a productive mentoring session, it is very hard to explain why it works so well. The best mentors have a way of feeling the edges of your knowledge and the nooks and crannies of the decisions you're about to make. Some mentors have a wealth of experience themselves that they can draw from, which is very helpful, of course. The truth is that as the company's founder, you are steeped in the industry, the specifics of the challenges you're facing and the full knowledge of the customers you are serving. The problem is that because you're laser focused on the day-to-day of your startup, it can be hard to take a step back and get the full context of what you are doing. Getting the perspective of an outsider is invaluable. If that same person can also break you out of your well-worn thought patterns and unlock new layers of innovation, creativity and problem solving, you've found the perfect mentor for you.

I've lost track of how often I've had my mentees tell me at the end of a meeting that our 30-minute chat changed everything. However, it was rarely my specific idea or advice that moved the needle. They knew the answers to the problems they were facing. They just needed someone to help nudge them towards the answers that were already there.

Now you are in the same place. You've found a way through your first startup. You've slayed the dragons, you've laid waste to your enemies and you've rescued the fair maiden from a distant tower. Maybe your company was tremendously successful and you're headlining conferences around the world. Or perhaps your company left a dinosaur-extinguishingly large crater in the ground. It doesn't really matter. The important thing is, you have created your first startup(s) and you have the battle scars to show for it. Now it's time to pay it forward, and become a mentor yourself. You'll learn from it, and it's the right thing to do. But how?

Being a mentor is an oddly intimate thing; in the best mentor/ mentee relationships, people tell each other things that they tell few others. In business, you'll no doubt come across sensitive, complicated situations that need to be handled with finesse and respect. Getting advice on these types of things means that you have to open yourself up. Seeking advice can feel like a position of weakness and giving advice has the connotation of strength. In my experience, it is often the other way around. Realizing that you need help with something isn't a weakness. It takes a huge amount of self-awareness and strength to formulate the things you don't know and reach out to another person for help.

Giving advice, on the other hand, is extremely hard, too. It is good to want to be a mentor, but I have seen it done poorly many times. You may occasionally come across extremely experienced entrepreneurs who seem to be completely incapable of listening. They will listen to the questions, but seem to be listening only for keywords. "Hiring," they hear, and are ready with an anecdote about that one time they hired a rockstar coder. "Problem with compensation," they catch, and are ready with a story about how they once successfully talked a potential team member out of a large salary. The problem is that mentoring doesn't work like that. In fact, most of the time, entrepreneurs coming to you for advice will be asking the wrong questions. You need to listen to the question, of course, but it's possible that when they are asking about hiring, they are really wondering about operational efficiency. Maybe when they say they have a problem with compensation, they are actually having a challenge with the stock option pool or melting cash. This is where the perceived "strength" of offering mentorship is such a misnomer. The best mentors are incredibly humble, and know very well that what they know is only applicable to another startup in a limited way. Giving generalized advice only goes so far, and learning to listen carefully to a founder in order to correctly identify what an underlying problem is will take time.

Of course, as an advisor you will want to cheer on your startups and see them thrive, but it's also important to stay honest and give constructive criticism. Early-stage startups are often gemstones in the rough. They will be polished over time and they will eventually turn into beautiful jewels... or they won't. Many startups need a little bit of tough love and painfully honest feedback to try to get them on track, and that's one of the most valuable things a good mentor can offer. Of course, even painful feedback has to be handled with compassion and care, but just like good friends will tell you when you're making a mess of things in your personal life, your mentors will do the same for your company.

Great mentors will spend time researching and exploring the company they are mentoring and the industry it operates in. They will converse with their own mentors and friends in order to gain a deeper understanding of the startup. Taking a mentoring relationship lightly is the best way to undermine it. I try to mentor as few companies as I can. It is tremendously hard work to be a great mentor, because I feel that whenever I offer to help a company, I need to be able to be there for them. I need to be able to show enthusiasm for what they are trying to accomplish, I need to have knowledge about the field they operate in and I need to be able to offer my network as assistance. In effect, by taking on a company as their advisor or taking on a founder as his or her mentor, I am investing a bit of my social capital in that company. In other words: a company will be judged in part on who its advisors are. And I will be judged in part on the companies I advise. That is a good thing in both cases, but the corollary is that you do have to be careful about which companies you decide to invest your time in.

As an mentor, you shouldn't be charging money for your services. Of course, if the company wants to fly you out to an event, they should probably offer to pay for your expenses, but ultimately, mentorship isn't something you do for the money. To understand why, think about alignment of interests. If you get paid by the hour for mentorship, there will be a natural temptation to spend as much time mentoring a company as possible. In some circumstances (say, the company is in the process of raising money), working full-time on a startup might make sense, but as I mentioned, the distance from the company is part of the value you have as a mentor. If you get your hands dirty in the day-to-day operations of a startup, you're not a mentor. You're a team member. Also, there's a word for a paid advisor: consultant. There's a place for consultants in startups, of course, but the expectations for a mentor and a consultant relationship are very different. Creating a mix of the two is rarely helpful. Finally, the most important argument against paying advisors is that your advisor should know better. Early-stage startups have extremely limited resources, and every penny should be invested in growing and developing the company. If an advisor is arguing that the services he or she offers are in alignment with that goal, they are probably offering consultancy services rather than mentorship or advisory.

In general, the accepted way for advisors and mentors to work with startups is on an equity basis. The Founders Institute has created a great template to help formalize the relationship, known as the Founder Advisor Standard Template (FAST). It's free to use and it's fair and balanced both for the startup and the advisor. The FAST agreement gives an advisor between 0.1% and 1% of equity in the company, based on the stage of the company and how involved the advisor gets. For much the same reason that paying for advisors is a bad idea, equity works great. Early-stage startups are equity-rich but money poor. Far more importantly, a mentor who is paid in equity has the same incentive as the founding team. If the company gets hugely successful, the advisor can see a decent return on his or her investment, and is therefore incentivized to work hard to help make the company a success.

I normally operate on a 2.5-meeting rule when I advise startups. That means that I'll take two meetings free of charge with no commitment. Beyond that, we're going to have to formalize the relationship somehow. After two meetings, I'll hopefully know whether the startup is doing things I can add real value to. The startup, in turn, will hopefully realize whether or not I can be helpful and whether they can work with me. The next half-meeting is about finding out how we continue to work together. This agreement is extremely important, because it crystallizes the expectations we both have for this relationship. What am I expected to do? How often?

Against what compensation? Getting all of this down on paper helps keep things clear and simple. Ultimately, as an advisor or mentor, you'll be investing in the company. Not necessarily with money, but you're investing an even scarcer resource: time.

As a person, you probably have strengths and weaknesses. We all do. Those qualities will be reflected in who you are as a mentor, too. Some people look at a spreadsheet and they can feel their will to live leaving their bodies. Others look at the same spreadsheet and are filled with insight, inspiration and excitement. Similarly, some people love selling, hiring, motivating, strategizing, creating processes, building relationships, creating partnerships and so forth. Having skills that can help extend and develop those of the founders is crucial to having a good mentorship relationship.

The final question is, "Why spend your time advising startups?" We're all standing on the shoulders of those that came before us, and helping the startup ecosystem develop further by helping the generations that come after you is simply the right thing to do. There are a lot of other benefits, too. Personally, I love the feeling of pride that comes from watching a startup that I helped find its way in the world take off. It's not quite like the kinship I feel with my children, of course, but there's a definite parallel there. The other huge benefit is that you'll learn a lot from providing advice. Being subjected to a lot of different ways of thinking and interesting ways of solving problems will help you become a better problem-solver, too. It'll help you develop new ways of looking at issues and new angles from which you can attack problems and challenges that come up in your own companies.

Finally, there's the network effect. You'll invariably get pretty close to the startups you're advising and the founders behind them. These relationships often continue long after the company has been bought, sold or folded, and I have more than a few great friendships to show for it.

Epilogue

Some Final Thoughts

Thank you for joining me on this journey through the world of startups. I hope it has been helpful, and that you're just itching to get started on your next big venture. In this final section, I will leave you with a few thoughts.

As I'm sure you've noticed throughout this book, I've highlighted that the journey you're about to embark on isn't going to be a walk in the park. Running a startup is hard, and even if you have a lot of experience from working at large companies, it turns out that many of the hard-won skills from working on the corporate side of things don't necessarily transfer all that well.

Choosing to take a turn off the road and into the heavy jungle of the startup world is a decision you have to make carefully. Just like negotiating a forest, you'll probably have to carve your own way through. What worked for those that came before you might not work for you. That is true on several levels. Even if someone has already cut a path through the forest, they may have done so several years ago, which may as well be an eternity in startup land. Tools and methodologies change so rapidly that by the time this book ends up in your hands, chances are that some of the things I mentioned will be out of date. That's OK. Your mentors and peers will have strong opinions on what the right platforms and tools are.

Your friends and family may think you're nuts for giving up the relative security of a corporate job. The accepted way forward among our parents and peers is a pretty standard path of getting good grades, going to a good university and getting a good job at a nice company. You go through a series of regular promotions, and eventually you retire, you play golf and you die. The golf bit is optional, and replaceable with fishing, playing chess, collecting stamps or whatever else gets you through the days. That career path seems perfect to some, but you've read this far, so I'm willing to bet it doesn't sound perfect for you. You want to make your own way. What your parents might not understand is that as a true entrepreneur, this is all you want to do. You'll probably falter along the way, and you might even get burned a few times, but ultimately, this is a lifestyle you choose for yourself. If it were easy, everybody would be doing it... and you aren't like everybody else.

A lot of the overnight successes you hear about sound sexy. The company was founded, and six months later they raised a million dollars. A year and a half after that they raised a $15 million Series A. And a year and a half months after that, Google bought them for a bazillion dollars. That sounds easy, but it isn't. It never is. A lot of journalists love telling the story of an overnight success (it makes a great story), but the truth is that most overnight successes had a long run up. There were turns down the wrong paths. There were problems. They had their own share of issues before they hit their stride and became successful. The overnight success myth isn't helpful here. In my experience, it takes about a year to fully develop an idea and another year or two to see if anybody cares enough to give you money. Then it will likely take another three to five years to see it through.

That's an average of an eight-year commitment to something where nobody is really able to tell you whether or not it's going to work. It takes a special kind of human to decide that this is what you're going to do with your life.

If we agree that you're potentially embarking on a near decade-long project here, that further illustrates my earlier point. Solve something that is worth solving and that has its roots in the future. If you solve a problem that is immediate in the here-and-now but is likely to be a non-issue by the time you've spooled up your company and are ready for the big leagues, it's obvious that you're running at high speed towards disappointment. The company you found today has to keep inspiring you and your team for a long time; if it doesn't, you're going to run into some serious challenges sooner rather than later.

Founding a company will take a toll on you. You will experience stress, your relationships may suffer and you will almost certainly be making less money than you were in your old job, at least for a while. Don't let it stop you. Don't even let it slow you down.

The one thing I would like to highlight, however, is something I've alluded to a couple of times already. Money is a renewable resource. You can raise more through revenue or through investors. Your time isn't renewable. Work only on projects that are worthwhile, and that have a place in the future. If you find yourself working on a project that used to make sense, but somehow doesn't anymore, there's no shame in bailing yourself out, brushing yourself off and throwing yourself at a new project. From an energy and health point of view, let's be honest: you may have three or four startups in you. Make them count, and only invest your life in projects that you feel are worthwhile even if they don't turn you into a billionaire. If you're solving problems you feel passionate about for customers you care for, it will feel great whether your company turns into a commercial success or not.

THE END

Acknowledgements

First and foremost, I want to acknowledge and thank my parents Mark and Yelena Golomb, who were incredibly brave to upend their lives, move our family to Silicon Valley and offer amazing opportunities to my brother and me. Our refugee journey was far from easy and deserves a separate telling. Perhaps if they had chosen to move us to Southern California, this book would have been about becoming a rockstar instead of a startup star. C'est la vie. My brother Michael, who has always set the bar high in our sibling rivalry.

My kids Ari and Sophia, who are my greatest inspiration to improve the world no matter how incrementally. Their mother Joyce, for all the sacrifices she's made to pick up the slack while I learned many of the lessons in this book the hard way.

Haje Jan Kamps, Jake Widman, and Nora Oravecz, without whom this book would never have gotten out of my head. Andrew Romans, your advice has been invaluable in putting this project on the right track. Sridhar Solur and John Biggs, your expertise and insightful guest chapters added value on topics I could never have done justice. Your friendship means the world to me.

Over the years, I've always been fortunate to find mentors who were willing to let me vacuum their brains for invaluable knowledge. Alex Pachikov, who has been my sounding board and consistent sanity check since we were kids. Stepan Pachikov, who allowed his son to bring along his best friend to hang out at ParaGraph, where the startup bug first bit. Jennie Matt, who in retrospect was crazy to hire me as a teenager and is still a friend to this day. Michael S. Malone, who I witnessed write the premature obituary of Apple, Infinite Loop. Mahesh Rao, who asked me to take time off from college in exchange for a seat on his rocketship. That year and a half of the dot com era is responsible for a good chunk of the experience I've been able to pass down in this book. Howard Lieberman, who has been my professor, innovation coach, musical partner and friend. Steve Goldberg, who was always willing to make time to meet with me while I was building companies and later getting ready to switch to the other side of the table. Jim Dvorkin and Bennet Goldberg, who are my faithful board members and business coaches. Ullas Naik, who was one of my first investors, a patient sounding board and an under-the-radar powerhouse VC. Dave McClure, who is the hardest working man in venture capital, and who not only believed in me as a founder (and penned the foreword of this book), but also let me look over his shoulder and always reminds me of the positive impact entrepreneurship can make on this planet.

Armen Gasanyan and Mike Reiner, who are great business partners and friends that have put up with my BS and always made me look good. My friends around the world—many of whom are in the startup world—who have given me their support and encouragement. My whole team at HP Tech Ventures, who are quite possibly a group of stand up comedians who mistakenly ended up in an office.

And my dear Kate. She always keeps me grounded when I get ahead of myself, and motivated when I (often) bite off more than I can chew. She is my muse and laser-sharp mental sparring partner who gives me no choice but to keep growing and becoming a better version of myself.

This book started out as an idea supported by eager backers in a crowdfunding campaign, without whom it wouldn't have made it into your hands:

Official Sponsor: TechCode

Patrons: Chris Warren, Darryl Siry, Gennadii Nissenbaum, Guy Vincent, Vikram Lal, Vitaly Soldatenko and Xuan Li.

Early Supporters: Andrew Gaule, Cerina Zhang, Dmytro Bukhantsov, EJ Dieterle, Jean Kropper, Jeroen van der Putten, Julian Zegelman, Andrew Bolwell, Andy Wilson, Anthony Catt, Augustin Jarak, Brandon Cusick, Brend Kouwenhoven, Chantalle Dumonceaux, Dvorah Graeser, Elaine Wherry, Leonid Ganapolskiy, IdaRose Sylvester, Jot Toor, Justin Hall, Matija Šošić, Nagla Gaafar, Paolo Lombardi, Scott Gillespie, Stuart Schmukler, Terry Cox, Yaroslav Mudryi, Christophe Fraise, Alex Pachikov, Heather Russell, John Gower, Lee-Hong Lau, Louis Lehot, Tim Shiple, A. Lester Buck III, Anthony Kim, Artur Furau, Darren Meredith, Francine Gordon, Hubert Grealish, James Caldwell, Jarosław Sajko, Jenny Chau, John Conkle, Jonathan Romley, Kiran Kotresh, Lison We, Mohamed Aboshady, Oleg Khazanov, Piotr Wilam, Riccardo D'Amico, Viacheslav Kachur, Viacheslav Davidenko, Alberto Haddad, Andrea Gaiardo, Cris Doloc, Diego de Jódar, Emil V, Francois Montegut, Greg Pichard, Ismail Berkan, Jim Dvorkin, Joe Diaz, Madhu Sudan G, Manoj Subramaniam, Marcos Mueller, Matt Cartagena, Rémi Grosclaude, Sydney Lai, Todd Flynn, Travis Gilkey, Viktor Kompaneyets and Ziv Gillat.

CPSIA information can be obtained
at www.ICGtesting.com
Printed in the USA
BVOW08*2028270317
479361BV00002B/2/P